THANKSGIVING SERMONS

THANKSGIVING

SERMONS

BY
CHARLES WADSWORTH

This text was originally published in the United States
The text is in the public domain.
Modern Edition © 2024
Word Wise Books

The publishers have made all reasonable efforts to ensure
this book is indeed in the Public Domain in any and all territories
it has been published.

"Our Thanksgiving is partly in view of the ripened fruits of the earth; but mainly in view of other and higher blessings. And in this regard, as well, it is properly — a feast of harvest."

—*CHARLES WADSWORTH*

PREFACE

In the tapestry of American religious history, few threads weave a more profound narrative of gratitude and spiritual insight than the sermons of Charles Wadsworth. As we embark on this literary journey through his Thanksgiving Sermons, we find ourselves drawn into the eloquence of a man who dedicated his life to the pursuit of gratitude, encapsulating the essence of the Thanksgiving season in profound and timeless ways.

Charles Wadsworth, born in Philadelphia in 1814, emerged as a prominent 19th-century American preacher and theologian. Wadsworth's ministry unfolded against the backdrop of a nation grappling with its identity, navigating through the turbulent waters of the Civil War, and seeking solace in the face of profound social and spiritual changes.

Wadsworth's journey to becoming a celebrated preacher was marked by an unrelenting pursuit of understanding, compassion, and a deeply rooted appreciation for the transformative power of gratitude. His sermons, delivered with a compelling blend of erudition and heartfelt sincerity, reflected his commitment to drawing individuals closer to the divine through the lens of gratitude. Thanksgiving, for Wadsworth, was not merely a seasonal observance but a guiding principle that shaped his theological outlook and pastoral approach.

But his views of Thanksgiving were not limited to personal motivations. He looked beyond home and hearth, to the role of Thanksgiving in the building of a young and growing nation, at that time less than a hundred years old and experiencing tumultuous waves of immigration and territorial expansion.

The pages that follow offer a glimpse into Wadsworth's fiery pulpit eloquence and unique perspective on Thanksgiving, inviting readers to reflect on the timeless relevance of gratitude in their own lives. As we explore the sermons gathered in this collection, it becomes evident that

Wadsworth saw Thanksgiving not as a perfunctory annual ritual, but as a spiritual discipline capable of transforming hearts and communities.

Central to Wadsworth's theology was the idea that gratitude serves as a bridge connecting the finite with the infinite, the temporal with the eternal. His sermons delved into the human experience, exploring the complexities of joy and sorrow, success and failure, and the constant ebb and flow of life. Through it all, Wadsworth's sermons resonated with a steadfast belief in the transformative power of a grateful heart.

Wadsworth's impact extended beyond the pulpit; he was known for his compassionate pastoral care. His sermons were not detached theological treatises but rather intimate conversations with congregants, offering solace and guidance in times of uncertainty. As we peruse his Thanksgiving sermons, we glimpse the empathetic shepherd who saw the importance of fostering gratitude in the human soul, recognizing it as a salve for wounds and a source of strength in adversity.

As we reflect on Wadsworth's life and ministry, it is impossible to ignore the historical context in which he preached. The Civil War loomed large, challenging the very fabric of the nation. Wadsworth's sermons during this tumultuous period carried a distinctive message of hope and resilience, urging his congregants to find gratitude even in the midst of chaos. His words were a balm for wounded spirits, a reminder that, even in the darkest hours, gratitude could be a guiding light.

In one particularly poignant Thanksgiving sermon delivered during the Civil War, Wadsworth spoke of the transformative power of gratitude in times of crisis: "Now, this thought we will pursue through the remainder of our discourse — that these afflictions are designed for our good — that this war is not God's destroying axe, but His beneficial pruning-knife."

Wadsworth's ability to draw spiritual sustenance from the well of gratitude is a theme that runs like a golden thread through these sermons. His words resonate with an enduring relevance,.

As we embark on this journey, let us open our hearts to the wisdom contained within these pages. May his insights inspire us to cultivate a spirit of gratitude, not just during the Thanksgiving season but as a perpetual wellspring of joy and connection with the divine.

CONTENTS

I.	A SERMON.	11
II.	RELIGION IN POLITICS.	33
III.	POLITICS IN RELIGION.	51
IV.	AMERICA'S MISSION.	75
V.	THANKFULNESS.	99
VI.	CHARACTER.	115
VII.	THE FEAST OF HARVEST.	139
VIII.	THE JOY IN HARVEST.	161
IX.	IN EVERYTHING GIVE THANKS.	185
X.	WAR A DISCIPLINE.	205
XI.	A CALL TO PRAISE.	227
	About the Author.	243

1

A SERMON

PREACHED IN THE ARCH STREET PRESBYTERIAN CHURCH, PHILADELPHIA, ON THANKSGIVING DAY, NOVEMBER 25, 1852.

"Let them sacrifice the sacrifices of thanksgiving."

PSALM 107:22.

"The sacrifices of God are a broken spirit."

PSALM 41:17.

"Present your bodies a living sacrifice unto God, which is your reasonable service."

ROMANS 12:1.

Our gathering in God's sanctuary this morning, viewed in any of its various aspects, is peculiarly beautiful. Beautiful in *itself*, for it is the setting apart of secular time to the services of divine worship; beautiful in its occasion, for it is at the call of the civil authorities, and it seems like a green spot amid deserts under a government reiterating its pretensions to be an economy separated from all religion, to find the finger of executive authority pointing the multitude to the temple of God; beautiful in its *peculiar observances*, for it is a day hallowed to friendship, when many a severed family reunites for a season in the beloved circle, and the very words of the sanctuary are not of indignation, but of love; beautiful, too, in its thoughtful associations, for it comes linked with visions of Plymouth and the pilgrims, and the simple names they so honored living, and the hallowed graves of their immortal dead; beautiful, above all, in the spirit of its *memories*, for they are all joyous—all of life's sunshine and gladness—all of a Father's kindness and a Father's care; we stand today on a high mount flung up in the path of our pilgrimage; and, looking back along all our journeyings, have no eye save for the *Ebenezers*—for the green spots fresh in their verdure, and shaded with bright palms, and sparkling with sweet waters, wherewith a bounteous God has chequered all our path.

As a religious service, thanksgiving is an expression of gratitude for divine favors. As a duty of creatures, it has its foundation in the very nature of things. For as we can by no equivalent recompense God for his favors, it seems entirely unnatural that we should not entertain a lively sense of his goodness, and give utterance to our gratitude on fitting occasions in appropriate forms. It has, moreover, the sanction of the highest authority, in the example of all holy men, and in the manifold exhortations and commandments of Jehovah. And while it may not strictly be denominated holy time, yet, as in the exercises of a most holy service, it becomes us to gather statedly in this holy place—our hearts swelling with grateful emotions, and our lips breathing the beautiful language of Israel's king: — *"Bless the Lord, oh my soul, and all that is within me, bless his holy name."*

It becomes us, however, to enter upon such a service intelligently; to understand what we are doing, and how we are to do it; and the object of our present discourse will be to consider most simply our duty of thanksgiving in the two aspects of its Occasion and its Character.

Attempting nothing more than to answer these two questions simply and briefly—

I. WHY *are we to be thankful?*

II. HOW *are we to be thankful?*

Now in reference to both these topics you will expect us to discourse rather on general and national blessings, than on those strictly private and individual: by a beautiful understanding among our rulers, the old separate State thanksgivings have given place to united National thanksgivings. And although, each man for himself, we are bound this day to remember with deep gratitude God's special mercies to ourselves and our households, yet when gathered thus at once as a whole people in ten thousand temples consecrated to Jehovah, it is becoming that our thoughts should dwell more prominently on God's distinguishing benefactions to our land and nation. Regarded, then, mainly in our aggregate national character, what is today *our Occasion for thanksgiing?* (i. e.) *what are the great national benefits we have received from our Maker?* Now to answer this question fittingly were to occupy your attention till the sun goes down. We can of course only glance at the subject. *For the American nation what hath God wrought?* Why the question should be rather —*what hath God NOT wrought?* What hath God not done for America? Unto what people, not excepting even the covenant descendants of Abraham, hath God ever manifested so wonderfully his loving kindness? We are disposed to set up for these United States no invidious claims to precedence. Anniversary harangues have exhausted all the strong words and metaphors of the language, until *"eagles"* and *"star-spangled banners"* have become the shibboleth of fools, and should be held consecrate to bathos. America is, after all, neither the old Eden by the Hiddekel, nor the New Jerusalem by the living water. We acknowledge our imperfections and our diadvantages. We are frank to confess our rudeness and obscurity in comparison with the high culture and ancestral renown of older and transatlantic nations. We have many lessons of social refinement and political wisdom yet to learn from the empires beyond the sea. Nevertheless, no American heart can ponder the records of the past or the conditions of the present, without a very over-burden of grateful emotions.—Truly "In pleasant places have our lives fallen." If, borne on angel's wings, you could take flight over the world today, you could find no realm to rival it. A *territory* of two millions of square miles, embosoming immense resources, and capable of sustaining a most dense population. A *mighty munition* of thousands of miles of great waters, protecting us from foreign aggression upon our rights, and foreign interference with our glorious experiment of self-government. A *climate*, judging from its observed influences, as well fitted as any on earth for the finest development of physical and intellectual life. A *soil*, whose fertility, even under all the imperfections of American tillage, has rendered it already the granary of the Old World's starving millions. *Natural scenery* so bold and beautiful, that God seems to have cast our continent in a rarer and nobler mould than all lands beyond the ocean. *Institutions*, civil, literary, religious; yet indeed immature in the necessary imperfection of experiment and infancy; nevertheless, even now boldly challenging the oldest nation under heaven to show us their equals. Our *Literary Institutions*—inferior, confessedly, in the reach and refinement of their individual culture, yet vastly superior in the advantages for education they afford to the multitude, and the universal culture they put forth on the great national intellect. Our *Civil* institutions—confessedly imperfect in the friction and mal-adjustment of a great national experiment; yet even now the envy and admiration of the world for the harmony of their play and the optimism of their productions. Our *Religious* institutions—discordant, indeed, in the bigoted and unseemly antagonisms of Ephraim against Judah, and Judah against Ephraim; nevertheless, this very hour confessedly the only hope of a lost world; in the glorious brotherhood wherein Ephraim and Judah go forth, bearing in generous rivalry, and together, unto the nations sitting in darkness, the gospel's peaceful and everlasting light.

And, my brethren, in these and a thousand other particulars, how wonderfully blessed is the American lot! If the inspired Psalmist, looking forth over his beloved Judea—a land whose whole extent was scarcely one-fifth of our own single state—felt his whole soul swelling in thanksgiving unto God, who had granted to Israel a heritage so goodly—how does it become every American to bring his thank offering gladly, at the survey of an inheritance so vast in extent, so fertile in soil, so friendly in climate, so immense in its resources, so free in its institutions, so matchless in its religious privileges, so sublime in the march of its present progress, so lustrous in the hope and faith of its great future promise—standing out in unquestioned prominence on the map of the world as the most magnificent dwelling-place for man on the face of the globe.

Now by this we are brought to the other aspect of the duty of thanksgiving, viz., *its character,* i. e., to a consideration of the other question to be answered—

HOW *are we to be thankful? What return are we expected to make to the Lord for all these great benefits?*

Now on this point, be it at once and for ever remembered, that thanksgiving is not merely, either an inward emotion of gladness, or an outward expression of lipservice. Our text speaks of "THE SACRIFICES *of thanksgiving."* Such sacrifices were required under the old Hebrew economy. The fed beast was slain, and the incense burnt, and earth's most precious things were consecrated to Jehovah. And though the cumbrous machinery of types has given place to a simpler and more spiritual worship, yet the reality and necessity of constant and costly offerings has not ceased, and even from us God expects "the SACRIFICES *of thanksgiving."*

And the last two clauses of our text explain the nature of those sacrifices: the first, *setting forth our general and national duties;* the last, *our duties special and individual.* Let us consider them in their order:

"The sacrifices of the Lord are a broken spirit:" i. e. *an acceptable thank offering unto God is "a broken heart."*

Now, in respect of nations as well as individuals, it is the designed tendency of God's goodness to lead to repentance. And in view of that constant goodness, God has *a right* to expect of us this day, as a *great* and *glorious* nation, and God *does* expect of us, as a *sinful* and *short-coming* nation, the thank-offerings acceptable in his temple—of *"a broken heart"* and *"a contrite spirit."*

Ah, my brethren, God is a jealous God, and he will not accept a single hour of thoughtless psalm-singing in his temple as an equivalent and atonement for years of hard-hearted forgetfulness and rebellion. This is as true of man in the aggregate as of man in the individual; and it is therefore that there seems to me, in the attitude of our great nation united in the religious services of this day, something almost sublimely and terribly *ludicrous.*

We have termed it a *national* thanksgiving. As it were, the whole people of the land unitedly offering thanksgiving to God in his holy temple. The incense is going up to the skies from ten thousand altars, and millions of voices are joining now in the swell of one magnificent hallelujah. And yet, *actually,* as manifested in the tenor of our national character and conduct, what is our real attitude this day in regard of Jehovah? Why that of a nation trampling God's laws under foot in giant scorn: in the very boldest attitude of blasphemy and defiance. Is there a single precept of the divine law we observe as a nation? Ah, go ponder these precepts at your leisure, and learn how our land is in armed rebellion against Jehovah. Just begin with the first, and go on in their order.

"*Thou shalt have no other Gods before me.*"

And do we keep that law? Alas, no better than the poor idolaters of Israel: for, like them, no sooner are we out of the Egypt of bondage, than we forget the God who hath brought us forth with a strong hand. *Riches*—individual and national wealth—seem to us the Gods who must go before us to our political Canaan; and so we have torn off our individual and national ornaments, our jewels of honor, and honesty, and pure patriotism, and noble philanthropy, which our fathers brought with them through the sea, and have cast them into the raging fire of covetousness, and behold, there have come forth—a calf;—and we have bowed down and worshipped, and men have brought peace-offerings, and children have shouted hosannahs, and maidens have gathered with timbrels and dances, and young men have eaten and drank and rose up to play. "*No other Gods before me!*" Why verily Jehovah might as well have been buried ages agone in the great grave Geology seeks for him, for any influence a thought of his being has in our great national councils, or on our great national operations!

"*Thou shalt not take the name of the Lord thy God in vain.*"

Keep we that law? Alas, so foul are the blasphemies blistering this day in high places, and low places, on the American tongue, that the American Jehovah seemeth nothing else than a great God to *swear by.*

"Remember the Sabbath day to keep it holy."

Keep we that law? Why you cannot petition your legislature against a Sabbath breaking railroad. You cannot send your remonstrance to your great national council against Sunday mails; so that your own letters to beloved ones may not be an offence to God by their Sabbath journeyings, but the nation scoffs at you as priest-ridden. And the American mind seems concentrating all its energies, and arraying all God's great elements unto one great purpose—the wind, and the water, and the very lightnings of heaven, working together to murder God's holy Sabbath, and transport the very carcass thereof out of the universe.

"Honor thy father and mother."

Keep we that law? Why verily there seems nothing in the midst of us like the old-fashioned relation of parent and children. Babes spring from their cradle "young gentlemen" and "young ladies," and the travestied rendering of the old-fashioned commandment is, "Thou shalt obey thy daughter, and honor thy son."

"Thou shalt not commit adultery."

Keep we that law? Alas, it has come to this: that while under the very shadows of our temples pollution flaunts in radiant apparel, and the miasmata of the cities of the plain ascend to heaven, mingled with the incense of our holy offerings. Yet woe be to the indelicate man of God who dares lift a light in the den of the monstrous iniquity; and the priest in his holy robes utters hurriedly and shrinkingly the very words of the precept God thundered from the skies.

"Thou shalt not bear false witness."

Keep we that law? Why, my brethren, there walks not the breadth of this fair land today a creature of our race whose heart hath not bled under the serpent tooth of slander. And the whole newspaper press, which may justly be called our great national tongue, what is it—with many noble exceptions—but a mighty machinery for the utterance of foul calumny, and the martyrdom of personal character?

"Thou shalt not kill."

Keep we that law? Why the blood of men murdered in our

highways and our city streets cries out against us unto heaven. And while we do not say that there may not be wars justifiable by Revelation; and do not believe that the time has yet come when our land should cast away sword and spear, taking only to ploughshare and pruning hook; yet we do believe and do say, that some of our later military enterprises are a bold violation of this divine precept; and while men may call them a vindication of national honor—as if, forsooth, a thief's honor were vindicated by defending his stolen property. Yet, call it what you will, God calls it murder.

"Thou shalt not steal."

Keep we that law? Why I do not know what new synonyms may have been introduced into our political lexicons; but morality has been wont to regard the largeness of the plunder as only enhancing the foulness of the felony; and though men in high places may speak of any high-handed encroachment upon the territory of neighbouring nations as a simple Annexation—*yet God calls it* THEFT!

"Thou shalt not covet."

Keep we that law? Alas! make the best of that desire, and call it what you please—a desire to enlarge the area of freedom, or to diffuse more widely the principles of our peculiar institutions—yet if that desire be, in violation of all the courtesies of national intercourse, and the whole spirit of ancestral negotiations—to wrest, without money and without price, whole islands or provinces from the control of any rightful sovereignty, then God calls it COVETING. Why we are as bad this day as the very haughtiest of the victorious Cæsars; and having cast our covetous eyes over the whole round world that God has made, would fain have God make us another world, that we might covet that also.

Oh, my brethren, what need of demonstration on this most obvious point of our national disregard and violation of all God's commandments; and with our great sinfulness so apparent, did I not say rightly, that our national attitude this day is almost ludicrous in its seeming of bold, and transparent, and most terrible mockery? We are standing up as a mighty people, singing a loud and ambitious hallelujah of thanksgiving unto the Eternal

Jehovah, and yet the while, mark you, like a giant heated with wine, trampling in dust under our feet every commandment of God in mockery and despisal. And do ye think, and can it seem to you that Jehovah will accept, such an offering as an expiation for such wickedness? I tell you *nay!*

"*The sacrifices of God are a broken spirit.*" The "*penitential heart*" of this great people must be laid as "*a sacrifice of thanksgiving*" on his holy altar; else the very smoke of its incense will be an offence to the Eternal One! Nothing less than a national reform, a great national repentance, "*a broken heart*" and "*a contrite spirit*" will be acceptable to Jehovah. God has been very good to us—oh, how wonderfully has he blessed us! It is his great hand, and not the hand of sagacious statesmanship, that has gathered round us this day so many testimonials of the working together of American institutions for the American welfare.

The forth-bringing of the Spirit of our peculiar national liberty was amid the fierce throes of the great Reformation. *God gave it birth.* It was cradled amid the fierce storms of early Protestantism. *God rocked its cradle.* It rose into youth, abandoned and outcast amid the heartless dynasties and despotisms of the Old World. *God* smiled upon it lovingly in its loneliness, and opened for it a Canaan of hope in a new hemisphere. The child grew well and wondrously amid the solitudes of the forest sanctuary; for it was *God* that girded its loins with strength, and fed it with the wild meat of the wilderness. The savages of the desert looked scowlingly upon the boy's slumber, but the shield of their Great Spirit seemed bright on the bosom, and they recoiled from the death-stroke. The enemies of the elder world sent against him their Gath-like champions; yet there met them a youth on the shore with a shepherd's armor, and *God* guided the pebble to the giant's brow. And now, grown mighty in stature and in strength, standing, like the Apocalyptic angel, upon land and sea, his right hand grasping the very lightnings, and his voice speaking to a world with the sound of many waters, he stands—alas! alas! forgetful of all past deliverances, in proud scorn of his Everlasting Protector—tearing God's great statute book into fragments, and trampling it under his giant feet in despisal and blasphemy. And standing thus, I say, do ye think God's anger will be appeased, and God's great love conciliated—Think ye Jehovah will be deceived, and feel himself honored, and smile graciously back, like a carved image at the shrine of a Hindoo, if the gigantic rebel, with his very foot on the broken commandments, just look up into his face for an hour, with a half-glance of reverence, and sing him one psalm as a majestic thanksgiving? Nay, nay, my hearers: I tell you *nay!* Jehovah hath too much respect for his Godhead to accept such a mockery of sacrifice.

The *heart—the great national heart—penitent for sin, broken under a sense of iniquity*—this is what God asketh: this is what God will have. And just so sure as Jehovah is immutable, and holds not with a palsied hand and a heartless power his sceptre over nations, just so surely must America make between two issues her great national election. Either turning from this warfare with Jehovah, and flinging down spear and shield, and laying a penitent and obedient heart all consecrate on God's altar, she must go forth as a divine almoner of good unto a world, on her great national mission of purity and peace to all nations, in the strength of a protecting God, glorious and immortal: or else she must gird herself more mightily for the battle, and, rushing like a giant on the bosses of God's buckler, go down as a reed in the storm's path—*a wreck and a ruin, and a desolation forever!*

Thus much, then, for the fitting character of our *national* thanksgiving.

II. But, passing from this to consider briefly the text in its more individual and personal application, we would have you reflect upon the return God expects *from each one of us by himself,* for these great national benefactions: and enquire *of what nature today should be your sacrifices and mine, of thanksgiving.*

Now the last clause of our text just answers this question:—*"Present your bodies"*—i. e., as the original means—*"Present your entire selves living sacrifices to God, which is your reasonable service."* You will understand at once that we are taking these words only in their national bearings and aspects. Arbitrary as may have seemed at first the whole system of sacrifices among the Hebrews, there was nevertheless a beautiful appropriateness in the selection of special offerings for special occasions. Cain was a *husbandman*, and he brought of the fruit of the ground. Abel was a *shepherd*, and brought the firstlings of his flock; and so is it ever,—our required sacrifices are a *"reasonable,"* an *intelligent*, and *appropriate* service.

Our sacrifices are to be *in kind* the same as our benefactions. Are you thankful for *wealth?* Then your *wealth* should be consecrated to Jehovah. Are you thankful for *health*, or *intellect*, or *children?* Then your *bodily* and *mental faculties* should be used for God's glory, and your *beloved offspring* should be early consecrated unto and trained up for Jehovah. And so as well in the *direction* of the consecration. Our thanksgivings for *religious* privileges should be something for the advancement of religion; our thanksgiving for social beatitudes should be something for the purification and perfection of the great social system. And so in the case under review, our sacrifices of thanksgiving for our great national privileges should be *our bodies*, i. e., our entire selves, consecrated afresh to the perpetuation of our great national interests. We are, therefore, here in God's house today, not merely to lift our voices in hallelujah to God for his great blessings to us as a people, but to consecrate all our powers to his service, and a service whose direction shall be to perpetuate unto our children's children our great social, and political, and religious privileges. Our sacrifices of thanksgiving are to be *our living selves*: and therefore, the solving the question, *What sort of consecration God requires of us individually?* is involved in the solution of this other question, *What kind of men our nation needs in times like the present?*

Now on such a point time would fail me to attempt an extended illustration. Let me suggest a few qualities that should enter as essential elements into our character as citizens, at such times, of such a nation, and leave the wider range of the thought to your own private meditations.

And, *first* of all, not only in its appropriateness to the sacredness of this occasion, but in its absolute importance to the welfare of our country, we observe that the citizen of such a country should be *personally religious*. And this for the twofold reason, that such piety will lead him to love his country more, and will incite him to greater efforts to secure its highest welfare. It will produce in his heart greater love for his country, because it will give him a truer and loftier conception of that country's great design in God's economy of providence. To an unbeliever in the Bible's revelation, all earthly interests end with the present. Ask him what a man is, and he will tell you that he is a compound of bone and blood and animal fibre; or, descending to a finer chemical analysis, that man is, chemically speaking, a mixture of about fifty pounds of carbon and nitrogen with some ten gallons of water. Ask him what a nation is, and he will answer, that it is an aggregate of some twenty or more millions of such organisms, together with certain accumulations of gold, and landed estate, and household furniture, and mines, and cotton mills, and agricultural and commercial machinery: in a word, a simple political organization, whose loftiest purpose is to bring the highest species of animal, with the least misery and in best condition, to an everlasting grave.

But to a *religious being*, man seems an immortal creature, made in God's image and hastening to eternity. And this American nation seems the mighty wheel in the great mechanism of the Evangel, whose movements in the wide economy of God's providence are working out the restoration unto Jehovah's sovereignty of this revolted world. So that a Christian's love for man; and for American nationality, as the highest realization of associated manhood; will be, in comparison with the infidel's, as a love for a marble statue, in contrast with a love for a winged and crowned archangel. And thus, excited to greater efforts for the welfare of his land, religion will equip him most efficiently to labor in behalf of it; for it will send him out to seek the smiles of divine providence in a life of well-doing: striving to outroot in our midst all those great national iniquities which excite God's anger:—and knowing that a religious morality is the only safeguard for free institutions, will urge him so to diffuse the principles of personal and political virtue throughout all our borders, that our national foundations shall rest on righteousness and equity; and the Omnipotent Power that sheltered American infancy so lovingly, shall brood over our loftiest maturity in protection, almightily and forever.

But, passing from this general thought, and descending a little to those particular qualities which enter into the character of a man *nationally,* or in this reference *practically* religious, we observe.

Secondly, That a citizen of such a country, in such a generation, should be eminently *a practical and common sense man.* The days of theories have gone by, and a man that will dream over hypotheses and abstractions, either religious or political, is a dead fossil, make the most of him. Even Genius, so long delighting in roseleaves and reveries, has sprung from the day dreams of its youth, and gone forth to the substantial enterprises of its manhood. Imagination hath itself become practical in its energies. Poetry is not dead, for the word "poet" means a *creator,* and its powers will cease only when a progressive race has attained the loftiest height of its possible strivings. Nor does poetry sleep even. Spite of all sentimental lamentations over the homely utilitarianism of this age, it is, after all, the most poetic and imaginative of all ages. But then imagination hath become practical. Samson hath sprung from the lap of Delilah, and gone forth against the Philistines. The poet, the creator of these later times, brings forth, not day dreams, but realities. The steam engine is a mightier epic than the Paradise Lost. The magnetic telegraph is a lovelier and loftier creation of true poetry than Spenser's Fairy Queen or Shakespeare's Tempest. Genius hath flung the flowery garlands off, and gone forth with a bronzed cheek and a hard hand, to work for a race in the very van of advancing civilization. The age is emphatically common sense and practical; and whether it be in literature, or politics, or religion, the man of dreaming speculations, and subtle metaphysical theories, is at best a mummy of a by-gone generation, and ought to be secluded from the busy world in a glass case, as a remarkable specimen, a monstrous curiosity. A religious man, who would do good to his country, must go forth with his religion as a political light, a great national savor. What we want is, not so much these good men who will mourn over our national degeneracy, and fast over our national sins, and pray for our national prosperity; as those *better* men who will rise up from their fasts and prayers, and go forth and work for the reformation of our national morals, and the securance, through practical righteousness, of our national well-being. The time has come for the diffusion of practical piety into our whole national politics: when the selfishness of personal ambition, and the low intrigues of partizanship, and the whole ruffianism of demagogue statesmanship, should be cast out, and the spirit of honest patriotism and religious principle abide as the conserving presence over the whole national and political economy.

And so we remark, *thirdly*, as that without which all this must be for ever impossible—

That a citizen of such a country, in such a generation, should be emphatically a bold man. I do not mean a blusterer, a man of ruffianism and sham-chivalry, who talks loudly of his honor, and resents insults, and practices pistol shooting, as if to let out a fool's blood were essentially to edify a fool's reputation. By bold men I do not mean swaggerers, Quixotic politicians, who project interventions and invasions, as if the American eagle were only a game and gaffed fighting fowl. No! the land has already enough of them. Our entire political organization, from the lowest ward meeting to the highest national council, swarms with them, till one would almost suppose that every tenth American mother were a giantess, and had brought forth a Goliath.

But we do mean that our age requires men of true and tried courage men who, taking ruffianism by the beard, dare to do right and stand by the right: men who fear neither to explode an old dogma, though adored for centuries, if it be a falsehood: nor to stand by an old custom against a world, if it be honorable and truthful; who are afraid neither to tear the religious vizor from the face of a false reform:—nor to turn the back on the old Sphynx of conservatism in the direction of a true progress; men that, understanding what is best for man's welfare and God's glory, will rend as the flax on a Samson, every *tether* of party or sect, that would withhold them from seeking it; doing their duty manfully themselves, and leaving Almighty God to take care of their reputation.

We observe, therefore, *fourthly*, that of course such men should be *educated* and *intelligent*. We do not mean that they should be literary men or classical scholars : men competent to construe Plato's Greek, and to calculate eclipses delighting to quote Horace at dinner tables, and vapor about old republics on rostrums. University education is well enough in its place. But by *education* and *intelligence*, as needed by our country, we mean *plain common sense* and *a knowledge of human nature;* an understanding of the operation of human governments, and the philosophy of human society an acquaintance with the history of the past, not for the sake of classic quotations and encyclopædian statistics, but for the recorded development therein of a progressive humanity. We want men who understand the wants of our great country, and can take warning from the beacons that blaze over past political disasters. Republican franchises are tremendously fearful prerogatives. The principle of representative *instruction*, yea, even of representative *accountability*, must be forever ignored in our politics, or else every constituency must be educated and intelligent enough to instruct its representatives wisely, and hold them to their account discerningly and justly. The time has come when no paltry cabal of intriguing demagogues should select our executive and settle our national foreign and domestic policy. But when every man who casts a vote should be able not merely to read it and to understand the party it goes for, but to know as well for himself, who ought to govern him, and how he ought to be governed.

Consequently we remark, *fifthly,* that an American in this age should be eminently *a comprehensive* man. I mean a man of large views, and broad sympathies: a man neither of half a heart, nor half an idea: not one of those mongrel and monstrous good men even, who will have slavery to be the only evil on earth, and total abstinence from strong drink the only virtue out of heaven. But men whose minds half an idea cannot satisfy in whose great souls half a world would leave half a vacuum; whose piety is breathed in no sectarian shibboleth; whose patriotism becomes not an exotic if it pass a state line, or cross the Potomac ; whose morality vapors not everlastingly about some one isolated cardinal virtue; whose philanthropy reaches more than one caste or one color; who find in every creature of our race a child of the same great Father, and in every religious sect a fellow band in the same army of Immanuel; and in every tribe and nation under heaven a part of the same mighty world, already redeemed by Divine blood, and bound resistlessly onward to a glorious regeneration.

And as following from this, we remark, *sixthly*, that an American of our generation should be *a man of progress:* a man fit for the nineteenth century, and baptized with its baptism. I do not mean that he should despise old things because they are old. We have enough of such men already, the world knows: men who would put out the sun that they might introduce gas lights, and ignore the principle of physical life, that they might walk and digest food by the application of electricity; men everlastingly parading themselves in the march of mind, though the direction be that of a wandering star—outward bound, into black darkness: as if man's intellect were a high-pressure locomotive, and the true human progress, the swaggering of a blinded giant, yearning to swim stormy seas, and to leap great precipices. But by men of progress I do mean men who see in the mighty movements that go on around us, indications that as yet the race is in the infancy of an oncoming and magnificent manhood: who have no sympathy with old things, just because they are old; who are something more than overslept watchmen—coming out with their lanterns when the east is flashing with the day spring: whose type is not Lot's statuesque wife, looking back everlastingly to Sodom, but the rather Lot himself, with his face lifted to the mountains and urged on by archangels.

Meanwhile, and *seventhly*, we observe that the American of this age should be emphatically *an earnest man*. I do not mean that he should be excitable. We have enough of this, the world knows. The American character, altogether discordant and chaotic in its multiplicity of elements, yet holds all these elements in combination, by the principle of a hot fusion. In the universal furor with which we enter into all opposite and antagonistic pursuits—of politics, and money making; fanatical piety and frenzied scepticism; magnificent church building and expensive theatricals; hero-worship, and hyper-religious bigotry; infidel socialism, and great moral reforms;—the intense excitability of our national youth is a mystery quite incomprehensible by the stolid and superannuated philosophy of the Old World. But then, excitability is not earnestness. Earnestness is not a spasm of furious feeling, but the constant inspiration of a mighty master passion; not a whirlwind on the sea, raising a waterspout, but the steady sweep of a trade wind, rousing the whole sluggish ocean into billowy and resistless life. And this is what our age needs. It is an age such as this lost world never saw before. The three score and ten of our years are worth more in these tides of earnest and efficient life, than the whole nine hundred and sixty and nine years of the old patriarch.

It is a time not to be dreaming and theorizing, but to be up and doing. The fact that American nationality is yet in its infancy, is the mightiest of all inducements unto American Christians and patriots to be mightily earnest in bringing the infant up in the ways it should go. The present generation of men will leave its character as an impress on our national character unto all generations. If the young eyes that are just opening on our national glories look out, in the dimness of age and the gathering darkness of death, upon America, and behold us, a great people—honest and temperate, and law abiding, and united in tried fellowship, and loyal to God in practical obedience to his great statutes, and working efficiently out, in the temporal and eternal interests of the whole world, the manifest purpose of divine providence in our national existence and progress; then there is no influence under the broad heavens that can darken thenceforward our promise, or lift up in our great progress, hindrance or disaster. For the fused metal in the mould will have cooled into iron and hardened into adamant; and the statue in its standing place shall be magnificent and forever.

And from this simple thought, how impressive the exhortation to be at work for our country; to consecrate our living selves as a divine offering in our national service. Earnestness will come too late if it come only to baptize with its spirit the coming generation. Now, at least, nationally is the day of salvation. In the great cradle beyond the mountains sleeps the giant infant, and with all its young Herculean strength, it hath yet the docile heart of earlier childhood. Send now the spirit of true piety and earnest patriotism to mould its forming character for a world's good and Jehovah's glory, and all its future life shall be in the mighty championship of human rights against every ruthless oppression. But leave it alone, as ye are this day leaving it alone, to grow up in the ways of a wild and untutored and infidel youth, in contempt of its God, and careful only for its own personal aggrandizement, and it will spring in its unbaptized strength from that cradle, and rush forth to its destiny trampling all sacred things under its feet, and taking hold like a blinded Samson on the pillars of the palaces of the world, will rock them into ruin, and die itself beneath them.

Now I may not consider this point further, nor detain you on other points longer. This is but a most rude. and imperfect cartoon of the character of the man whom our country and our times need to stand up in our midst as our great national bulwark. You can complete the picture for yourselves, and consider it at your leisure.

The main point we have been considering is, that a fitting sacrifice of thanksgiving for our great national privileges should be, the consecration to God—in endeavours to perpetuate those privileges—of *our whole selves* in such style and stature of moral and intellectual manhood.

Simple gratitude and gladness, we insist on, is not what God requireth. He hath showered upon us, as upon no nation under heaven, the riches of his wonderful and adorable goodness; and a single annual gathering to chant anthems of praise to his name, is not all that such benefactions deserve, or Jehovah requires of us.

My text speaks of *"sacrifices"*—of the giving our whole selves to the great work of our national welfare, as an acceptable and reasonable service. I have not thought to speak to you as religious men, but only as patriots thanking God for your great social and civil beatitudes. And I say such benefactions alone, deserve at every one of your hands sacrifices—contrite spirits bowed unto God for our past unfaithfulness, and new consecration to his service in this great national direction.

Such, and such only, is an acceptable thanksgiving. The custom of this anniversary had its rise with the Pilgrims: of it were they alike originators and examples. And how did they keep it? Oh that I could roll back for centuries the tide of time! That I could close your eyes for a moment on the glories that constitute your present nationality, and open them on those earlier days and ruder forms of Americanism for which our fathers offered so earnestly *their* sacrifices of thanksgiving. Oh that for a little hour these towns and cities, with their mighty population, and their hum of busy life; and these blessed homes, with all their luxurious delights, and their cherished affections; and these sanctuaries, with their Sabbath bells, and their sacred and undisturbed services; and all these countless and invaluable sources of present comfort, and of future hope, which make us this day in our borders the freest, and happiest, and most wonderful and glorious people the world ever saw. Oh! That for one little moment these might all seem to disappear, and in their stead the primeval forest, with its mighty aisles and its awful solitudes, might rise up around us, and we listen as our fathers listened to the rush of the mighty wind, and the roar of the wild beast through the wilderness, and the cry of the red hunter in his path of battle. I should love to stand with you on Plymouth Rock, just as Plymouth Rock was at the landing of the pilgrims, two hundred years a-gone, and show you how at the first, in the midst of all their darkness and trial, American hearts kept festival, and offered unto their God the *sacrifices* of thanksgiving. There they gathered in their lonely and untempled worship. The blonde homes of their childhood, and the precious sanctuaries wherein they had learned to worship Jehovah, were far away in their blessedness and their beauty; and behind was a wide and tempestuous sea, and before them the mighty depths of an untrod and awful wilderness; and beneath their feet the bleakest soil of the rock-bound shore; and above their head the cold and cheerless azure of a stranger heaven: and yet even thus and there, *their thanksgiving* was more than the burst of hallelujah, that pealed startlingly out through the aisles of that rocking forest, and rose exultingly up through the depths of that bending firmament. It was, indeed, the tearful, and yet entire and joyous, laying of their very selves, body, and spirit, and soul, on Jehovah's altar. The offering of themselves and their little ones in an everlasting covenant unto God: the spirit contrite, the heart broken, in acceptable service.

And what, then, oh, tell me what ought to be our thanksgiving for our amazing national beatitudes. Oh beloved, beloved, the spirit of the old pilgrims, of which this day is a memorial, shames our smaller consecration. We do but mock God's great love by any half-hearted offerings. Gathering in his temple to thank him for our great national blessings, and yet not devoting ourselves here to the great political and religious welfare of that nation, we mock Jehovah with lip service. Yes, coming as individuals to offer words of acknowledgement for the great temporal and spiritual mercies of another blessed year, and yet not devoting ourselves with earnestness, yea, with an entire consecration, to God's renewed service, alas! We put open scorn upon our Divine Benefactor. The crown we bring to our Maker is a crown of thorns; the cup of thanksgiving we tender is of the gall and the vinegar.

Thus —thus speaks the text of God's prescribed thank-offerings. It shows me a great temple flung open for sacrifice. The priest stands at the shrine, the fire burnt on the altar; and behold, he that would worship acceptably, brings not of the fruits of the earth, nor of the firstlings of his flocks; nay, he cometh, earnestly bringing, and lovingly offering, *his contrite spirit, his broken heart, his living self,* in everlasting consecration.

And tell me, beloved, will ye offer this day such a reasonable service? Ah, I call on you, and I call on myself, by the memories of God's past goodness, to obey this commandment. How fully does our Heavenly Father deserve this at our hands! In all our forgetfulness he has never forgotten us; in all our disobedience and our scorn, never hath he withheld from us all the depth of his infinite tenderness. And, standing thus this day, amid these wonderful memorials of his abiding affection: surrounded by ten thousand influences making life beautiful and blessed, and yonder crowned immortality attainable through Him who has died for us:—yea, gathered in God's own sanctuary professedly to offer unto him anew these sacrifices of thanksgiving—Oh, I tell you again of God's exuberant and almighty goodness: I point you again to this beloved altar, all kindled with its untorturing and holy fires: and I pray you, in Christ's stead, to lay your own selves upon it, a living sacrifice, with *"your contrite spirit,"* yea, *"your broken heart."*

2

RELIGION IN POLITICS

A SERMON, PREACHED IN THE ARCH STREET PRESBYTERIAN CHURCH, PHILADELPHIA, ON THANKSGIVING DAY, NOV. 24, 1853.

"Render to Cesar the things that are Cesar's."

MARK 12:17.

THESE words, you will remember, are part of our Lord's answer to the Herodians, when they sought to entangle him in the political controversies of the times. I have not, of course, selected them as a theme of usual scriptural and Sabbath-day exposition. You have come here expecting to have your meditations turned into channels beseeming the occasion. That occasion, owing to the agreement of so many of our United States, to celebrate it simultaneously, *is a great National Thanksgiving*. And to turn from its *national* or *political* aspects, and confine ourselves to what are called technically, *"religious"* considerations, were to do evident violence to the proprieties of time and occasion.

And yet, here, at the very outset, are we met with the outcry of the whole howling pack of Infidelity and Irreligion, as they hunt in couples for Christian inconsistencies; claiming meanwhile for themselves, the whole body politic, as a carcass from the shambles, to be cast to their kennel. "Do not bring politics into the pulpit," say these men. "Do not desecrate God's sanctuary. A preacher's business is to minister to the gospel,—God's pure and peaceable gospel. And beware how you desecrate and pollute it by interfering in State matters." Verily, these be most wonderful men! Blaspheming, and reviling, and trampling under their foul feet, for the whole three hundred and sixty-five days of each year, this very gospel; and then overwhelmed with a holy awe, lest some preacher, once in a whole annual revolution, should happen, in their apprehension, to forget its high sacredness. Ah! most astonishing men! Most wonderful zeal for the gospel! Nevertheless, we agree with these men in the assertion that a preacher's business is with the Gospel of Christ, and its religion. only. But, then, what is RELIGION? *Religion, as revealed in the gospel!* Is it an influence so ethereal and unearthly, as to require to be shut carefully from common life into Sabbath days and sanctuaries, lest its white garments should become soiled by a contact with worldliness?

So, indeed, these men tell us. And here we are at issue with them. Religion is not merely a *sentiment,* but a *life.* Not merely *affections God-ward,* but *activity man-ward.* It renders a man not merely a singer of psalms, and a partaker of sacraments, but, indeed, renders him mainly a kind friend, an affectionate father, an estimable citizen, and an honest man. And, therefore, a religion that does not pass beyond the region of technical sacredness, and pervade the whole economy of the social and secular—entering as a living power into the commerce, and the literature, and the magistracy, and the politics of a man—is a mutilated and a monstrous religion, make the best of it.

In the text, our Lord sets forth one great part of Christian duty. It is not only *"Rendering unto God the things that are God's,"* but, as well, *"Rendering unto Cesar the things that are Cesar's;"*—a principle taking as vital an interest in a human, as in the Divine government. And, if you will remember, that in Christ's time the form of civil governments, and their practical administration, were as imperfect as they ever have been; and that the Cesars were, with few exceptions, the veriest of tyrants, you will perceive how emphatically we are taught in the text—*that a man's religious duties are not only unto his God, but as well unto his country;* or, more simply stated—*that a man should carry his Christianity heartily and wholly into the politics of his country.*

And this, then, is the theme of our present meditation. *The duty of every Christian man to go forth in the face of all this infidel outcry, and carry his religion into his politics.*

But, then, what do we mean by *Politics?* Do we mean the paltry chicanery of placemen for power? A working out the low artifices of party in pursuit of offices and spoils? Would we have a Christian minister, or a Christian man, go down to the shameless and undisguised corruption which pervades what is called the peculiar moral code of politics? Would we have such a man sit face to face with the brutal ignorance and ruffian vice, which, hidden from the face of honest men, distribute the parts of the great play, and shuffle, and cut, and deal the dirty cards wherewith partisan gamblers are to play a game, whose great stake is our civil and national welfare? Oh no, no. By Politics, as we would have them mingled in by Christian men, we mean—*"The science of government; that part of ethics which consists in the regulation and government of a state or nation, for the preservation of its peace and prosperity; comprehending the defence of its existence and rights against foreign control or conquest; the augmentation of its strength and resources; the protection of its citizens in all their rights; and the preservation and improvement of their manners and morals;"—and involving therefore every religious, patriotic, and domestic interest that is near and dear to us.* And in such—as the only grand and just idea of Politics—we would have every Christian and good man mingle religiously and wholly. And this, for several reasons, we will now go on to consider.

And this, first of all: *Because such political privileges and blessings as we enjoy, deserve at our hands, as God's great gift, such a public, religious consecration.*

This is indeed the very *"sacrifice of thanksgiving"* we are met in God's house to offer this morning. In all times have religious offerings been *discriminative and appropriate.* The *"husbandman"* has brought of the *"fruits of the ground."* The *"shepherd"* has brought the *"firstling of his flocks."* And one *appropriate* sacrifice of thanksgiving for national and political blessings, is not a mere expression of gratitude in hallelujahs, but a consecration to God of our powers, in a service which shall perpetuate unto children's children our great social, and political, and national privileges.

And surely such privileges as ours deserve such an offering. Truly, a goodly and glorious gift is our American birthright! I know men tell us it is grandiloquent, and in bad taste, and savors of arrogance and vanity, and is wanting in national courtesy and good breeding, to be everlastingly glorying in our *"Eagles"* and *"Star-Spangled Banners,"* and exulting in our national consciousness of political superiority, and our national hope of a sure, and limitless, and magnificent future. But for our very lives we cannot help it. *"How can the children of the bride chamber mourn, while the bridegroom is with them?"* We look at the nations of the old world—gigantic, if you please, but manifestly in the wrinkle and decay of a hoary age; and we look at our own land, just springing in glorious and gigantic youth, with flashing eye and iron sinews, to run such a race of honor and power as the world never saw. And we cannot—shame on us if we could—repress the thrill of pride from the heart, and the exulting words from the tongue, as we think of our own matchless land as it is now and shall be.

Oh! I see it! I see it! A nation that shall be unto all other nations as blessed old Israel was to the Amorite and the Philistine. A nation stretching from ocean to ocean across this whole continent. A nation of freemen, self governed; governed by simple law, without a police or a soldiery. A nation of five hundred millions of people, covering the sea with their fleets, and the land with great cities. First in learning, and science, and arts, and every great product of industry and genius. Ay, and better and higher and holier,—a virtuous and godly people; bound together in one tender and beautiful brotherhood; and luxuriant with fruit and flower, in the bloom and aroma of all Christian graces. The refuge of the oppressed. The protector of the downtrodden. The home of the exile. The terror of despotism. The victorious champion of earth's wronged tribes, against tyranny and outrage. The almoner of God's great grace to the wounded spirit and bleeding heart of a redeemed humanity. I see this, and more than this, in our safe, and dazzling, and limitless future. And my tongue would cleave to the roof of my mouth, if I thought to check the joyous words that swell up in hallelujahs.

We have—we have a magnificent birthright. And what is it all, but God's gift—God's gift through the Gospel? All it is—all it shall be—A RESULT OF CHRISTIANITY—and so all it is, and all it shall be, but *an ascension gift of my Lord* unto his disciples as Christians. And are we then as Christians—as the very men for whom it was projected and for whom it is conserved—are we, as religious and Christian men, to stand back from this glorious nationality, and let fools and ruffians—the filth, and pollution, and offscouring of moral life,—creatures bought and sold for a price, as cattle for the shambles—the wrecks and the rotten-wood that float with every shifting tide of infidel and irresponsible political opinion,

—are we to stand altogether aloof, and let creatures like these mar and mutilate this great national machinery? Shall the insane fanaticism of the North, and Southern sham-chivalry, bluster about the dissolution of the Union, and hew with a fool's axe at the root of the tree of our Liberty? And must I, as a Christian man and minister, not smite them with all the strength God has given me, lest I should pollute my Christianity by a contact with worldliness?

Away with such shallow and hypocritical reverence for Christianity. I owe it to my Gospel and my God, as all the return I can make for a birthright so glorious, to fling myself as a Christian man, into the defence of that birthright, and bare my bosom, as a religious being, to the infidel and accursed tide, that would sweep all those good and glorious things away, as wrecks upon a deluge. And we have come up this day as a rejoicing people, not merely to praise God, but to consecrate ourselves to this very work in a sacrifice of thanksgiving. And go forth in the performance of our Christian work, *"Rendering," not only "to God the things that are God's, but as well rendering unto Cesar the things that are Cesar's."*

Now this leads me to remark, *Secondly,* That as Christian men, we are bound to this duty; *because our nation needs this day for her own preservation, the mingling in her politics of this religious element.*

She needs it, indeed, at all times. On all principles of national and governmental policy. There never has existed—and never can exist a nation, without this pervading element of religious influence. Even the heathen and unenlightened rulers of the elder world, all perceived and acted on this common-sense maxim. History has no record of a single legislator, who attempted to enforce obedience to law on the sole ground of its civil sanctions, and its *temporal* penalties. They universally perceived the insufficiency of all such motives, if unstrengthened by the higher motives drawn from *religious* principles. And if they were strangers to *Divine Revelation*, they found a substitute in their *Mythology*, and applied it as skillfully as might be, to the prejudices of the people. Lycurgus, Solon, Numa Pompilius, Mohammed, and indeed, every legislator at all famed for the wisdom of his institutions; were compelled to have recourse to religion and in fact, derived therefrom their mightiest motives to enforce obedience. And in all this, they acted on an accurate and extensive knowledge of human nature; and with a wisdom that will remain true, so long as sinful passions and affections have such an influence on mankind. For whenever, as in France, the attempt has been made to loose all religious restraints from the minds of a people; then have the whirlwind and the storm, and the great waves dashing into shipwreck, made eloquent proclamation that for the preservation of every great national and political interest, there is need of a GOD, to ride upon the whirlwind and direct the storm.

Now, if all this be evidently true, even of nations held in check by the armed power of despotism, how emphatically must it be true of a free and a self-governing people. Our free institutions were created, and are conserved by the Christian religion. The two grand pillars whereon the whole edifice rests, are—*The Equality of Human Rights*—and—*Brotherly Love equal to Self-Love*. And these great truths we have learned from *the Gospel*. Take them away, and our peculiar nationality is destroyed in a moment. We may still exist, indeed, as a power on the earth. We may exist still *united* under an armed aristocracy, or a great military despotism. Or we may exist a *fragmentary* and *dissevered* power, as a hundred petty and belligerent principalities. And *this* Continent may be parceled out like the old, unto rival conquerors. And our miserable descendants "increase and multiply, and vegetate and rot," in ignorance and bondage. And go forth in fierce feuds, marshaled under rival banners of the Bear, and the Lion, and the Lilies, over the very fields where their fathers marched united and triumphant, and free, under their one glorious Eagle. But sure I am, that if the religious element be taken from our politics, our *Republicanism* is gone, at a stroke, and for ever.

I have not the limits here, to enter into the argument of the manifold advantages to a free people of Gospel piety. Time would fail me, to tell you how it increases national wealth, by diminishing the popular tendency to luxury and extravagance, and by inculcating temperance, and industry, and frugality. How it operates as a mighty check on all those corruptions which weaken a free people. How it educates into truth and tenderness the popular conscience, without which, just laws must remain dead letters in the statute book, unenforced, and without influence. How it destroys all those selfish and sectional animosities, whereunto demagogues always appeal when they would break in pieces great governments. How, in short, by restraining in the human heart the vices that weaken, and regenerating into nobler life the virtues that strengthen, it makes ever manifest the great truth, that free, and prosperous, and united, and *"blessed is that people whose God is the Lord."*

This, and all this, we take in our argument for granted. And based upon it, our plea is, that we are called on as religious men to rise up, and cast more of this salt of godliness into our national character. We are this very day, in God's sight, going backward from our old moral landmarks. We are even now as a nation swarming with drunkards, and Sabbath-breakers, and profane swearers. The emissaries of the old foreign Ecclesiastical despotism—the tool and the mainspring of all European despotism—are among us, foul and frequent as locusts of the Nile on the green things of God's husbandry. Fanatics at both ends of the Union are toiling might and main at their fiendish work of dismemberment. Our national compact itself, founded on the compromise of local interests, exposes us more and more to sectional jealousies and competition, and to the heartless assaults of ambitious agitators of popular passions. We are entering confessedly on stormy times. New forms of infidelity, and political atheism, and false philanthropy, are rising in strength in the midst of us. While Christian men stand aloof, fools are heaving at the pillars of our great national temple. And the whole tribe of the Philistines are twisting at the cords, while God's Samson sleeps in the lap of the Enchantress. It is time, high time, then, for Christian championship to awake. By the men of the present generation is the great question to be settled, whether there can be maintained in the midst of us, enough of an enlightened and tender moral sense to keep us a virtuous, and free, and united people, in face of all these assaults of infamy and irreligion. By the Christian men that now worship in God's temples is the uncertain problem to be solved,— Whether the light of liberty that shines on us this day, is of a sun bounding gloriously from the Orient, or already sinking sadly and slowly to the sepulchral clouds of the west. And, therefore, the call comes to us loud as the voice of prophets in the glorious days of Israel of Judah, to stand forth against the enemies of hearthstone and altar for our God and our country; casting religious salt into the polluted fountains of our national conscience; pouring religious light along the troubled seas of our national politics; *"rendering unto Cesar the things that are Cesar's, as surely as unto God the things that are God's."*

And by all this are we brought to remark, Thirdly: That we are urged to this duty *by our regard for all the great interests of the Race and the World.*
Disastrous as would be the destruction of our peculiar nationality in regard of ourselves—more disastrous and appalling still would it prove in regard of the human race everywhere. Speaking only *civilly* and *politically,* and there is no sign of hope for a world's popular liberties, if our republicanism fail us. Unto America are turned this day the regards of all nations, as the last practical experiment of popular self-government. From America goes forth this day the only light of hope to fall on the heart of an oppressed race as a joy and a consolation. *For* this great work were we raised up, and this great work *are we doing.* Talk as men will about the sanctity of international law, as preventing on our part with the old world, interference and intervention; yet spite of it all, with the whole power that is given us we are *interfering* and *intervening.* As surely and constantly as the blazing sun interferes with the prowling night-beasts, are we interfering with the oppressions and despotisms of the world's farthest nations. There is not a Cabinet in Europe that does not look upon this great Republic as the real author of all the revolutionary movements on that whole broad continent; that does not plot and pray for our ruin, as the mighty disturber of the peace of their haggard and hoary oppressions, and the only formidable and gigantic obstacle to the perpetuity of their foul despotisms hereafter and forever. The grand and simple principle that unites us as a free people, is a principle actively and essentially at war with the whole spirit of European nationality. And we are this very morning, by the never-ceasing and omnipresent influences of our free institutions, more powerfully and offensively interfering with the despotic policy of those European Empires, than if a hundred thousand armed men stood marshaled under the American Eagle on the banks of the Danube, and our whole naval power, three times told, were cruising on those European seas, sweeping a despot's fleets from the waters, or thundering with a thousand guns against the bulwarks of a despot's capital.

We are interfering, and, what is more, we are bound to be interfered with!

We may let European despotisms alone—and, doubtless, we shall let them alone, as to all armed aggression—but then the plain and simple fact is, *they will not let us alone.* It is a mistake altogether to imagine that the whole popular sympathies of the old world are with popular freedom; or that the masses of those oppressed nations are prepared for, or ambitious of, our free institutions. The political movement of the whole East is backward manifestly to feudalism. Those favored empires; that with a constitution limiting the monarch, we have rejoiced over as already half free; and gloried in as marching in the van of advancing civilization; are already in the wane and wrinkle of dotage and decrepitude. Great Britain is tottering already under the hideous burden of a bloated aristocracy; and the Lion that once roused itself to shake the world with its roar, if a breath of offence stirred the folds of its banner, now crouches tamed and spaniel-like at the tread of the great Eastern despotism. France, that looked unto the world so like a winged creature of liberty, by a monstrous recoil has gone back to a chrysalis, and is bound, as God lives, to come forth a worm again. Spain is already a dead thing in the grave; and Austria, that fouler thing than a despotism—the despotic tool of a despot. And if princes seem building for freedom and the race on the banks of the Rhine, and along the blue Italian seas, they build, alas, on a volcano—the crater already ablaze, and the whole mountain shaking.

Yonder continent has indeed this day but one united—one advancing and absorbing power; and that the great Northern, and naked, and unmitigated military despotism. A despotism, too, be it ever remembered, not resting in, and trusting to, popular ignorance, but where industry is stimulated; and the arts encouraged and fostered by all possible appliances; and commerce steadily and strenuously advanced in every possible direction; and where the subjects are not held in an unwilling bondage, but are the rejoicing and enthusiastic abettors of despotism. And thus firm on her foundations, and terrible in her might, is Russia aspiring and advancing to the conquest of the world. And prescient of the far future, she sees in the whole wide world today but one mighty obstacle in her path—this young Republic—the everlasting light of our popular freedom in the dark places of tyrants. And so the momentous signs of the times are now proclaiming a coming conflict, when amid such terrors of antagonism as the earth never saw, there shall go on under the rival banners of the Bear and the Eagle, the last great battle for freedom and the world! But if in all this we read not aright the programme of the struggle, sure we are, at least, that the great conflict of this and the coming generation will be of Freedom against Tyranny. And sure we are, therefore, as well, that in the preservation and perpetuity of our free institutions there rest the only hopes of oppressed humanity; and that in the terrible hour that is coming on all people, our own civil and religious liberty must furnish the only championship for man's heart and soul against the despotisms of the world.

Now, if to this thought of our *civil and political influence* upon the nations, you add the other thought, of the *religious* AND EVANGELICAL *influence* we are manifestly designed to exert upon a lost race, the thought under consideration will appear most impressive. Even if for the civil franchises of mankind there were to rise up other than American championship; yet whence, save from the American *Church,* can go forth the light of a redeeming gospel to the dark places of the earth? If there be any philosophic reading of a historic Providence, then from *God's past and present dealings with us as a peculiar people,* and *from the evident signs of the times,* as displaying the powerlessness of all other nations for evangelizing a world; from these, I say, is the truth as apparent as an oracle of Revelation, that unto us, as stewards of the grace of God, is awarded the magnificent service of sending forth a full and free gospel over all the benighted continents of our globe—that from our beloved land, glorious in its scenery, and its broad boundaries, and its new growth of civilization, and its loftier type of civil and religious manhood, the Angel that hath the everlasting gospel to preach, is already pluming the wing for flight over the nations; and that the hopes of the race, therefore, not merely for *Time,* but for *Eternity!* Not merely for *Earthly Freedom,* but for *Immortal Glory,* do, under God, suspend themselves upon the perpetuity of our Union, and the permanent progress and development of our free institutions. So that to give up our national character to the spoiler, were not only to quench every light on the altars of Liberty, but to quench for the world the fires on God's altars—to shiver the great wheel in the mechanism of a triumphing Evangel—and so to cast the race back, not merely to the iron thralldom of despotism, but to the more monstrous bondage of superstition and infidelity.

And I say you have only to remember all this, and consider it, and you will get an impression of the unspeakable importance to a whole world of mankind, of the perpetuity and progress of our free institutions, which will make you jealous with an immortal jealousy of any stain upon our national character as a wisely-governed, and intellectual, and moral, and religious people; and send every man of us to stand proudly up in his place as an American Christian and patriot; carrying our piety as an inspiration into the duties of our citizenship, and lifting up in great faith Christ's redeeming Cross as a bulwark more powerful than all else to roll back the tides of iniquity, and corruption, and infidel legislation, and the whole wild deluge of ruffian and irresponsible politics, which would sweep all these glad and glorious things away as wrecks upon the waters. For we shall perceive how God himself has linked all the great interests of our race with these American politics, so that in this whole matter, by *"rendering to Cesar the things that are Cesar's,"* we are most surely, as well, *"rendering unto God the things that are God's."*

Now this leads me to remark, *Fourthly,*—and lest we should weary you,—*Finally:* That we are urged to this duty *by a due regard for our* RELIGION *itself.*

We have already said that it is a false notion of religion which supposes it to be polluted, and thus injured, by every contact and concern with merely worldly interests. And we now go further, and declare, that we should do very much to honor and magnify Christianity, were we to carry it forth as an energizing principle— yea, as a vital and controlling power—into our whole practical life as American citizens.

You are all of you familiar with the infidel clamor of the times— *that the Christianity of the Gospel has proved a great failure.* That while it did good service as a pioneer of civilization, and a rudimental teacher of the alphabet in the great school of humanity, nevertheless, that now, when the race has progressed from its nomadic life, and the great man-child has flung off its swaddling bands, and mastered the rudiments of knowledge, and entered the higher forms of intellectual culture—that now Christianity must surrender its great charge to the higher teachings of Philosophy, and be flung aside as an effete engine, whose work has been accomplished, and whose day gone by. And we are fain to confess, that this outcry is not without plausible arguments—arguments drawn with irresistible force from the narrowness of the field, and the feebleness of the power, wherein professing Christians have themselves developed their Christianity. For we most frankly admit, that a religion that remains shut away from the common business of life, into the pure regions of spiritualism, as a thing of ecstasies, and sentiment, and psalm-singing : appearing statedly on Sabbath days, and in sanctuaries, and seen no more abroad during the six days of the secular and the social—We confess, I say, that such a religion, be it Christian or Pagan, is altogether out of place, and imbecile amid the restless and earnest tides of an age and a life like our own.

But then quite as confident I am, that if Christianity have not hitherto acquitted herself to the full of all her secular and social duties; the secret lies not in her inadequacy to the work; but in the smallness of the sphere which Christians themselves have assigned her, and the class and kind of labor they have committed to her hands. Sure I am, at least, that as an intellectual and moral system, Christianity was designed for all nations and generations; and is divinely adapted to the exigencies of all nations and generations. Her credentials to our Race, are not merely as a fitting and tender nurse for its unsteady infancy; but more fittingly still, as the earnest tutor of its hot youth; and the glorious guide and guardian of its magnificent manhood.

Embodying, as Christianity does within itself, the mightiest and most practical moral influences to be found in God's universe. And revealed as the master contrivance of Infinite Wisdom, to restore man from his ruins, and bring back a wandering world to the light and the liberty of God's own children. It has only to be inaugurated in its place of rightful authority. Only to be brought forth from the cloisters of contemplation, and the chairs of academic speculation. Only to take hold in its strength, on the great practical questions of the race and the age,— and the scoffing world will acknowledge as they see, that an influence so long despised as a thing only busy with creeds, and ceremonies, and sacraments, can yet work gloriously and with a strong arm, as man's practical benefactor—that its fostering is of every influence which makes up civilization—that its calling is unto the patronage of the arts, and sciences, and literature, and commerce, and trade—that its place is as truly in the cabinet as in the conventicle, in the senate-chamber, as at a sacrament—that it can acquit itself vigorously of all Social and Civil, in a word, of every secular duty; and is gloriously equal to all the exigencies of the times, and every possible emergency of the day and the generation.

And we say, such an inauguration to a high sway over things merely temporal, Christianity deserves today, at the hands of its disciples. It deserves to be justified openly from the suspicions of the world, that it is after all, but a low, and paltry, and driveling fanaticism. It deserves to be brought abroad from the closet and cloister, to enter as a living power into the philosophy, and speculation, and the earnest life, and all the high enterprise of an uprising Humanity, *"Rendering unto Cesar the things that are Cesar's,"* as steadfastly, *"as unto God the things that are God's."*

Religion has, indeed, its most glorious place in the recesses of the redeemed spirit, and an honored throne in the Sanctuary, with its praises and sacraments. It is the joy and glory of its great prerogative, that it abides in the sancities of the heart, and the household; and brings heavenly comfort and peace to the secluded hut of the poor child of want; and sits in seraphic love at the hushed bedside of the dying. Nevertheless, it is its other prerogative, and should be its joy and glory as well, to take care of man's *temporal* interests as wisely as his spiritual. And, walking abroad as the conserving spirit of the day and the age, to pour its divine light upon the speculations of philosophy; and to bathe with its heavenly dews man's learning and genius; and to lay its strong hand on the energies of trade, and of commerce; and to lift up its heavenly, yet resistless voice, in the halls of legislation; and to stand in meek, yet mighty glory, in the haughtiest presence of monarch and noble; and to fling from its radiant loveliness a resistless moral power, that shall pervade the world's arts, and sciences, and literature, and jurisprudence, and economy of politics, and machinery of government. *"Rendering as wisely and as well, unto Cesar the assisting tribute that is Cesar's, as unto God the adoring worship that is God's."*

Christianity, I say, *deserves* this honor at our hands. What we are as a nation this day, we owe, under God, to its blessed influences. Our very *National existence* is a miracle of the Gospel. The Genoese navigator and the German reformer,—the one opening a new world; the other evolving a new Humanity to enter in and occupy,—were rocked in the same cradle, twin-children of Evangelism. The strong sifting of all nations for God's chosen seed, to scatter in glorious husbandry on this virgin soil, was a Gospel winnowing. That almost heavenly refinement of taste and love; that found earth's noblest kingdoms but an intolerable wilderness, without a pure altar, and an open Bible; but could make a blessed home with the storm, and the sea-eagle, and a God to worship; was an inspiration of the Gospel. That patriotism and courage, and self-sacrificing toil, which battled fearlessly unto death for hearthstone and altars, were all upshoots from the Gospel. The matchless wisdom of a Constitution, whose great central truth of *"human equality"* was in direct antagonism to all principles of known governments, and startled the old despotisms of the world as the light of a coming judgment; was a direct revelation of the Gospel. Yes, and then all the subsequent beatitudes, which, as if flung from angel wings, have been scattered along all our path to national immortality—our accumulating wealth—our enlarging commerce—our vast increase of population—our progress in arts and manufactures—the magnificence of our practical charities—the increasing harmony and strength of our political machinery—the enticing beauty which our land bears today, to far away nations amid the sobbing agonies of their downtrodden children—and the glory, and honor, and power, which the world accords today, to the wing of the American Eagle, in its flight through the skies. This, all this, and more than this—all, in short, which makes the American eye flash with pride; and the American heart beat with rapture; and gathers us this very hour in God's temples with loud hallelujahs of praise, an exulting and thanksgiving people; we owe under God to our glorious Christianity.

And, amid such results of magnificent accomplishment, CHRISTIANITY DESERVES *at our hands,* a justification from the slander of the infidel, that it is at best an imbecile and worn out and dreamy sentimentalism. It deserves to be lifted up as the conservator of the glories it has created; and since by the breath of its inspiration, life's great ocean has been roused from the dead calm of. ages into billowy and exulting play; it deserves to be sent forth in a divine glory, visibly to ride upon the whirlwind and direct the storm. Christianity *claims,* AS A DIVINE RIGHT, the acknowledgment in the face of the universe, that *"while it renders carefully unto God the things that are God's, it renders as carefully unto Cesar the things that are Cesar's."*

Such then, most imperfectly put, are some of the reasons why American Christians should carry their religion with their duties of citizenship. That they have not done so hitherto is a fact which needs no argument. So manifestly devoid of all Christian principles is the whole moral code of American politics, that to prove a man positively religious or even severely and Puritanically a moral man, were to destroy all his chances of political popularity and preferment. And this, too, at a time when the great balance of power in this matter is confessedly in the hands of the virtuous and religious. But when, strange to tell, these virtuous and godly men; either from unfounded fear of dishonoring their religion. by so earthly a contact; or, from an unutterable contempt of the whole business of such desecrated politics; have stood in their dignity aloof from it altogether. Leaving the matter of popular nominations for office, and the arrangement of platforms, and the projection of great national and state *policies*, and, in short, the whole real working of our great political machinery—(and mark me here—I am not speaking, nor will I be misunderstood as speaking evil of our Rulers, and Magistrates, and Representatives; in regard of whom religion itself enjoins reverence; and who, for aught we know, are models of all that is honest, and pure, and lovely, and of good report. But I am speaking of that ubiquitous class of irresponsible, yet efficient men, whose calling is to pull the wires of partisanship, and mingle the seething elements in the great political cauldron; and who virtually, at least, color if they do not control our whole national politics)—leaving it all, I say, to the moral outcasts of our social system; to men, bankrupt of all virtuous reputation; to wily demagogues, who would flatter the foul fiend for the sake of his influence; to fawning menials, who would crouch at a despot's feet for the smile of his patronage; to blustering ruffians, whose only elements of moral power are blows and blasphemies; to vaporing patriots and brawling philanthropists who would freely barter their country and their race, and their own souls, for the profits of an office or the outfit of an embassy; to the blind fools of fanaticism, who would trample the Union and Constitution under their feet, and deluge this blessed heritage with flames and blood, and bring down upon their own wives and little ones a worse than Ethiopian bondage, for the sake of the phantom of an abstract and selfish principle, whose practical outworking were a cruelty and a curse. Leaving it, in short, I say, to such things as these—to the low, mercenary, Machiavellian herd that gather in the dens of darkness and sin—to project the programme and distribute the parts of that great play, whose sublime issues are; the glories of our country, and the welfare of a world.

This, and worse than this, is the sad truth about the matter. Pardon me, my brethren, that I feel constrained to stir up with so foul a picture your pure minds by way of remembrance. I confess that to a refined taste it is coarse and revolting. But the *pitch was on the canvass! I but touched it and am defiled.*

Nevertheless, the picture is neither caricature nor exaggeration; but the sorrowful truth colored too faintly. And all this, too, at a time when as sincerely as ever before private virtue and morality are revered and honored throughout the land; when the great mass and majority of our population; north and south; east and west; of every party, and every state; are proverbially honest, and intelligent and law-abiding, and patriotic, and earnestly desiring the application of a pure and religious morality to the whole complex machinery of government. And when it needs only a religious courage and consecration, to take hold on those great interests; and this whole vampire brood, that fatten on the nation's heart would hide their heads in shame, as serpents from a sun-burst.

It is time, then, we say—high time that religious men roused themselves to a sense of their political responsibilities. Moralists, indeed, tell us—from the pulpit, sometimes—that Christianity claims no power over a State, and no official connexion with it. But what, I pray these men, is a State? *An abstraction—an idea!* No, indeed! Simply an aggregate of individual and immortal men; and with every one of these men Christianity should have an immortal connexion; and over them it has a claim, pre-eminent and eternal. It is time, then, that the precise bearing of Christian principles upon legislation, and the administration and general policy of our government, were understood and acted on. Not that Christianity may be established by law; but that our laws may be established by Christianity. Not that the Gospel asks alliance with the State, but that the State sorely needs the conserving influences of the Gospel. It is time that Christianity came abroad from its cloistered sanctity, to acquit itself of its great *civil* and *national* responsibilities. And spite of the whole howling herd of infidelity and irreligion, (who in this, are only true to their instincts, and do after their kind)—it is time for Christian men, and Christian ministers—now so busy with the minutiae of *private* and *minor* immoralities. Uttering fierce denunciations against slight heresies in a man's creed, and trifling inconsistencies in man's conduct. Seeing well to it, that a little child does not laugh loud on the Sabbath, and that a man's face does not graciously smile at any questionable amusement. Loud in the outcry of "heresy" and "hypocrisy" against men, honestly striving to walk in the ways of godliness. I say it is time for such Christian ministers and men, to walk forth to a broader field, and to a loftier standpoint; to cast an indignant glance over our civil and national short-comings; to launch the fiery denunciations of our blessed Redeemer, as "serpents" and "vipers" against irresponsible placemen and their unprincipled tools; and to pour the glorious light of the Gospel of God, into the whole hideous den of political abominations.

And this, then, is our religious business this day, in this temple of Jehovah. We have come up, with one common thank-offering unto God, for our great national beatitudes. Beatitudes so wide and so wonderful, that the eye moistens and the heart bounds, as we contemplate our great birthright. God's great gift to us, not merely as men, but mainly as Christians. For, whatever we are, or may be, we owe to the Gospel. All our social and national influences—all the canvass of our commerce—all the enterprise of our market-places—all the breadth and wealth of our husbandry—all the machinery of our trade, and the pomp of our great cities. All! all! have grown up to us under the shadow of this Cross, and owe all their goodness, and glory, and power, to the sprinkled Blood from Mount Calvary. And coming with some sense of the greatness of our blessings—God claims at our hands, as the only fit *"sacrifice of thanksgiving,"* such a consecration of ourselves to his service, as shall send us abroad in our strongest endeavors to keep the blest fires of liberty bright on these altars;—and transmit, undimmed of one glory, our free institutions to an hundred generations that shall come after us.

Such a religious consecration can, and can alone, save us from the tides of infidelity, and corruption, and moral death, that are rolling in upon us. Let Christian men go bravely forth, carrying their religion as a light, and a power, and a conserving influence, into our political machinery, and nothing out of Heaven can impede or weaken us. Who speaks in fear of *foreign aggression?* Why, sirs, Gibraltar is not more steadfast and secure against the dash of its sea-surges, than we against the wildest assaults of the banded war-power of the world's every despot. Who talks about *"disunion"*—and the *severance of this great national confederacy?* Why, sirs! the fanatic and the fool who thinks to accomplish it, might better think to sever the mighty bond that unites the Solar system, and blow with his foul breath those glorious stars away that march in God's great law of gravitation round the blaze of the sun.

Ay! ay! If borne radiantly abroad as the light and the savor of our earnest lives, along the vales, and by the streams, and athwart the great hills of our blessed land, this heavenly Gospel have free course and be glorified; then, spite of every storm upon the seas, and every cloud upon the firmament, are our foundations as the everlasting mountains, and our blessedness as the immutable love of our Heavenly Father. And so, upon the sincerity of our religious consecration on such festal days as this, depend, under God, these momentous issues.

Oh! we are here today, not merely to unite in a great national hallelujah, but to work out a great prophetic problem in the face of the universe. To bring forth the data for the solving the solemn question.— Whether this national hallelujah of thanksgiving hath to God the character of a *birthday gratulation* over our luxuriant youth—or a *funeral wail* over our already smitten and departing glories.—Whether these shadows that brood today along our national landscapes, are passing away from a *rising,* or lengthening and deepening with a *descending* sun.—Whether the giant Babe which God's hand, amid tempests and storms, has rocked into majestic strength in this great cradle of the West: imbued with the gentle spirit of the Gospel; and filled, as to its great heart, with Divine Love; shall come forth to its earnest manhood, sandaled to walk the round world as a deliverer; and safe, therefore, under God's own shield, to mount to the loftiest summit of national glory. Or, alas! alas! whether, with the madness of a fool's atheism within it, shall leap from that cradle like a roused giant, to rush in mad strength on the bosses of God's buckler, and perish as a reed in the crashing fire of God's thunderbolt.

3

POLITICS IN RELIGION

A THANKSGIVING SERMON DELIVERED IN THE ARCH STREET PRESBYTERIAN CHURCH, PHILADELPHIA ON THURSDAY MORNING, NOVEMBER 23, 1854.

"And render to God the things that are God's."

MARK 12:17.

We have thus divided the verse, because, in our last Thanksgiving service, we considered more particularly its first clause, and we propose now to consider particularly its last.

The whole passage is a fine specimen of the inimitable practical wisdom of our Divine Master, uttered as an answer to some artfully disguised enemies, who sought to entangle him in the political controversies of the times. They came to him in the beguiling attitude of sincere inquirers after truth, and addressed him in the honeyed words of a most sagacious flattery. And they said —

"Master, we know that thou art true, and carest for no man: for thou regardest not the person of men, but teachest the way of God in truth: Is it lawful to give tribute to Caesar, or not?

"Shall we give, or shall we not give? But he, knowing their hypocrisy, said unto them, Why tempt ye me? bring me a penny, that I may see it.

"And they brought it. And he saith unto them, Whose is this image and superscription? And they said unto him, Caesar's.

"And Jesus answering, said unto them, Render to Caesar the things that are Caesar's, and to God the things that are God's."

Now this answer is altogether matchless in its consummate sagacity. It establishes the limits, regulates the rights, and distinguishes the jurisprudence of the two great governments — the earthly and the heavenly. The image of the earthly potentate on the coin, denotes that the things which that coin represents belong specially to his earthly jurisdiction; while the image of the Invisible God, stamped on the immortal soul, denotes that its immortal faculties and powers belong specially to His higher jurisdiction and are to be employed in His higher service. To temporal governments man owes obedience and tribute: obedience to its laws, tribute unto the expenses of its maintenance;—while to the Divine government men owe as well the whole heart and soul in reverential love—the whole mind and strength in religious consecration.

But, then, over and above this great and matchless aphorism of obedience, there is apparent in the purpose of our Lord — *a divided application of the broad truth to the two antagonistic classes of mankind before him.* To the *Pharisees,* who holding their Roman rulers in abhorrence were stirring up the people to refuse the tribute money, his expostulation is, *make not God's holy religion a pretence to justify sedition*— "Render to Caesar the things that are Caesar's." While, on the other hand, unto the *Herodians,* who out of compliment to their conquerors were disposed to do things forbidden by their Divine law, his expostulation is — *sacrifice not religious principles to the will of worldly rulers* — "Render to God the things that are God's."

Now on the former occasion we insisted entirely and at much length, upon the first clause of this answer, striving to show that all true Christians had a duty to perform towards their earthly and temporal governments, and are bound to *carry their religion into politics.*

We turn now to consider, at some length, the converse of this — as set forth in the last clause of the answer — *that all men, apart from their Christianity, and regarded only in their political character, have as well a great duty to perform toward the heavenly and divine government, and are hound to carry their politics into religion.* Then, we showed that the Pharisees should "render to Caesar the things that are Caesar's." Now, we desire to show that the Herodians as well, should "render unto God the things that are God's." *"Religion in Politics"* was our former theme, *"Politics in Religion"* is our theme to-day.

But here, as before, we must keep distinctly in mind the true definition of *politics.* We use the word only in its widest and noblest sense, as denoting the practical science of government; or rather, we use it here in its last analysis, as denoting positively the *government itself.* We wish to show that a man's political power and influence should be exerted, in all proper ways and to the fullest extent, in support of that religion which constitutes the tribute man owes unto God. And this definition we wish you to carry with you through our argument, else you will be quite sure to misunderstand us most sadly.

There is a common, and indeed a popular sense, in which to carry *politics into religion* is a curse and a sore wickedness. Take the word politics in its vulgar and most perverted meaning, as denoting the paltry chicanery of placemen for power — the low artifices of prostitute and false statesmanship for office and spoils — and the man who would seek its coalition with any great moral and religious interests deserves at our hands an indignant rebuke, and will, at God's hand, surely meet a most sore retribution. And yet, alas for us! just such coalition is frequently sought by good men in the midst of us. Yea, more emphatically alas! even *in the sacred desk* it finds advocates and patrons.

I need not tell you that it has come to pass in these latter days, that these standing places of God's messengers to a ruined world, become ofttimes the mere platforms for political harangues. These altars of our God, where the broken heart is demanded as a sacrifice to Jehovah, become ofttimes only "seats of custom," where the worldly tribute is rendered to Caesar. The precepts of the Divine law, thundered from Sinai; the promises of the Gospel issued in the death-cry from Calvary; alas! they are all set aside and forgotten, that these ambassadors of God may discourse political declamation upon moot-points that divide our great political parties. Either because these men find the duties of their sacred profession so light and their consequent leisure so abundant ; or because they regard the care of souls so trivial a concern in comparison with the general enlightenment of society on these political questions; or, it may be, because they regard themselves as men of such prodigious powers and special inspiration, as to make it their extraordinary call to leave to their humbler and less gifted brethren the care of the ark in the fields of Bethshemish, while they strive about the golden mice with the lords of the Philistines.

Certain we are that for some reason, into their religion, such as it is, they carry some of the veriest abominations of ruffian and radical politics. Their pulpits become platforms, where all questions of practical morals are discussed as side issues with some aim of the demagogues. The cross of Christ is taken down from its high place, as the crowning glory of the sanctuary, and in its stead — as an engine of reform — is lifted the ballot box; and the popular passions are lashed into storm, that with their suffrages as freemen they may carry a Maine Law or defeat a Nebraska bill. And with this advocacy and patronage in the Church's high places, it has, not marvelously, come to pass that the edification of the audiences should be after their kind. Certain we are at least of the fact, that many a Christian man looks today to the foulest machinery of partizan politics as an efficient auxiliary in a reformation of morals. Temperance — moral reform — religious education — universal brotherhood — indeed all things that are true, and pure, and lovely, and of good report, are — to speak technically — by a species of moral log-rolling, linked as twin issues with the foulest aims of ruffian demagogues seeking preferment and place. Nay, verily, alas ! these heavenly moral virtues, that as white robed angels on radiant wings should be all unsoiled by dust and soaring sweetly in God's sunshine, are harnessed side by side with bank charters and tariff provisions, to drag the chariot of some unprincipled placeman into honor and power.

    I am not, of course, condemning, nor will I be misunderstood as condemning, any conscientious endeavor to legislate crime out of a community. Oh, no. I hold it to be my right (and I will not insult your understandings by attempting proof of such a truism) I hold it to be my right, nay, I hold it to be my most bounden duty, to seek all honorable legislation to aid me in the suppression of popular iniquities. Intemperance, — oppression, — sabbath-breaking, — profaneness, — these, and the whole great catalogue of flagrant immoralities, are as very felonies on a man's civil rights, as are highway robbery, or adultery, or murder. And as an integral part of society for whose widest welfare the government is only created, I can come to that government, not asking as a favor, but claiming as a right, that it protect me and my beloved ones from such foul felonies on my interests.

    But then, as Christian freemen, in a high-minded and manly way, to seek legislative action in maintenance of these great interests, this is one thing — but another thing is it altogether, to enter into foul partnership with political partisans for the sake of such legislation — making temperance and Sabbath-keeping, and the Bible in schools, and all or any great practical morality twin-measures, co-ordinate and co-equal issues, with the charter of a Sabbath-breaking rail road, or a swindling banking house, or a monopolizing gas company. The first is only a goodly, and lawful, and noble *carrying the grand science of government into religion;* while the last is manifestly an ignoble carrying of *politics* — politics in its most vulgar and abhorrent sense, with all its monstrous shapes and gigantic abominations— *politics* — *politics into religion!* Oh, no, no. The beautiful chariot of God's moral government — wheel within wheel, all lustrous with the colors of the beryl of heaven — is not to be dragged triumphantly on by a team of foul monsters. The strong and stormy passions of bold and brutal ruffianism are not things to be appealed to in an attempt to spread abroad over God's lost world the glory of a high and a heavenly regeneration.

Taken in its common and most perverted meaning, and politics should be held an outcast from the whole household of religion. But in the high sense already insisted on, politics should be welcomed, and indeed claimed, as a handmaid of religion.

What we mean, then, by the proper carrying of *politics into religion,* is the duty of the political power, as embodied in government, to take care, in its lawful sphere and exercise, of the interests of religion. And in discussing this subject I have no time nor occasion, as surely I have no taste, for entering at length into the great church and state question. We will admit at the very outset that of all unions abhorrent to an unseared conscience, this church and state union is the most monstrously abhorrent. We will go, indeed, on this point the whole length of the rankest infidel legislator, admitting most frankly that human governments were never designed for the propagation of Christianity. They were created for a different end and a different object; and to strive by any false logic to make the salvation of men's immortal souls an end or an object of human governments, is as foolish as to pretend that the soul's salvation is an end for which we charter a bank, or a hospital, or a college. The corporation of a hospital, or a bank, or a college, may indeed have peculiar facilities for propagating the Gospel; nevertheless they were never designed for any such purposes. And just so of government. Its grand end is, beyond all controversy, *the protection of the temporal interests of person and property.* And although a man's immortal interests are confessedly vastly more important than his mortal interests, yet it is after all the mortal interest of which the human government takes care, leaving the immortal interests in care of the higher government of Jehovah.

Now all this we admit — nay, all this we insist on. Temporal prosperity is, and must be, the grand end of all earthly government. Nevertheless, if it appear, as it surely will appear to every philosophic mind, that the Christian religion is itself at least a mighty mean of this temporal prosperity, then, as an efficient auxiliary in the attainment of its great end, should the earthly government, in its lawful influence and sphere, take earnest care of the interests of such a religion. And so the right, and indeed the duty, of human legislation, — not perhaps as its great end, but as a mean unto that great end, — to guard carefully the vital interests of Christianity, can never be questioned by any thoughtful and honest man, whether he be truly a Christian, or only soundly a philosopher.

The "Pharisee" unquestionably should render some things "to Caesar." But as unquestionably should the "Herodian" render some things unto God. And this very claim of religion upon government is admitted as a principle, and demonstrated as a power, in the very proclamation of the Executive which has called us together. For what is this day of Thanksgiving, but a religious service, appointed by government? — and so only a governmental provision for a great interest of religion. And on such a day, and after such explanations and definitions, I am surely justified in insisting on this duty of carrying *politics into religion*, and dwelling desultorily on those things which the Herodian should render unto God.

What, then, without surpassing its appropriate sphere, or transcending its peculiar prerogatives, can an earthly government do for the interests of religion?

And I answer, first of all — *That a government can, in its own 'peculiar and appropriate sphere, advance the interests of religion by manifesting as an example the power and goodliness of all Christian graces.*

The aphorism that corporations have no soul, and so no moral character, so that men may do in associations what they would not for their life dare to do as individuals, is, alas, a truth deduced from the very "widest observation. But then it ought not to be so. Shame on us that it is so. Corporations should have both soul and heart. They should have a lofty and lovely moral character.

A civil government, in its union of legislative and executive functions, is as verily bound as any of its individual officials, or subjects, to make exhibition before the world of a character adorned with all qualities that are pure, and true, and lovely, and of good report. I speak not here of any positive legislation in behalf of good morals. I speak only of that mighty power of example which goes along with the general character and acts of a government, almost irresistible in its influences either for good or evil.

Over and above the peculiar power which men in official stations exert in the exhibition of personal moral character, the government itself has the same powerful moral character, and is bound by every possible motive of good unto the government to make its example a savor of moral purity and life to its individual subjects.

A government, in a word, is bound to be virtuous: By a public and unvarying manifestation of a reverence for every principle of high-minded morality. By rigidly maintaining in every legislative and executive act all that conscientious regard for truth, and mercy, and impartial justice, and enlarged philanthropy, which are reckoned as radiant adornments of individual character. By an exhibition towards other governments, and foreign powers, of all that moderation, that sincerity, that magnanimous uprightness and honesty, that mingled beneficence and justice, which, on the one hand, refrains from all unfair advantages; and resists steadfastly, on the other hand, all unfair encroachments. An exhibition, I say, of all these fine moral qualities which characterize the conduct of an individual man at once benevolent and brave in his intercourse with his fellows. By manifestations such as these, of a heart, and a soul, and a conscience, should a government cherish in its every subject a moral sense of his own dignity as a man — and as well of his brotherhood with the whole human family.

Governments have a moral character as patent and as paraded as the device on their banner folds. The elder Rome was an unscrupulous robber. The elder Greece was an exquisite voluptuary. Russia to-day is a sturdy and selfish churl. France is an ambitious and unprincipled man of fashion. Spain is a wasted and wrinkled and scorned courtesan, in the decay and decrepitude of her dissolute living. England is a cross breed between the Pharisee and the prize fighter. And America is a well trained yet most passionate youth, of whom it is altogether a problem whether the manhood be a fine Christian gentleman or an unprincipled ruffian.

Governments have such moral character which in the influence of an omnipresent example is almighty either for evil or good on the moral character of their subjects. And I say then first of all, and by no means least important of all, that in its appropriate sphere a government should make exhibition of all that truth, and purity, and loveliness which are so graceful and goodly in individual character.

Meantime, over and above all this silent and negative influence of example, should a government do much for religion — positively and powerfully — *by precept and penalty.* And so we remark —

Secondly. That every government is bound to put forth its appropriate power in the suppression of public vices.

Sin, indeed, as a principle of our nature latent in the heart, is subject only to the higher jurisprudence of Jehovah. But sin, when it becomes sensible, developing itself openly in flagrant iniquities — becomes a legitimate object of earthly jurisprudence — and should be met promptly and resolutely by the sternest rebuke of executive authority. While the great end of all legislation in regard of public vices should be — the prevention of crime and the reformation of the criminal; and so should be always characterized by great moderation and mercy: nevertheless, such legislation should be powerful and prompt ; at once impartial in its application and unyielding in its enactments. *It should be impartial in its application.* And here, perhaps, more than elsewhere, is the short-coming of our criminal code. It bears unequally upon the castes of society. Its type is too truthfully a spider's web, strong as a hempen cord around the wing of a poor fly; but weak as gossamer to the golden plumes of the hummingbird. It punishes without mercy the shivering beggar who makes theft of a coat to keep him from freezing; but smiles graciously on the fraudulent bankrupt who, out of enormous robberies, can rear a palace of marble and crowd it with the magnificence of an oriental monarch. It is all iron to the poor drayman who happens to jostle your carriage and mar a wheel or a panel; but only poppy and rose-leaf to a titled commander who, in mad race upon the water, runs his bark into shipwreck — the ruthless murderer of your beloved ones. It has fetter and dungeon for the poor coiner who utters a spurious shilling; but only ottoman and cologne for the swindling officials of a banking-house, flooding a whole land with utterances as worthless. Verily, the criminal jurisprudence of our times has the Pharisee's moral conscience; straining out with shuddering recoil the poor *goat* of iniquity, yet swallowing without shrug or contortion, hump and all, the whole monstrous *camel*.

Government should legislate impartially, *and then execute impartially.* It should frown as severely on the rich and the noble, as on mendicant and menial. Indeed, as crime committed in high places has less to excuse it, and reaches further in its mal-influence, so should its punishment in high places be more sternly inflexible. And instead of the monstrous judicial iniquities so paraded in the midst of us, whereby the richer villain goes free and the poorer villain suffers — instead of this, I say, only the more lacerating for the fine garment should be the law's iron scourge — only the heavier for the pampered flesh, the iron links of the fetter. In a word, a government owes it to its subjects that its laws against crime should be few and simple — based on justice, but tempered with mercy — impartial in their operation, and inflexibly executed.

But with no further limits to enlarge on these general principles which should characterize legislation in the suppression of iniquities, let me dwell in illustration, for a moment, on a few of the many public immoralities a government should set itself to prevent or punish. Of course, in these illustrations, I shall select only such as are not sufficiently regarded in our land's jurisprudence.

I. Take then, first, as an example, the vice of *Intemperance.*

Now you are all aware how this vice has come to be regarded rather as a misfortune to be pitied, than a crime to be punished. But all this is manifestly most unwise and most wicked. The intemperate man, say what you will of him, is not, like a robbed man in the street, the poor victim of another's cupidity. He is a most bold and brutal violator of all social and domestic rights. He commits high felony on the property and prerogatives of his neighbors. He robs his children of their rightful bread. He lashes his wife with a sorer scourge than a scourge of hot scorpions. He brings down to the grave with a very murder, his gray hairs who begat, and *her* broken heart who bore him. He racks with more than inquisitorial torments those hearts that are bound to him by love's deathless affections. And comes, therefore, as directly and manifestly into the legitimate province of severe criminal law, as a man who commits arson on his own house, or murder on his own family.

And as of the intemperate man himself, so as well *of the man who makes traffic of Intemperance.*

As observed before, I will not insult your understanding, with an argument to prove that government has the right to rule out of the land this whole infamous commerce. I would sooner spend breath on the proof that the law could restrain me from importing whole herds of lions, from the Indies, to let loose in our forests; or whole dens of deadly serpents from Africa, to scatter abroad in our gardens. Government has, indeed, already and always assumed this right as its prerogative, in its whole system of license laws. *Its right to license presupposes its right to restrain.* But then this license system is not sufficient. It works partially and imperfectly.

It is, indeed, nothing better than a legislative re-enactment of the grotesquely horrible old *Bull of Papal Indulgences.* Written fairly out as a business transaction, and how would the doings in this matter by a Board of Excise read? Why something like this:

"Know all men by these presents, that on this day of this year, Anno Domini, —, because Mr. A. B. seems morally qualified for such a business, and in consideration of value received, we hereby license him to destroy property, to bring misery into families, to take away bread and raiment from small children, to make parents childless and wives widows, to fill poor houses with paupers and prisons with criminals, to send bodies to the grave, and souls to damnation—"

This — this, and this only, is the moral significance of our license system. And I say it works at best partially and imperfectly. I am not thinking here to speak of what would be in this matter a wise and wholesome legislation. I am not satisfied that as yet any proposed system of enactment meets the case's great exigencies. I am as heartily sick as any man can be of all that ruffianism of moral reforms, which will link temperance as a twin issue with the foul ends of political partisanship. I am not projecting the provisions of a bill. I am only insisting on the grand principle of prerogative. That it is the *manifest right*, and the *bounden duty*, of all human governments to rise up each in its place, and put its heel in all its omnipotent strength on this monstrous Hydra of modern civilization.

II. Take next as an example the vice of *Sabbath-breaking*. And we say it is the duty of the government to prevent or to punish it.

This hue and cry of *"Church and State,"* which is ever boisterously raised when we seek aid from executive power for such sanctification of God's Sabbath, is as little countenanced by our Federal or State Constitutions, as it is by common sense. A public recognition of the Sabbath, as holy time, has from the first been accorded to the day by our Federal Constitution. On that day, the high civil functions of the Chief Magistrate of the nation — the business of the Supreme Court— the sessions of both houses of Congress — the operations of the War and Treasury and Navy Departments — all are suspended by constitutional provisions. And so all the individual States of the Union, in their capacity of sovereign powers, do provide for the Sabbath's sanctification, by precept and penalty.

And that, in such legislation, governments have acted only in their appropriate sphere, needs surely no argument. The Sabbath is man's spiritual blessing not only, but his great temporal blessing. Confessedly, Sabbath breaking, as a crime, is the grand source of all crimes. Philosophically considered, the Sabbath is the world's great public recognition of the being and sovereignty of a God, whose laws are over us. And so to degrade it from its sanctity, is to fling a loose rein on the neck of all the wild passions that spring out of Atheism. And as a fact of observation, just as you blot out the Sabbath you blot out civilization. How was it with France? Why as long as the Sabbath stood untouched, so long there rose a strong bulwark of adamant to stay and beat back the wilder flood-tides of iniquity. But so soon as with insane hands they blotted that hallowed day from the calendar, and enacted a decade to the Goddess of Reason, just so soon was the roused ocean let loose from its bounds, and a tide of crimson and fiery desolation overwhelmed the whole nation. *The Sabbath is not merely a Saint's day of religion, it is God's gift to the race as a great temporal blessing.* The Sabbath was made for man, for every man, his nature craves it, his constitution requires it. It is identified with his pursuits, and with all his moral tendencies. And, therefore, is as manifestly the prerogative of earthly governments, to legislate inexorably for its observance — to see to it that no breath of blasphemous infidelity breathe a stain upon its shining garments — to guard it carefully from every rolling wheel and every trampling foot. As manifestly, all this, the prerogative of human governments, as to protect my dwelling from an incendiary's torch, and my fields from an invading enemy.

III. Take again — and lest we should weary you, finally, for example: *Any one or all of that great class of public vices, whose unpunished influence in our midst, is to lower the standard of Christian morals, and destroy the moral purity of the rising generation.* I need not pause here in an enumeration of these vices, their name is legion. Profane Swearing, Blasphemy, the Race Course, the Card Table, Libertinism, the Polluted Utterances of a Licentious Literature — the monstrous shapes of sin that link themselves with our Theatres, the bribery in Jury-Boxes and Elections, these — and such as these — are but specimens of a great class of public vices, whereby morality is stricken down in our streets, and a wounded Christianity lies bleeding at her own holy altars.

And we say it is the prerogative of civil power to suppress such iniquities. I know how these men say that the civil power is only for the protection of temporal interests. But be it so — and what then? Do these temporal interests, which Caesar's jurisdiction guards, include only the pecuniary and personal well-being of our estates and our bodies? Hath the man no purely temporal interests that pertain to the home, and the heart, and the social life of himself and his beloved ones? Shall the civil power punish a man who injures his neighbor's cattle, and yet leave that man free to injure his neighbor's children? May he rob me of my peace of mind, while he dare not rob my pork barrel? May he break my heart, while he dare not break my walking stick? Must a leper be quarantined lest he fill the breeze with contagion, and the poisoner of my well, go to prison — and all this because the civil power guards the bodies of my beloved ones? And yet shall the man walk lawlessly abroad if he fill God's pure air with pestilent blasphemies, and poison the sweet wells of the old Saxon tongue with libertine literature, till he destroy all the peace and the purities of my household, and bring the very *hearts* of my beloved ones as festering corpses to the sepulchre?

Ah! No, sirs! No, sirs! As a member of society, and a subject of government, I may have bank stock and a body, which deserve protection; but then I have a *heart*, too, and a *soul*, which deserve protection. And so all the temporal interests of my soul and my heart are as strictly under the guardianship of the civil law, as are my body and my bank stock — as are the products of my farm — and the property of my merchandise.

I cannot enlarge further on this point of the subject. Enough has been said at least to illustrate the proposition — *that civil governments are hound — on every principle of. right and prerogative — to put forth all their power in the suppression of public vices!*

Now we had designed, at this point of our discourse, to consider at some length—

Thirdly. The duty of the civil government to promote and provide for the religious education of its subjects. I say the *religious* education — because, to discuss such a duty in regard to education in general, were to waste words on a self-evident truism. Universal education is an obvious and absolute prerequisite to universal suffrage. The man who cannot read the ticket he votes at the ballot-box, has manifestly no suffrage at all, save that of an automaton. Of *all* civil governments the education of the subject is a duty, growing out of their guardianship of mere temporal interests. And of *our own* civil government — it is not only a duty to the subject, but an absolute dictate of self-preservation. Here, popular suffrage, without popular education, were not only monstrous, but positively suicidal.

But, then, not merely general education, but general *religious* education we claim as a right at the hands of our government. On this point, we have no space for extended argument. But in such an argument, we should claim such education, only, of course, on the ground of its temporal advantages. You are all of you aware of the infidel endeavors to exclude the Bible from our public schools — and such exclusion every patriot will resist on the simple ground of a *temporal wrong doing to society.* And this wrong doing is most apparent. If education be a duty of the civil power at all, it is because it fits its subjects for the duties of good citizenship. But, then, what are these duties? Merely physical — or intellectual duties? No, indeed, but in the main, *moral* duties — those duties, social and civil, whose performance requires an educated moral sense. And so every system of popular education, if it accomplish its designed ends, must have some standard, and universal text book of morals. Simple intellectual culture does not furnish a man knowledge as to the duties of citizenship. Will a man learn, what is only commercially right and wrong by the study of arithmetic? Will he learn the meaning of a judicial oath, and the power of its awful sanctions, by studying the grammar of language? Will he be trained to the obedience of civil law, by watching experiments in chemistry and natural philosophy? Will he be fitted to understand civil relations, and observe social proprieties, and compass the whole complex moral economy of good citizenship, by the mixed mathematics of navigation and surveying, or the speculative mathematics of calculus and geometry? Will you fit a man for the moral duties of society by training his intellect? Why, you might as well fit him for those duties by strengthening his muscles in the gymnastics of the athlete. Oh! no — no — moral duties presuppose moral culture — and popular moral culture demands a standard text book of morals. And the world has no such text book but the Bible. Find a better one — nay, find one as good — nay, find any one, however imperfect, which shall be chosen, (as the Bible is chosen,) by popular majority; and then let that be the great text book of morals in our State system of education. But till this be done, we claim, as a right, the Bible in our school system. Claim as a right! — nay, we claim it as a dictate of social self-preservation. Why, look ye! — where would be our whole social system, but for the sacredness of the *judicial oath*? But what is this oath? — what, but a simple imprecation of the vengeance, and a renunciation of the favor, of the *God of the Bible*, if the utterance be false or the official duties be unfulfilled. Yes, and this very oath administered on the Bible. But how then, I pray you, can the awful meaning of such an oath be understood without a full knowledge of that Bible, wherein its sanctions are alone defined, and on which alone it is administered?

Administer oaths on the Bible, and yet not require the subject of such an oath to understand the Bible! Why the world has never heard of a parallel to such suicidal absurdity! All as safely to your liberties, might you inaugurate a president or empanel a jury, by pressing to the man's lip some old volume of Pagan mythology, which the man had never read — whose gods he did not know — whose authority he did not recognize. Alas! alas! the outcry against the Bible in our schools of popular education, is a war cry against our whole social system. If general education be — as it confessedly is — a duty of civil government — it must be such an education as prepares for our peculiar franchises. It must educate *the whole man* for the functions of good citizenship. Not merely the man's body — that might make him only a strong limbed giant. Not merely his intellect — that might make him only a cold blooded demon. Over and above all this, it must educate as well, his *whole moral nature*. So training his sensibilities — so refining his manners — so directing and establishing his principles — his feelings — his habits of thought. In a word, so elevating and educating his moral sense into an understanding of what, as a good citizen, he owes to society — that, together with a strong body and a trained mind — a trained and tender conscience as well, may fit him for honorable citizenship in this freest, and fairest, and noblest nation on the face of the earth.

The grand plea of these men, that the Bible should be excluded from our schools because it may be perverted in the hands of sectarian teachers into a sectarian text book, is just as logical, as a plea against teaching penmanship in our schools, because some unprincipled instructor might teach his pupils how to commit forgery. When a man dares to teach sectarianism out of the Bible, then displace that man as unworthy his office. But destroy not in the midst of us a great social right, on account of some possible or actual abuse of it. Do not cut off every man's right arm, lest some men should commit murder! Do not annihilate the whole atmosphere, because it has sometimes been a vehicle for the malaria of pestilence.

Alas! alas! either for the common honesty or for the common sense of these men. For without the length of the argument we had intended to pursue, we hold that it only needs the smallest share of both common honesty and common sense, to perceive and to feel that from every consideration of *duty* and *self-preservation, a civil government should provide for the religious education of its subjects.* We pass then to observe—

IV. *That it is the duty of government jealously to guard the religious liberties of its subjects.* After what has been already advanced, we can not be honestly misunderstood on this point. We have already abundantly acknowledged, that earthly governments were not designed for the propagation of Christianity, nor for the establishment of religion. Nay, more — we have conceded it. That being established for special temporal purposes, they have no more to do with the strictly religious expressions of a people, than they have with a people's dress — or equipage — or domestic arrangements and social customs. But then to legislate in religious matters, is one thing. And to protect religious rights, is another thing altogether. And while, though not legislating in such matters, yet governments do guarantee to their subjects the widest liberty in regard of dress and equipage and social conventionalisms — so should they in religion. Indeed, in respect to our own government, this protection of religious freedom, is, in the constitution — our great bill of rights — guaranteed to its subjects, as a special provision.

Religious liberty as distinctly as *civil* freedom, was a grand end for which our fathers bled in the battle, and legislated in the Senate house; and its protection is indeed *part of the specific purpose for which our government was established.* I am not pretending that the civil power should recognize any religious sect — or establish any system of Bible doctrine — or form a national creed. On the contrary, should the time ever come — which God forbid — when bigoted sectarianism, or even bigoted Protestantism, shall seek to lay the lightest finger of legislative oppression upon either Catholic or Jew — upon either Infidel or Pagan — then will every true-hearted follower of Christ be found as the first man to resist the wrong and roll back the iniquity. All we ask at the hands of our government, is the largest religious liberty for ourselves and for all men. We insist only on a free Sabbath — a free sanctuary — a free Bible — a free conscience — a free Christianity, in a word, that shall walk forth untrammeled and untouched, by all these waters, and through all these valleys, and athwart all these hills wherever and whenever it listeth. That shall enter as a thing rightfully at home, into every high place and low place under the shadow of our eagle. And while it asks not, nor will receive one morsel of sustaining bread from the hands of civil authority, yet brooks not, nor will bear one spider's web of restraint from such civil authority.

Meanwhile, this protection of religious rights which the government guarantees to its every subject at home, we claim as resolutely from that government *in all our wanderings abroad to the very ends of the world!* And on this point do we often blush for our country. This religious freedom is part and parcel of an American's birthright, as patent among the provisions of the Constitution, as the freedom of his limbs, and the right to his life. And go where he will, he should carry it abroad guaranteed by his government. I say *guaranteed*, for this government has the power of such guaranty amid the farthest tribes of this world, where its pilgrim subject may wander.

Our eagle does guard jealously and well our *civil* rights. Let a man — I care not how unknown — I care not how insignificant— from the banks of the Connecticut or the ridges of the Alleghanies — let him go abroad to the ends of the earth with merchandise for commerce, and with the stars and stripes waving over him — woe be unto the prince or potentate who dares to lay ruthless hands on one cord of his tent, or one ware of his traffic! Touch but his pilgrim staff, or his sandal shoon, or his scrip, or his garment, and then beware! The eagle! the eagle! How he swoops and screams! But now let this same man go abroad as a *religious* being, pitching his tent as a sanctuary for the living God, and opening therein his blessed Bible as bread from heaven. And then let oppression rock his dwelling into dust, and burn his heavenly treasure into ashes, and alas for the eagle now! It will swoop you as gently as *"any sucking dove"* and scream you as softly *"as it were any nightingale."*

And I say, shame, shame, on the eagle! thus to care for the meanest right and neglect the noblest — thus to guard the small fraction of a man, but forget his whole manhood. To sit as an omnipotent protector on a barber's pole by the Rhine — and be scared from a heaven-pointing spire of God's temple in Italy. To flash his eyes in wrathful fire when men dare to shiver my wine flask — and doze like an owl in the sun when they tear away my Bible. Shame! Shame! on the eagle!

Why, sirs, the Christianity of this Bible, was that eagle's nursing mother. When overborne in long struggles for freedom in the Old World, it fled across the ocean. Then did this Heavenly Spirit open shelter and eyrie in these great forests — and as its bright eye grew dim, and its strong wing fainted, did she take it gently to her bosom, and cherish it with bread and sweet water, till the eye flashed again, and the plumes strengthened, and the heart bounded; and as a marvel and a terror to its old tyrants, it soared again to the sun. And now to forget, in its glorious flight through heaven, this, its only protectress, in the hour of its homeless desolation! Shame, shame, shame on the eagle. — Yes, yes! — a thousand times yes! do we claim as a part of an American birthright, protection here, and everywhere, and always, for every religious interest of our being. Here, and everywhere, and always, a Free Bible — a Free Conscience — a Free Sanctuary — a Free Sacrifice — a Free Spirit. Free to go forth on benevolent ministries to men's perishing immortality. Free to worship the God of our fathers, in spirit and in truth.

Now there is more, much more that we had designed to say in illustration of our subject; but our limits are exhausted, and we may not enlarge further. These are only specimens of a large class of duties, which all governments, and especially our government — so founded, so furnished — can perform, and are bound to perform, for the interests of religion. These are but several items in the tribute which the Herodians of politics should render unto God.

While, confessedly, was no government established for the propagation of the Gospel, our own government, at least, most certainly was established in the broadest recognition of its entire subordinacy to the higher government of the Eternal. In theory we never were an Infidel government; and, God helping us, we never will be an Infidel government. The baptism in tears and blood of our young giant of nationality was a *Christian* baptism — a *Protestant* baptism. And it is not in American motherhood to send the young babe from her bosom to the unnatural and monstrous nursing of Infidelity and Anti-Christ. No, no. True to that baptism shall the nation grow up, Christian and Protestant. And if die it must, it shall die and be buried Christian and Protestant.

The framers of our constitution recognized their obligation to act as in the everlasting presence of a higher than human authority. And they did act as in such presence. Protestant Christianity is positively part of our common law, and part of our constitution. The civil law of this land lifts a Protestant Bible in every official inauguration — and proclaims the Sabbath as consecrated to God, alike in the halls of our higher national council, and in the rudest hut of the borderer. Thus recognizing God's authority as supreme over all the nations on his footstool. And whatever we might be in truth compelled to say, were our vine planted amid the ancestral despotisms of Europe — yet sitting safe under its blessed shelter in Christian America, we do say — not as Christian sectarians, nor as Protestant bigots — but we say simply, as free born American citizens, that while *"rendering carefully unto Caesar the things that are Caesar's,"* we are bound *"to render as carefully unto God all those things that are God's."*

Verily, my brethren, as a great and free people, we *owe something unto God. Something?* Ah me! how mighty — how magnificent should be the tribute Christian America rejoices to lay at the feet of Jehovah! What has God done for us? Alas, I have no strength and no words for the argument. You know what God has done; the whole world knows the story by heart. Look at America this day as she is. Behold her broad boundaries — her glorious scenery — her new and noble civilization — the breadth and wealth of her husbandry — the pomp of her great cities — her seaboards, the market places of a world — her canvas of commerce whitening all oceans — her matchless progress in manufactures — and the arts, and literature, and science — the spread of her mighty population — the strength and style of her magnificent specimens of manhood. Oh, look at America today, as the world looks at her. Amid the nations of the earth that are moaning under task-masters, and lying down under burdens, and heaving and tossing, and passing away in God's anger — she, sitting like a fair child crowned for holiday, all peaceful and prosperous, and law-abiding and blessed. The Ararat, whereunto moves the Ark of the Race from the sweep of the Deluge. The glorious Jerusalem, unto which all earth's scattered tribes look from their exile and home-sickness. The purest, the fairest, the most joyous, the most hopeful, the most magnificent dwelling-place for man on the face of the globe.

And *whence* all this? Why from God, and God only. No statesman lives, or has lived, who dare say, "My wisdom has done this." No political party dare utter the bold blasphemy, the transparent falsehood, of pretending to have been even God's "hewer of wood" in this magnificent temple building. Old Nebuchadnezzar, had he lived amid these cities, would have sunk to a fouler beasthood than he did, and instead of eating grass as an ox, would have crawled, eating dust, as a veriest reptile; had he dared to say of such glory as this, *"Behold this great Babylon which I have builded."* No, no, it is *God's* work, all of it; the wisdom of his counsel, the work of his Omnipotence. And tell me then, if you can, what should we render, as a nation, unto God for all His great mercies? If the *tribute money unto Caesar* — what, what unto God?

I need not tell you how little we are rendering, I have indicated already how greatly we come short in our duties toward Jehovah. I have spoken of God's broken laws — of God's murdered Sabbaths — of God's forgotten presence — of the crimes that go unpunished through the midst of our streets, and the iniquity that rolls as a flood over all our high places. And alas for it all. I am afraid for my country, when I think of God's munificent gifts, and God's terrible justice. As "Herodians," at least, "we do render to Caesar the things that are Caesar's." We have demanded for our civil rights the exactest "tithe of mint, and anise and cummin." Our government has been great in its *little things*. Like little Zaccheus, climbing into a tall sycamore tree, to show himself the chief of the tax gatherers. It has been a worthy "publican," sitting amid the farthing boxes, at the receipt of custom. All praise unto our great statesmanship! We have made magnificent battle for cod-fish on the Banks — and guano in South America. We have blustered for the Black Warrior's cotton in Cuba, and thundered with great guns for national honor at Grey-town. We have bearded all Europe on the grand question of diplomatic costume, and maintained, in the face of all creation, our inalienable rights to wear either broadcloth, or velvet, or homespun, as we will, everywhere and always.

Glorious things are spoken of us! We are accomplishing feats of statesmanship, such as Washington never dreamed of. The "stripes" — at least the stripes are belted broad on our banners, be it as it may with "the stars." *Caesar, at least , ought to he satisfied.* We have tithed all the meanest herbs of the earth in tribute to his treasury. The eagle has gathered straws for his eyrie, if he have not soared to the sun. *The Eagle!* nay, henceforth paint me an *Owl* as the blazon on our banners. A bird that can see every reptile in the midnight, but not even Mount Blanc or Niagara in the blaze of the sun. Alas, alas for our greater things. *"Woe, woe unto us, for roe tithe mint, and rue, and all manner of herbs, and pass over judgment and the love of God."*

This, this unto Caesar, but then unto God! Our great and glorious Preserver! Our Benefactor! Our Rock in every storm! Our great shield in every battle! What, what unto God has America rendered? I have said, and said truly, that in theory at least, we are a Christian people; that our very Constitution recognizes God's authority as supreme over the nations of his footstool. But then practically, as God requires, can we call ourselves a Christian people? Well, then, commend me to Christianity as the choicest livery of the menialhood of the Evil One. We acknowledge God's authority, theoretically and in general, but trample it underfoot practically, in each and all its specific requirements. Our national religion is very much like the old Hindoo's, who worships the great white elephant, once a year, with great ado of prostrations and burnt incense. Meanwhile, though, keeping their divinity carefully guarded in the temple, lest he should break forth and set foot on some practical field of the secular and social. *We*, a Christian people! *Ours* a religious government! *We, "keep God's commandments!" We, "have no other gods before Him!" We, "make no graven images!" We, "take not the name of the Lord in vain!" We, "keep the Sabbath holy!" "not coveting," nor "killing," nor "stealing," nor "committing adultery," nor "bearing false witness!"* Alas, alas, every specific precept of this Divine Law answers, in the headlong course of Young America, about the purpose of a hedge in a steeple-chase, to show with how high and daring a leap the horseman may go over it! Our national Christianity is a strongly distilled compound of the Mosaic and Levitical. Moses shivering the divine tables, and Aaron at work on the calf! And on the whole the divine law in the midst of us fares worse than did God's holy ark, when the Philistines brought it on its way from Ebenezer to Ashdod.

Oh, I sicken — my heart breaks over the whole subject. We bring our tribute to Caesar, but what bring we to God? And, my brethren, believe me, it is full time, and on this day of national recognition of Jehovah's Being and Presidency, it is fitting time to count carefully the cost of such disloyalty to Jehovah. In ceasing to be nationally religious, we have ceased as well to be nationally philosophic. The relations of divine government to republican institutions have not been studied well by our legislators, as involving the principles of a higher statesmanship than is busy with the expedients of a present necessity. The man who thinks it safe for us to withhold our national tribute from Jehovah, has not studied well either the past history of moral causes or the present signs of the times. I cannot enter on the argument — I but tell you in a word — that the great machinery of Divine Providence, while leaving ample room in its economy for the widest play of human free agency, has yet always wrought out its great purposes of *casting clown every high thing that exalteth itself against God.*

Practical and political atheism has been the worm at the root of all national glory. Look at Babylon in her grandeur! Who came forth against her as the Angel of Desolation? A conqueror with his bannered armies? No, a *poor Prophet of God?* Look at *Jerusalem* in the magnificence of her glory! Who uttered the "woe!" "woe!" that made her a scorn and a hissing? Caesar on his throne? Nay, *a poor Nazarene on Mt. Olivet!* So has it been ever. And are we more omnipotent, that we can play harmless with God's thunderbolts? May not *our* house too be left unto us desolate? May not the satyr dance and the wild beasts howl in *our* glorious palaces?

Oh! thou Eagle, hear the word of the Lord! Oh! thou Eagle! *"Thy terribleness and the pride of thy heart have deceived thee: thou that dwellest in the cleft of the rock, and boldest the height of the hill, and sayest in thy heart, who shall bring me down to the ground? Though thou set thy nest among the stars, thence ivill I bring thee down, saith the Lord God Almighty?"*

Oh! thou Eagle! From the death-dust of every nation that hath gone down to the grave — from the sepulchres of Nineveh and Tyre, and Egypt and Edom, rise shadows for the plumes of thy wing, if thine eye look not full on the Great Sun of Righteousness!

We are met in times, never so solemn, never so momentous with magnificent and awful issues! If there be truth in the signs of the times, then is the Seventh Trumpet already on the angel's lip — and the last of God's vials lifted up over the nations — and already are there lightnings and thunderings, and great voices, and a sound as of the great hail falling from heaven! and as of the rush of every island and mountain fleeing from the face of an angry God!

The year we are now ending has been a year full of the power of the right arm of Omnipotence. Under other nations is already awake and a-move the great earthquake; and upon us, amid all our amazing mercies, there have fallen the seemings of a frown from the face of the Great Father. Ours have been a parched and blighted soil; the wide desolation of pestilence; the awful calamities of a devouring ocean; the dark judgments consequent upon gigantic frauds and dishonesty, deranging and paralyzing our whole commercial machinery; the grinding of our Golden God into powder, and the strewing it upon the water, till the whole land today is sick as Old Israel in the compelled drinking of its bitterness.

And what mean all these things, I say, but the shivering plume of the Seventh Angel, as he lifts the last trump and pours forth the last vial? Sure I am, at least, my brethren, that it is time to gather ourselves solemnly to our reckoning with Jehovah! Not to think less of Caesar, but to think more of Jehovah, — to take tithe if we will of all herbs, but to regard meanwhile the Love of God and the great things of Judgment — to turn from the mere tithing of mint, and rue, and anise and cummin, unto that world-wide and glorious ministry for our race and our God, unto which God has called us, and for which he has equipped us — to hearken to the voice that for a down-trodden humanity and a groaning creation is summoning us as with a great trumpet, to be doing our peculiar work on this broad theatre of our National Life — in the Spectatorship of the Universe. *To be rendering unto Caesar the things that are Caesar's, and unto God the things that are God's!*

Oh! my Country! hear the voice of thy God! Oh! thou *Eagle!* — thou of the flashing eye! — thou of the strong pinion! — hark to the sweep of the mighty winds, as they lash the great seas and rock the deep forests! Oh! thou Eagle! it is God's summons from the slumberous eyrie to the broad empyrean! The night is passing; the day dawns; open that eye; fling abroad that pinion, and away from the dream in the heath-bells, soaring up to the sun!

4

AMERICA'S MISSION

A SERMON PREACHED IN THE ARCH STREET PRESBYTERIAN CHURCH, PHILADELPHIA, ON THANKSGIVING DAY, NOV. 22, 1855.

"And who knoweth whether thou art come to the Kingdom for such a time as this?"

ESTHER 4:14.

WE have not selected these words with an intention of dwelling at length upon their original reference. You have assembled on the morning of your National Thanksgiving, expecting to have your meditations led in directions beseeming the occasion—and we call your attention to this particular text, because we judge it to contain a great principle, entirely appropriate to our present circumstances.—The occasion of its primitive utterance is familiar to you all. It is the message sent by Mordecai unto Esther, when the machinations of Haman were hemming the Jews in unto destruction, in which he urges her to the performance of her duty to her people, from the consideration that, apparently, God had brought her to the queenship of that great oriental kingdom, with the very design that she should work out their deliverance—as if he had said—"Divine Providence has not distinguished thee, raising thee from poverty to a throne for thine own sake merely, but rather for the express purpose of counter-working a great scheme of wickedness formed against the whole people of Israel;" and this argument is prefaced in the context by a prophetic intimation, that if, for any reason, she shrank from the accomplishment of this purpose, her own destruction, as one not achieving the end of her political elevation, would inevitably follow. And herein is manifestly and strikingly set forth the great truth: *that God, in His Providence, raises up special instrumentalities for special purposes; which instrumentalities will themselves be destroyed, if they subserve not those purposes.*

Now, we need not pause to prove to you that such is a principle of the Divine administration. Such is, indeed, a principle of every wise administration, however finite and imperfect—and reason and revelation conspire to affirm it a great and pervading principle in the government of God. We take it, therefore, on the authority of Revelation it receives in the text, and go on, at once, to a practical application of this principle to ourselves as a nation, in our peculiar circumstances this morning.

It is the morning of our National Thanksgiving—a morning when the heart of every American patriot and Christian, swells high in rapture over the glories of his birth-right, and the voice of a nation lifts to God grateful anthems, as a befitting sacrifice of thanksgiving, in return for our distinguishing religious and political blessings; and yet, a morning when, in view of our national short-comings, every Christian and patriotic heart in the temples of Jehovah confesses a foreboding, as to what shall be the future of such a people, in the Providential outworking of a Divine purpose, alike all righteous and omnipotent. And this is the peculiarity of our circumstances, which renders the great principle of the text most appropriate, and we go on at once to consider and apply it.

This principle, in this application, involves two simple thoughts.

First, That God seems to have raised us up as a nation as a great instrument of Civil and Religious benefit to the world.

And, *Secondly, That our own national prosperity and indeed, national existence, for the future, depend, under God, on our diligent outworking this grand purpose of Providence.*

Let us consider these two thoughts in their order.

We say, then—*First, That God seems to have raised up this American Nation as a great instrument of civil and spiritual salvation to a world.*

This truth, will, we think, be made manifest from several distinct considerations.

Foremost of all, as in the case of Esther, in her relation to the Jews, we would have you observe—*The indications of a most marked and wonderful Providence in our national rise and progress.*

This fair world was not rounded into beauty and hung amid the stars, to remain forever a stronghold of the apostate. In the first hour of its disloyalty to Jehovah, it was, *a priori*, to be expected that God would either sweep it out of being, or redeem and restore it; and with an eye carefully observant of its past history, we perceive how God's system of providence has all been tending to one great end—*The restoration of the race to its original condition, through the institution and extension and triumphs of the Church.*

Nations have flourished and fallen—and the eye of Christian philosophy, looking back upon the convulsive workings of human passion, that have rocked the cradle and dug the grave of progressive empires, traces distinctly the operation of a grand Providential economy, working, indeed, in that great majestic patience, and those circles of immense sweep, wherein Omnipotence ever achieves its purposes; yet working steadfastly and surely ever, turning and overturning old systems, for the establishment, on their ruins, of an everlasting Kingdom, whose Monarch shall be God. And, if it be ours at all to judge of Divine designs, from Providential indications, then this American nation constitutes, so to speak, a great spring, or lever, or wheel, in that vast and complicate machinery whereby Omnipotence is outworking this magnificent result.

To the eye of skeptical philosophy the phenomena of our rise and progress as a people, may well appear marvelous. It is a marvel that, until the fifteenth century, in the enthrallment of his moral nature, man should have remained but half a man—his noblest prerogative unrecognized. It is a marvel that until the fifteenth century, the world should have remained but half a world, its noblest continent undiscovered, yea, undreamed of. And greater still seems the resultant marvel—that in the march and movement of God's providence, the self-same fifteenth century should have developed man in his majesty as a whole man—and the world in its magnificence as a whole world. I say, the eye of *skepticism* sees, in all this, the greatly marvelous; and so every preceding and attending circumstance of our national being—our early preservation—our glorious revolution—our subsequent progress, seem all, as well, things mysterious and wonderful; and yet the eye of philosophic *Faith* sees in them all—in the simultaneous invention of the mariner's compass and the printing press, the one lifting the curtain from the whole world, the other shivering the fetter from the whole man—in the simultaneous birth of the Genoese navigator and the German reformer, braving, in behalf of that world and that race, the one the tempests of the material, the other the tempests of the moral world—in the simultaneous rise of English literature and English intolerance, the one producing the English Bible, the Magna Charta of the American Church, the other driving forth that Church with this precious birth-right blessing, to set up the pillar of its Bethel on Plymouth rock—in all those stormy conflicts that rooted colonial religion like the oak tree, deep amid the foundations of the everlasting hills—in the altogether matchless, nay, almost miraculous success of our early struggles for nationality, as an unarmed child in the wilderness against the mightiest war power in the elder world—in the wonderful wisdom of a constitution—conceived amid struggles for hearth-stone and altar, and written, as it were, in the life blood of heroic hearts, whose great central truth of *human equality*, has set it above all other political systems as gloriously as the living man of today is above the dead fossils of the old geologic races—in all the march and magnificence of a subsequent progress, which, ere the forests have decayed that showered their foliage as the pilgrim's welcome, has laid deep the foundation, and reared strongly a national superstructure, whose height, even now, among the nations of the world, is as Mont Blanc amid mountains—in all this, I say, the eye of *philosophic faith* perceives the evolution of far-reaching and Omniscient design, more distinctly marking this nation as one of God's great instrument for the world's civil and religious redemption, than did the strange call of the Hebrew Patriarch, and the marvelous preservation of the Hebrew law-giver and the magnificent Exodus of the Hebrew people; show the descendants of Abraham to have been the objects of God's special care—and divine instrument for the diffusion over the Gentile world of the light and liberty that abide in the oracles of God.

Now this leads me to remark as the second reason for the thought under review—
That the political and religious aspects of the other nations of the world, and the signs of the times in regard of them, lead directly to the conclusion, that

the work of the world's evangelization, and man's social and spiritual redemption, if accomplished at all, must be OUR *national work.*

I cannot enlarge upon this thought, but I ask any man to tell me where, save within our own borders, can be found the necessary resources for the great work of the world's national or spiritual redemption?

Look at the people and realms of the transatlantic world. Over poor Africa broods the moral silence and gloom of the sepulchre—scarcely the whisper of a child's Hosanna—scarcely any thing but the death-sob of oppression in all the dwellings of the children of Ham. Upon the vast Shemite world there has come down a power of great darkness, the Churches planted by the Apostles have not even a name to live, and the tree of liberty, that under the long line of Prophet and King shadowed in strength the cities of the Hebrews, Alas! it has died root and branch in the very Canaan of the Patriarchs. A limited portion of Europe and our own Republic are, at this moment, the only portions of the world where real liberty, and true christianity, have even a nominal being. To them, therefore, is providentially committed the entire work of man's civil and religious redemption; but if truth can be read in the signs of the times, the period is not far distant when European christendom, if it do not become itself missionary ground, will require all its religious resources in the match of its own altars; and when European liberty, if it be not utterly swept away in the advancing tide of despotism, will seek, even at our hands aid in the strife; and build with the granite of this pilgrim land, fortress and tower in the great day of her trial.

The transatlantic world is yet to undergo mighty revolutions ere the principles of the Bible can flourish there in their power and purity. Its social systems are in manifest antagonism, alike to the spirit of diffused popular knowledge, and to the Gospel of Christ. Three mighty social changes, at least, must precede a European Millennium.

The monopoly of soil must be abolished.

Irresponsible and arbitrary power must give place to the franchises of the multitude.

And unrestrained liberty of conscience must be restored fully to the race.

And to suppose that such changes can be produced by processes of gradual melioration, is to suppose that a granite mountain can be leveled, grain by grain, without the heave of an earthquake. You cannot make Europe the home of religious liberty by emendations and additions to her old social edifice—for all your multiplied sweepings and garnishings she will remain the same prison-house of bondmen. No! no! it must be rocked into the dust, and another structure raised upon its ruins, ere Christianity and liberty can enter in and dwell there. Europe must herself become free, before she can be counted as the champion for freedom and humanity. Europe must herself become evangelized, popularly and thoroughly, ere she can be reckoned as an instrumentality for the world's evangelization. The gospel must enter her social system as an original element—European society must take its shape, and model its usages, and baptize its whole being in the genius of Christianity, ere God will make use of her prominently as the regenerator of humanity in the conversion of the world.

And, in view of all this, I repeat it—The eye of faith, looking abroad for agencies for this great work, rests, as its last hope, on beloved America; and the man must be a blind man, who fails to perceive how God hath raised us up to stand in the strength of these everlasting hills—the world's great asylum, and the gospel's great stand-point—in that period of approaching convulsion, foretold by prophesy, as a period that shall turn the sun into sackcloth, and the moon into blood, and shake the whole earth in the violence of her outraged and agonizing population.

Now, this leads me to remark, *Thirdly*, That the truth under review will appear still more apparent, if you carefully observe—

How the genius of American Institutions, and the peculiarities of American character, eminently qualify and equip us for this great work of man's social and civil regeneration.

The whole history of the rise and progress of our national character, cannot have failed to impress this thought strongly upon every philosophic mind. Not only in the original settlement of this country was there a sifting of all Christendom for the noblest specimens of manhood to go forth as colonists, but in all our subsequent progress has there been gathered into it every variety of national character, so that there is scarcely a solitary people in the whole earth which finds not its representative incorporated in our social system. The iron Saxon, the volatile

Frenchman, the grave Spaniard, the reflective German, the effervescing Italian, the warm-hearted Irishman; aye, and the member of the wildest clan and the extremest caste of earth's remotest continents, all speak of America as the refuge of their brethren; And as the celebrated Corinthian brass was only a rare amalgam of all other metals, so the American character holds in combination, all the available peculiarities of every people under heaven. While the original Anglo-Saxon is the controlling element of the mass, yet, so essentially have the highest qualities of other races modified the composite; and so warmly has the whole been fused and fired by the glorious freedom of American life; that our national character is, today, a new and nobler style in the development of manhood. And in this anomalous fact, you cannot fail to perceive how God has furnished us with the desiderata for one great mission to the nations, as well in the hold we thus have on the sympathies and affections of all people, as in those elements of ardor, and energy, and hope, which must render the Anglo-American the noblest representative of man.

Add to this, then, the mighty resources of influence and strength which our nation embosoms—the mighty and magnificent thing America is now on the earth—and the more mighty and magnificent thing she is to be presently, when, if true to herself and to her great mission, she shall stretch from ocean to ocean, athwart this broad continent; a nation of freemen, self-governed—governed by simple law, without a police or a soldiery—a nation of five hundred millions of people, covering the sea with their fleets, and the land with their great cities—first in arts and learning, and every great product of genius—and thus, even POLITICALLY, a power on the earth, before which the menial war-power of kings were as the Philistines before Samson. Aye, and more than all, RELIGIOUSLY, God's great almoner of the gospel to the race—the light of the benighted—the refuge of the oppressed—the home of the exile—the hope of the lost. Oh! I say, in view of what my country now is, and what she seems destined to be, in the march of God's providence, who can fail to recognize God's great purpose in raising her up as the one mighty instrument for the civil and religious regeneration of the world.

And this leads me to yet another point in the argument, which is just beginning to receive philosophic attention, and on which, though

it were not safe very greatly to rely, yet we would fasten your thought for a passing moment—we mean
> God's great Prophecies in Revelation having reference to America.

This argument begins with the assumption which has, at least, a plausible seeming—that it is unreasonable and unphilosophic to suppose that in a vast system of prophesy, detailing the grand features of the world's history to the end of time, and specifically and repeatedly predicting the rise of every nation whose existence was, vitally, to affect the church of God—that in such a system of prophesy, no mention should be made of a nation confessedly destined, more than all others, to affect the world—no allusion found to an epoch, an era, a nationality, more replete than all others with influences of good to man, and glory to Jehovah.

Setting out with this assumption, it confidently expects to find this American nationality fully foreshadowed in the ancient symbols of prophesy, yea, and it confidently declares it has found it in many a line of misinterpreted revelation.

It finds it *in Ezekiel's prediction of the restoration of Israel.* The unequivocal promise of future nationality to Israel in the Christian era, it interprets as fulfilled with wonderful particularity in the manifold parallelisms of American nationality.

It finds it in *the Fifth Kingdom of Nebuchadnezzar's vision,* thus interpreted by Daniel—"*And in those days shall the God of Heaven set up a kingdom which shall never be destroyed, and the kingdom shall not be left to other people, but it shall break in pieces and consume all other kingdoms, and it shall stand for ever.*"

It finds it in *Daniel's vision of the great ancient of days.* That sublime prophesy of Empires coincident throughout with this dream of Nebuchadnezzar.

It finds it in *Daniel's third great prophesy—in Michael the great Prince, who should stand gloriously at last for the children of God's people.*

It finds it, moreover, predicted *in the whole range of Apocalyptic symbols.—In the man-child of the woman crowned with twelve stars and fleeing with great wings into the wilderness.—In the man with many crowns, who with eyes as as a flame of fire, and vesture dipped in blood, smote the nations with a sharp sword, and ruled them with a rod of Iron.—In the sealing of the hundred and forty and four thousand.*

It finds it indeed in many of those mysterious symbols of the Revelation, which have heretofore been regarded as of different interpretation. And this prophetic explanation, involving, perhaps, much that is fanciful, yet is made to rest on a philosophic interpretation of symbols, and a plausible computation of the sacred and symbolic time of the Hebrew chronology, such as give it the seeming of much that is worthy a Christian's earnest study. And applying these specific predictions to America, it draws clearly and strongly the prophetic inference, that the grand design of this new and wonderful nationality is twofold, to *destroy all systems of Monarchical Government, and to restore and expand over all the earth the glory of a pure and primitive Christianity.* That the time hastens, when against this last popular embodiment of Divine power, the kingdoms of the world shall ally themselves in anger, and be dashed in pieces as a potter's vessel. And that then, rising up in its strength, this glorious nationality shall work out as God's instrument, the last great purpose of the present system of things: *A universally diffused Freedom and Christianity to all peoples, and kindreds and nations under Heaven.*

But, even ignoring this last point as altogether fanciful, we think we are not assuming too much, we think we do not greatly magnify the strength of our argument, when we declare that just as Esther was raised up for the salvation of the Jews, so, manifestly has God raised us up for the world's regeneration, and that in the very words of the text: *"For such a time as this have we come to the kingdom."*

Aye, and this is the thought, more than another, which fills the heart with great rapture amid the hallowed gratulations of our national thanksgiving. We love to linger even over the political promise of our loved land. To behold the first spring of the eaglet to the air, that in circles of amazing swiftness and power, will out-soar every bird of the sky on its strong wings to the sun. To go forward for years and behold America, the last born, but loveliest and queenliest sister in the family of nations. This, even this, is a prophet's vision at which the American eye kindles and the American heart swells in Thanksgiving.—But when from a thousand considerations, some of which we have suggested, the conviction fastens on us, that, we have been raised by God's Providence for the accomplishment of purposes more magnificent and mighty than any vision of Statesmanship. That in very deed the mountain of an ascending nationality has been flung up as a stand-point, whence the apocalyptic angel, with God's everlasting gospel of peace to man, and glory to God in the highest, is to take flight over the world.—Oh, then I say, our mortal joy as patriots becomes immortal joy as Christians—and our thanksgiving for civil and social blessings, partakes of the hallowed exultation of the old Israelite, when he stood upon the crowned heights of Zion, and beheld proselytes from remotest nations of the world—Parthians, and Medes, and Elamites, and the dwellers in Phrygia, and Egypt, coming up with the tribes to the great ritual jubilee of the Jewish year.

But it is time now to pass to the other part of the text's great principle, and consider,

Secondly:—*That our own national prosperity, and, indeed, national existence, in all future time, depend under God, on our diligent outworking this grand purpose of Providence.*

And on this point there is small need of an argument. It is a *sequitur* at once, from the principle involved in the historical context.

That a Divine Instrumentality will be displaced and destroyed if it subserve not its designed purposes.

This was the whole argument of Mordecai with Esther:—*That inasmuch as God had brought her to the kingdom for such a time and purpose, she, herself, would surely perish, if she failed in its accomplishment.* The principle is one common in its application to all intelligent operations, whether Divine or human, viz: *That any instrumentality will be displaced and destroyed, if, upon trial, it fail to answer its designed purpose*—and from this principle, patent in all the records of God's past administration, there comes, mingling with our rejoicing thanksgivings this day, a foreboding of disaster.

We are not looking at the data of political and patriotic argument, though, even in these might be found material for unpromising prediction. Ungracious as it ever will be, to doubt the self-perpetuating power of American Institutions, there are yet, unquestionably, premonitions of political disaster in the things that are around us. There is a manifest decay of sympathy between remote members of our great national confederacy. There is a degeneration in the healthy and hearty old party spirit, from a magnanimous struggle for great principles into a selfish stickling for local and sectional interests. There is a loathsome prostitution of statesmanship unto the artifices and dishonesties of the rankest demagogueism, so that the heights of our political ambition are attained as often by the sinuous winding of the reptile, as by the majestic strength of the eagle's soaring pinion. There is an increasing *furore* in the proverbial restlessness of American character—and a growing intolerance in the bigotry of American liberalism—and an enlarging distrust in the very optimism of the American system—and, more than all, there is an overleaping of those great moral and religious land-marks, which our forefathers regarded as the only barriers whereby the wild waves of political excitement could be hemmed in from an oversweeping deluge. Intemperance reels through our streets; and blasphemy and profaneness burden the atmosphere; and the public conscience has become callous, through the frequency of unpunished crime, and licentiousness stalks unblushing through the land, and the Sabbath is trodden down by the multitude; and an unholy lust of conquest is working, like hidden fever, in the pulses of the body politic; so that right in the path of our glorious progress, the seas are white around the rocks whereon the old republics rushed to shipwreck two thousand years agone. And in these things the eye, even of irreligious statesmanship, perceives many a sign of disaster to our peculiar institutions. But of such things, as we have just said, we are not thinking to speak—we only insist on the great principle of the text—*That God has raised us up for one great purpose, and if recreant to that purpose, however gigantic our march, we are yet rushing to destruction.* That prepared, manifestly, by God, as the great instrument for the world's civil and religious regeneration, such an end we must recognize and accomplish; or, if God remain immutable in the principles of His administration, the smoke of our burning will surely ascend, and the fragments of our shipwreck go by upon the waters.

And here we are brought to a grand principle of national self-preservation, which, though for the most part lost sight of, deserves our serious pondering—and that is, *That our safety depends in looking less inwardly upon ourselves, and more outwardly upon others.* We do not, indeed, pretend that to a nation, as to individuals, self-preservation is not the first law of life; we only do assert that this outward and world-reaching activity, is the great means even of self-preservation. We ought, of course, earnestly and vigilantly to take heed to ourselves. Esther was to seek to preserve her own life as carefully as that of her people. National life, like all other life, begins at the centre, and must be watched at the centre, as it works outward to the circumference. We must see that our civil and religious institutions are perpetuated and perfected. The Gospel of Christ must be given in fuller measure to our vast population. There is a practical and positive heathenism coming down on parts of the nation, which, as an influence undermining our national christianity, must be earnestly evangelized. There is an alliance of infidelity, and Anti-christ advancing with bold front, against pure and undefiled religion, which must be met by the championship of faith, and conquered for Jesus.

Meanwhile, our *civil* institutions, as well, must be conserved and strengthened. We must see that no root of bitterness spring up and trouble us. We must set our whole strength to crush under foot every reptile that dares to whisper of *disseverance and disunion.* The political demagogue, who, for any purpose of personal aggrandizement, dares conjure the phantom, we should brand with the mark of Cain, and drive forth from all political sympathy, a vagabond forever; and the professing christian, who, for the sake of southern bondmen, dares to preach and pray for disunion, should be pitied, indeed, as a poor lunatic, without enough of common sense to bear the heavenly graft of true piety; but, meanwhile rebuked from our presence as one lunatic, with a whole legion of devils.

In regard alike of our civil and religious immunities, we should, of course, first, take care of ourselves, remembering that it is a great law of our God—*"That he that provideth not first for his own, hath denied the faith, and is worse than an infidel;"* but, meanwhile, remembering as well that other law of our God, that the very preservation of life depends on the vigorous working of that life outward from the centre to the circumference—that *"There is, that scattereth and yet increaseth, and that which withholdeth more than is meet, which tendeth to poverty;"* and that alike in individual and national life, there is an extravagant self-care, which tends to destruction; and a generous forgetfulness of self, which results in preservation.

We may not and would not be blind to the dangers to which our land is exposed, nor to the political and anti-christian influences which seem at work for our destruction; nevertheless we have no right to be everlastingly declaiming, about their dangerous influence, as things to absorb attention. After all, we have no doubt but that these evils are all exaggerated—they are, in the main, only the symptoms of unimportant disease in a strong man, which will be only increased by over much attention, and disappear of themselves if he go bravely abroad to his ministry. One and all, we say these dangers are exaggerated.

Men cry aloud against—*The upgrowth in our midst of the Papal hierarchy;* but this danger we take to be, in the main, a phantom, conjured by religious demagogues, as a man of straw to be overthrown in Quixotic chivalry, in the face of an ignorant multitude. Now and then some impracticable and effeminate youth may profess conversion to Rome, seduced by Jesuitic arts, and thinking of the romance of a foreign college, or the mysteries of a confessional; but that this Anglo-American people are to go back in any considerable masses to the driveling mummeries of the Tiber's haggard superstition, is about as likely, as that our commercial marine will retrograde into the old Roman oar-gallies, and our Paixhan howitzer give place to the old Latin battering ram. The man, who in a land and an age like this, is honestly declaiming against the temporal influence of the poor Pope; and earnestly warning his countrymen against the political arts of the poor Catholics; ought to have lived at least in the last century, and followed the Spanish Cavalier in his crusade against windmills.

Nor have we any more to fear—*From the influx of foreign elements into our body politic, in the character and habits of the mingled races of the old world.* Though foreign emigration were increased a hundred fold, it would no more alarm a thoughtful man, for the safety of our free institutions, than do the thousand rivers, that pour their varied elements into the sea, alarm a philosopher for the purity of the mighty and assimilating ocean. This nation is already, in all its grand elements of character, permanently Anglo-American; and a wise man would just as sincerely fear to dine on a salmon, lest he, himself, should become a great fish; or to break his fast on a bird, lest he should sprout with feathers and wings; as have a fear lest this American nationality be essentially or injuriously modified by any foreign elements that may flow into it.

Nor, on the whole, have we any more serious apprehensions of disaster from that everlastingly vexed question of *Southern Slavery*. The cry of danger to our Federal Union, from this cause, is, at most, the false alarm of over-slept watchmen, who, in the somnambulism of a half-dream, mistake the sigh of winds through the banner, for the stealthy tread of armed men, or the far peal of trumpets. We do not say that this great confederacy can never, for any cause, be rent into fragments, and instead of one glorious commonwealth, there arise on its ruins, with all their anarchical and revolutionary accessories, two smaller confederacies, like the miserable military republics of South America. Causes may, indeed, arise in the providence of an avenging God, which shall rock our proud nationality into dust, and bury in the grave of our free institutions, at once the liberties of all people, and the hopes of a world. This all may happen, as we shall, presently, insist upon, from the operation of the principle of the text—that God will surely displace and destroy every instrument that works not out the purpose of its establishment.

We might say, indeed, that this Union can *never be dissolved;* because it is the result of a great organic law, which makes it, as the different members of a common body, by the great principle of a common life, one and indissoluble forever—not a conglomerate of States, but a great and composite Nation. Nevertheless, as violence may destroy a common life by a disseverance of its members; so this Union, while it cannot be peacefully *dissolved,* like an ice-hill in the sun, may yet be rent into fragments, as a mountain is rent by an earthquake. We do not say that this shall never happen, but this we do say, with the clearest, the calmest, and most assured confidence, that this question of Southern Slavery is not the earthquake that has power to sever us.

There has been, indeed, since Solomon's time, a regular descent of men, "from whom, though brayed in a mortar, among wheat, with a pestle, yet foolishness will not depart,"—Impracticable and malignant fools, who, like Herostratus, would gain for themselves immortal infamy, by the destruction of glorious structures like the Ephesian Temple of Diana. And such are the men, who, for the sake of the black men scattered thinly over the continent, would destroy this confederacy;—and for the abstract and imaginary right of a poor fragment of a race—to whom its exercise, if practicable, were destructive and disastrous—would madly destroy the last hope of a world's salvation, and bring down, upon all races the burden of ancestral bondage, adamantine and forever. Nevertheless, with such men, the great Anglo-American mind has no sympathy whatever. This question of slavery is, confessedly, a perplexing and disturbing thing in our body politic, and about it men do differ honestly and widely; but then there is one greater and grander question, about which the overwhelming and ever-increasing majority of this people never have differed, never will differ,—and that is *a steadfast and inflexible purpose, to preserve against all enemies, and with their heart's best blood, this glorious Union indissoluble and forever!*

Slavery is confessedly an evil, which no man more deeply feels and more ingenuously acknowledges, than the intelligent slaveholder, to whom the evil was a birth-right—and how to get rid of the thing without disadvantage to the two races is a problem perplexing all Christian philosophy. If true to ourselves, the God who hath relieved us from sorer evils will work out this problem, and in the end make manifest to the world, His hidden purpose of wisdom, and love in that mysterious dispensation whereby these children of Africa have been permitted to bondage. Meanwhile about expedients for removing this evil, so that the black man and the white man shall be mutually advantaged, there may be—and till God reveal his own hidden wisdom there must be—honest and hearty differences; and yet none but a fanatic or a fiend ever thought seriously, for one moment, of solving the problem by dissolving the Union; for, in the first place, such a dissolution, so far from freeing the slave would leave him more hopelessly, a bondman in a great Southern military confederacy. And secondly, even if it resulted in the abolition of slavery, it would be treating an evil on the old heroic plan of setting fire to a house to get rid of a broken sash, or cutting off a man's head to cure his arm of paralysis.

Oh, No! No! indeed No! Our national bark may be driven, by God's storms into shipwreck, but it will not be on this poor pebble of negro slavery, we break up piecemeal. We have already escaped a thousand mightier dangers. When the old thirteen colonies arose against British oppression they were three millions of people, scattered along a wild seaboard, and even then, they bore bravely the pressure of dissevered counsels—of party jealousies—of State quarrels—of sectional encroachments, on a strengthless central government—of destroyed cities—of stagnant commerce—of burned and blighted harvests—of paralyzed industry—of a crushing burden of debt, and of a disaffected and dissolute soldiery. All this great burden they bore triumphantly through the long conflict with the mightiest war-power of the world. And if thus and then, a nation only in form and name, with little of the vitality of her subsequent national life—America only grew stronger under this pressure in all those elements that now constitute her glory; tell me, if now, standing erect and mature in the full grandeur of her strength, she cannot, against the empty breath of a thousand fools, bear onward unbroken, nay unbent, this poor fardel of slavery. Oh! away with the doubt, let it come from what quarter it may, let it assume what form it will, of philanthropy or religion, it should be trampled sternly under foot as a hissing reptile; and the man who even in a whisper dares to speak of disunion as a possible and practical thing, should be spurned from the face of all honest men into infamy and exile, *as a traitor to his Country and an infidel to his God.*

We say then in a word, of all these evils, and of all such evils springing either from elements within us, or enemies without us, that we have no apprehension they can work us serious national disaster. Our apprehension, this day, arises only from the immutable operation of God's great law—*That every inefficient and maladjusted instrument will be cast to destruction.* We have been raised up by God, as the world's great regenerator, and we must accomplish thoroughly that work or be broken up as an effete engine.

This regeneration is to be at least in part SOCIAL and POLITICAL. We have, in our national capacity, a great work to do with the false social systems of old and haggard despotisms; not that ours is a call, (as the great Hungarian understood it,) to armed intervention. Kossuth's mission to this land was based on a great and true principle, and hence at his advent the heart of the nation rose up in glorious welcome.—But his fiery genius mistook the practical application of that principle, and hence the resistless ebb of his popularity. To suppose that America is to furnish war forces, and send fleets and armies to fight the battles of European freedom, is as wild a chimera as ever danced in the brain of a madman. The simple matter of fact is, that the age of fleets and armies, as means of human progress, and asserters of human rights, is passed away forever. The strongholds of despotism the world over, are not now camps and fortresses, but the living hearts of the populace.—With a universal desire for free government in the popular heart of Europe, every bond of oppression would fall off as the smoking flax from a Samson. And the coming war of redemption to Europe is not to be a war of arms, but a war of opinion; a war in which men will not conquer kings, but conquer the only support of kings, their own ancestral and ignorant prejudice. Our national intervention in behalf of the race, is to be in the intellectual field of man's prejudices and passions; and though we might do it safely and perhaps with success, yet to interfere as an armed power in European politics, were as philosophic, as to send an army to the Alps to manage the avalanches, or a fleet of gunboats to Naples to manoeuvre Vesuvius.

No! no! our mission in behalf of the nations is not an armed intervention. Indeed our mission, in its higher aspects, is in no degree military, and there is no falser and fouler slander than the everlasting utterance of a pensioned foreign press, that America is to be, or desires to be a great military nation, emulous of conquests and feats of arms. We have unquestionably the fiery and high heart of a brave people, and all the bone and sinew of a resistless military people; nevertheless, pre-eminently above every other nation on the face of the earth, are we a peace-loving, and a peace-abiding people.

Surrounded as we are by weak and helpless nations, and strong as we are in every arm and appliance of conquest. Yea, provoked, as we have been, by blustering foreign insolence—this country exhibits this hour a glorious spectacle of moderation and magnanimity, and self control, such as the world never saw. Verily, were America instinct with that fiery and unscrupulous martial ambition, which these slanderers ascribe to her, then, spite of all the paraded alliances of every empire under heaven, would the banners of her conquest be floating this day, over every province and island that from Hudson's Bay to Cape Horn belongs to this continent. Had we a single title of the martial spirit of the old military republics, then five hundred thousand of the bravest soldiery on earth would march under our eagles; and a navy, such as the world never saw, be whitening with its resistless canvass, every ocean under the firmament of heaven.

But we have not such a spirit. In the progress of the race, the age has gone by for the gone by for the supremacy of such a spirit. America has a nobler work to do than to play the poor brutal game of war with crowned idiots. If, as seems not impossible, these European Empires in their essential antagonism, and irreconcilable hate to our free institutions, should band themselves together, and come forth in their strength—the bear and the lion, and all the beasts of the earth, and the fowls of heaven, against the flight of our eagle, then indeed, for a little will it be our high calling of God, to stand up by these great hills and glorious streams, and sounding cataracts, and show what God's man-child can do, when he rushes into the last great battle for freedom and the world!

Nevertheless, such strife will not be of our seeking. It will come, if it come at all, in the fulfillment of the apocalyptic prophesy, whose vision was:—*"Of the Least and the kings of the earth, and their armies, gathered to make war on him on the white horse, whose eyes were as a flame of fire, and on whose head were many crowns."* And the grand issue of conflict is foretold in the vision, as well—*"The blow of a rod of iron!"*—and *"the flash of a sharp sword!"*—and *"the gathering of all the fouls of Heaven to eat the flesh of kings, and of captains, and of mighty men, at the last great supper of Almighty God!"* If God appoint us to such a war-path, then let the world be sure—will we walk it with a bounding heart, and a flashing eye, and a great and terrible glory such as the world never saw!

But of such conflicts, I repeat, I am not speaking when I proclaim America's Political mission to the nations of the earth; nevertheless, I am speaking of influences she is to put forth as positive and powerful. We are not to sit still with folded hands and frozen hearts, in full view of Political oppression and wrong unto Christ-redeemed humanity. No! perish the thought! perish the craven policy that dare to advocate or avow it. In all ways of practical and earnest wisdom, God calls us to interfere in behalf of the race. We have been equipped from the first for a mission of intervention. Our colonial establishment was an intervention; our Declaration of National Independence was an intervention; the march of our magnificent progress was an intervention; our enlarged commerce—our liberty-breathing literature—the opening wide of our gates to all exiles from despotism—the power and play of our political machinery—the majesty wherewith man, as man, walks this broad continent—and the radiant flash to the ends of the earth, of the stars that blazon our banners—these, all these are influences of resistless intervention wherewith God hath gifted us.

And the alarming thing about it all is, that we are not exerting these influences as broadly and strongly as the times demand of us. The period has come for one full working; our attitude in respect of the law of the text, is not that of an instrument in process of formation and adjustment, *but of an engine already coupled to a system of mechanism, and set a going for trial.* We are not on march to a kingdom for some period of future emergency. No! *"we are actually come to the kingdom for such a time as this."* The day has come when, even politically, American influence ought to be mighty in the earth as a blessing to all nations. Already do the Isles of the sea wait for us; the great Continents wait for us; Africa lies drowning in deep waters; Asia moans like a famishing giantess; Europe is hot and seething as a great caldron—her oppressed people are weary with the yoke, and expecting deliverance. These mad monarchs are wasting, in suicidal battles, the resources they should husband for the oncoming struggle for their own imperiled empires; and oppressed MAN watches and waits for the hour, when, with an equal stake on the great game, he may spring to the battle. Italy heaves already with the presage of an earthquake. Hungary rests like a weary giant, recruiting strength for a fiercer struggle. France has breathed one deep breath of freedom, and henceforth, every despot's fetters on her limbs, are as the burnt flax on Samson. Britain, with her great Anglo-Saxon heart, will cast presently, every burden of bondage off, as a lioness the raindrops. The great northern despotisms feel pulses like the beating of living hearts under their blood-cemented dynasties—"and for such times as this have we come to the kingdom." From our free institutions should be streaming abroad those mighty and manifold influences which shall destroy despotism, and establish and vindicate universal manhood.—For this was America born, and baptized with God's baptism; that in the embodiment of a vast moral power, and the movement of a tremendous moral machinery, she should solve the great problem of a world's freedom, and work out the glorious accomplishment of an emancipated race.

But, then for more than this, far more, are we come to the kingdom. These influences, *social* and *political,* though pertaining to our mission, are secondary and subordinate to our *evangelical influences.* When the world has been vitally christianized, then, and then only will its manhood be thoroughly emancipated. And especially for this evangelical work have we been raised up and strengthened. We stand today in the world in the place of old Israel—the chosen and peculiar people of the new dispensation—to be the almoners of God's grace, and the promulgators of God's oracles to the ends of the earth. And already has the fullness of time come for the accomplishment of our mission.

We have no limits to enlarge on the thought, nor does the thought need it. It is patent in the signs of the times, so that he that runneth reads it. On all sides it is deeply felt, that ours is an age most momentous in magnificent issues. Events that once required centuries for their accomplishment, are the result now of moments; change succeeds change with the startling rapidity of unnatural and extravagant drama. There is a restlessness abroad in the present system of things which seems the very throe and sore labor wherein the creature travaileth for deliverance from unwilling bondage. The nations of the world are waking from the long sleep of ages—the great heart of the race sorrows and throbs for redemption. False religions no longer satisfy its immortal longings. Paganism all in the East, holds its iron sceptre with a nerveless hand, senile and superannuate. The Mahommedan faith like the Mahommedan Empire is already wasted and worn in its death struggle. Popery is already tottering to the grave in the wrinkle and decrepmitude of dissolute living. The Ganges, the Euphrates, the Tiber, the Jordan—those ancestral rivers—are glassing in their flow the purpling dawn of a great day of redemption.

Then, too, the resources of the church of Christ and the implements all furnished to her hand for the diffusion of the true faith, are almost miraculously mighty—steam, the printing press, the magnetic telegraph, have equipped man for the rapid diffusion of truth, with the very pinion and power of an Archangel. And the canvas of christian commerce is whitening all waters, and riches vast as the treasures of kings, are in Christian coffers consecrate to Jesus. Surely the time has fully come for the aggression of a militant Christianity upon the tottering kingdoms of Antichrist The American church is called of God to be leading the van in the glory of her beautiful garments, flashing light from heaven into the dark places of a world in ruins. This very hour should there be an American missionary in every hamlet, and an American Bible in every home of a perishing humanity. The islands wait for us; the continents wait for us; the world waits for us. The hour has already come, when as a political influence, and a religious power, America should be fighting the great battles of God Almighty—not for future times, but for such a time as this have we come to the kingdom.

And here we say is our ground of gloomy foreboding. Are we accomplishing our mission? Are we acting well one appointed part in this majestic drama of Providence? Are we taking this whole round world into the sympathies of one great national heart, and pouring the light and loveliness of our political and evangelical beatitudes into the habitations of them that sit in the shadow of death? Oh! you can answer these questions for yourselves, any child can answer them. We are doing voluntarily and efficiently almost nothing for God and our generation. There stands the great enemy to be conquered for Jesus. Against which, with the wisdom of the children of this world, we ought to be hurling the forces of mighty armies, and our poor craven hearts and carnal passions, keep us back from the conflict and the victory. Avarice clutches its great keys in its skeleton fingers and cries—*"Oh, all this will require treasure,"*—and Selfishness lays hand on its shriveled and bloodless heart, and says—*"Oh! Charity begins at home."*—And Fear whispers with pale lips—*"Oh! I saw there the sons of Anak, tall men and mighty."*—and Sectarianism, with its hundred hydra heads and serpent voices, hisses, *"Oh! let us enlarge our own borders and make popular our shibboleth;"* and Pride—a devil in an angel's robe,—cries, *"Come let us build splendid churches, with soft seats in the middle, and costly melodramatic ritualism at either end thereof."* Till verily, verily, the carnal carries it so mightily over the spiritual, that the militant church looks like a peace establishment in its holiday parade, rather than a veritable war-power, armed and eager for battle.

Alas! alas! Called to conquer a world for Christ—we have not yet in the field even the semblance of an army. We are not as yet even successfully skirmishing around the out-posts, when we ought to be thundering at the great inner Citadel, and pealing the shout of victory in the mighty tide of the last great battle. We are not fulfilling our destiny. We are not upspringing to our high calling of God in Christ Jesus.

And here lies our danger: *In the patent law of God's empire against an effete engine.* We fear nothing but this. We laugh to scorn every thought of danger to our free institutions from internal fanaticism or external aggression. We will stand up here, in the glorious brotherhood of our fathers and our God, and trample, as a serpent under our feet, this foul spirit of disunion. We can gather by these sounding seas, and repel the mightiest war-power of an allied world, as majestically as Gibraltar rolls back the ocean surges. We can bear, unbent, all our national burdens, and walk, in the face of all people, our own ascending path to the loftiest summit of national glory. *But then, Omnipotence is too strong for us,*—GOD can palsy the right arm of this giant! and dash our crown of glory into dust, as a potter's vessel!

To a Christian, the question of our national perpetuity is not a mathematical problem as to commercial wealth and military resources—it is simply and purely a philosophic inquiry as to the success of an instrument in achieving the grand purpose whereunto God has called us. That Omnipotence will accomplish, in one way or another, that purpose, it were infidel to doubt. Deliverance was sure to the Jews, even if Esther forgot them; but then upon Esther herself, such forgetfulness would bring down destruction. And so of ourselves. The oppressed peoples of the earth are destined to civil liberty, and the kingdoms of this world shall surely become the kingdoms of Christ Jesus. Just as sure as God lives, this eclipsed orb in the firmament, shall become a new world of righteousness, and emancipated and redeemed man shall walk its radiant fields in the strength, and beauty, and gladness of immortality. We may forget our duty, and stand back from its burning wheels, yet scarcely the less will God's chariot of redeeming love rush abroad to all people. But if, recreant to our high calling, we go not forth in the march as God's fellow-workers, then do we cast ourselves into the play of that stupendous law, that dashes in pieces our effete engine. And the very way in which America may accomplish the redemption of a world, may be, alas! alas! by being rent into fragments by great national convulsion, and the scattering of her sons and daughters as fugitive missionaries of civil and ecclesiastical liberty to the end of the earth.

These, then, imperfectly set forth, are the two propositions we have had under review.

FIRST, That God has raised up this nation, as an instrument of the world's political and evangelical redemption.

And, SECONDLY, That by the principles of a great Divine law, our national safety depends on an earnest outworking this great purpose of Providence.

And, the result of the whole argument in our hearts, today, should be mingled emotions of the loftiest joy and the deepest sadness—loftiest joy in review of God's distinguishing love, manifested to us as a people; but deepest sadness at the indications in regard of us, that we are not achieving the great purpose for which that love has so distinguished us.

We ought to be joyous today. It is fitting and goodful to gather in these temples of God, in National Thanksgiving, And his soul must be infidel, and his heart adamant, who can ponder our past history or our present position, without a very overburden unto God of all grateful emotions. We stand, today, on this high mount of privilege, flung up amid the waste of ages. We look abroad upon the other nations of the world, some of them moaning in fetters, some of them lying down under heavy burdens, some of them heaving with wild convulsions, some of them in the wane and wrinkle of hoary decrepitude; and we look to ourselves—and lo! by these grand old hills and by these rushing streams, there stands, like the apocalyptic angel, upon the land and upon the sea, a gigantic form, in the fresh vigor and fair glory of trustful and exultant youth, all girt as a giant to run a race, all armed as with thunderbolts, to fight God's great battles—and the goodness, the grandeur, the magnificence of our American birthright overwhelms us. We cannot—we will not—shame on us if we could—repress one rapturous pulse of the grateful heart, or check one exultant voice swelling up in hallelujahs. Verily from these great cities, and these grand old forests, and these sounding cataracts, and these majestic mountains, should there go up to Jehovah, this day, such a hymn of exulting thanksgiving, as since the birth-song of the morning stars in the firmament, this world has not heard.

Nevertheless, enough of foreboding should nerve along the heart to remind us, that our acceptable thanksgiving for such national blessings, is not an indolent and sentimental emotion, but a living consecration of all our powers to God's service in that world-redeeming mission whereto He has called us.—And, verily, amid all our rejoicings, there are just grounds for such forebodings. Although, in the play of the intelligible and immutable law we have been considering; our future destinies are committed to our own care and keeping—yet, today, the prophesy from the signs of the times is of doubtful interpretation.—It is beyond our poor power to decide, whether this national instrument is to be kept a-going as approved in its play and adjustment—or displaced and destroyed as effete and abortive. It is a question our dazzled and tearful eyes have not a vision to answer, whether the chill shadows which fall from these mountains are passing away from a rising—or lengthening, or deepening from a descending sun. It is a point in musical expression upon which our listening ears are dull of hearing. Whether our thanksgiving-hallelujah today, hath the quality of birth-day gratulations over a giant's cradle, or funeral honors over an untimely grave. It is a burden of mystic and unfulfilled prophesy, which we are not inspired to interpret—whether this apocalyptic man-child, brought forth in the face of the devouring monster, and nurtured by God's hand in the wilderness—whether, I say—all instinct and earnest with grateful love to Jehovah, and armed in heavenly strength to redeem man from thralldom, and conquer the world for Christ Jesus, he shall walk safely to the end his majestic path of deliverance, and be caught up in fulfillment of the sublime vision—to the very bosom and throne of the Lord God Almighty: Or whether—alas! alas!—forgetful of his Divine calling, and recreant to his redeeming mission, and loitering in the race, and standing back from the battle, he be torn from his high place as an effete engine—and dashed into fragments—burned into ashes by the flash of God's thunderbolts.

5

THANKFULNESS

A SERMON PREACHED ON SABBATH MORNING, NOVEMBER 16, 1856, PRECEDING THE ANNUAL THANKSGIVING.

"Be thankful."

PSALM 100:4.

We have just read in your hearing the Proclamation of the Executive, enjoining upon this Commonwealth the observance of its accustomed day of Annual Thanksgiving. But, much as we like the custom, we are yet disposed, to doubt, whether the mere appointment of the day, with all its ancestral prestige and executive sanction, will render it to us individually, a truly religious festival; unless by solemn meditation we are prepared for its observance. It is rather an easy thing to omit for half a day our ordinary business; to assemble in God's house for rather a long service; and then retire to the enjoyment of rather an elaborate dinner. But this, we think, is not performing precisely the religious duty of thankfulness and thanksgiving. And, as preparatory to that service, we propose, at present, some very plain and practical observations on the duty in general.

The exhortation in our text—*"to be thankful"*—includes, of course, both *the inner emotion* and its *outward expression,*

A Subjective Thankfulness, and
An Objective Thanksgiving.

Now, I need hardly define the word *"Thankfulness."* It is already in its last analysis. It denotes a complete emotion, whose elements are, *joy for a gift, and love for the giver.* Differing from gratitude, not essentially, but only in form. The one being necessarily, a feeling only; the other that feeling both existent and expressed.

Passing then at once to its practical and personal consideration. What we have to say may be embraced, if not very logically ,yet we trust somewhat profitably, under these three divisions:

The Hindrances.
The Helps, and
The Reasons of Thankfulness.

Beginning with the *Hindrances,* which practically interfere with this great moral and Christian duty, we are struck with surprise that there should be any such hindrances. This experience and expression of gratitude for Divine favors, has its foundation, as a duty, in the very nature of things. For, as we can by no equivalent recompense God for his mercies, it seems positively unnatural, not to cherish a lively sense of His goodness, and give utterance to the feeling on appropriate occasions. Nevertheless, in this as in many another good thing, we are manifestly hindered. And setting ourselves to understand this strange thing, *unthankfulness,* we find, to our surprise, that the vice, like its opposite virtue, has its foundation in a very principle of our nature.

The old Saxon word, *"Grymetan,"* whence comes our Anglo-Saxon, *"to grumble,"* expresses only an original law of the human constitution. For analyzed carefully, an hope, or expectation of future good, will be found the grand element of the exercise. A happy feeling, indeed, in an unfallen spirit. But in a fallen, resulting in dissatisfaction with the present—and thus in *grumbling.* And so we find that this dissatisfaction began even in Eden. Eve fretting, fault-finding, grumbling, about the Forbidden Tree in the midst of the Garden. And thence as a true lineal exercise it has been manifest in all her descendants. The infant in its mother's arms—The school-boy on his way to school—The husbandman at the weather—The doctor at the night-call—The merchant about the markets—The lawyer about retaining-fees—The parson about his salary—indeed the whole human race, imitate their first mother, and complainingly grumble. It is a law of our nature, and like other laws has its uses. It will be found, upon careful examination, that even the bodily exercises, of *crying* and *groaning*, are grand operations whereby nature mitigates and allays anguish. A physician will tell you, that a patient who gives free course to these natural feelings, will recover sooner from accidents and operations, than another, who, thinking it unmanly to cry and groan, represses resolutely all such manifestations. He will relate cases, where violent cryings and roarings have greatly reduced excited pulses, and soothed the nervous system, thus preventing or allaying fever, and insuring in many diseases a favorable termination. And so he rather encourages these tears and groanings in patients while undergoing violent surgical operations. And, in regard of restless and hypochondriacal subjects, who will always be under medical treatment, he knows that they can do nothing better for themselves, than groan all the day, and cry all the night.

In this point of view grumbling is medicinal, — an operation whereby nature relieves sorrow. And as we do not find fault with tears, no more should we find fault with querulous words, spoken shortly and seasonably. They are escape-valves of anguish, they relieve sensibilities, and so do good as a medicine. Indeed, he that has nothing to grumble about cannot be comfortable, because he has nothing to complain of, and therefore nothing to desire, and having nothing to anticipate, can never be happy.

But then this genial, good-natured, medicinal, and so beneficial grumbling, degenerates almost universally into downright, malignant, everlasting fault-finding; and then — like all medicine taken as a daily aliment — it becomes positively hurtful. It impairs the freshness and healthfulness of the mind; induces morbid, rheumatic, neuralgic moods of thought; makes the man a torture to himself, and a curse to the neighborhood; weakens his influence; destroys his character; renders him a wretch here, and tends inevitably to render him wretched forever. And so, although we find this root of thankfulness in a primal law of our nature, yet its manifestations result from various things which we have termed obstacles to thankfulness. Of these I mention—

First. —The habit of looking too much at other people, and too little at ourselves. Quite manifest is it, that very much of our discontent arises from a consideration of our neighbors. Others are richer, or more honorable, or beautiful, or successful than ourselves — others treat us with neglect, or injustice — others are guilty of manifest shortcomings or overt iniquities; and so, our poor life-bark, overladen with other men's wares, labors painfully on the seas, signals of distress flying from its every mast, and the sound of its minute-guns making night a burden. Whereas, if the poor man would go into his own heart, and fling overboard all but his own peculiar cares and troubles, and sit down to feast on the rich viands God has gathered as his sea-stores, then his lightened and relieved bark would float buoyantly on the waters, and answer readily her helm, and with glad songs and bright skies go on her way rejoicing. But then, this looking too much at the things of others, is not our only difficulty, and we remark, therefore,

Secondly. —That in looking to ourselves, *we are accustomed to let the mind dwell too much on the dark side of our experience.* Rather upon *what we have not,* than upon *what we have.* Rather upon the *Divine chastisement* than the *Divine benefaction.* It is the *spots* upon the sun that the astronomer talks of. It is when under an eclipse, that the moon and stars are most carefully observed. It is the one river with the cataract, and not the thousand rivers with their unbroken water-courses that tourists throng to.

In contemplating the history of a year, it is impossible in a probationary life, that it should have brought only uninterrupted gladness; and so, the thought fastens on the fairer things that might have been, rather than the fair things that have been. The ten thousand daily blessings wherewith God has been rounding our lives, are lost sight of in the occasional clouds of difficulty that may have chequered our pathway. We think more of the one thousand dollars lost, than of the twenty thousand left us. More of the one month of sickness, than the eleven months of health. More of the one beloved friend dead, than of the many beloved yet living. More of the mournful silence in the one sepulchre, than of all the sweet voices of our happy households. Whereas, if just reversing this process, we would look more at the bright side of things — at the stars that are not eclipsed; at the bright streams that are not broken by cataracts; at the profits of our business, and not at its losses; at the seats filled at the board and hearth, and not at the seats vacant. Then these earthly homes, which we are filling with mourning, and over whose portal we have written in black capitals, *"Rooms to let to the Sorrows,"* would flash again with festal lustres, and resound with festal songs; and seen to all who go by, the sweet and fair homes of God's happy, thankful children. Nor is this indeed the whole of it, for observe—

Thirdly —That even while considering our mercies, there is a habit of thought which hinders our thankfulness. I mean that—*of regarding the first gift of a good thing as alone demanding gratitude, and its subsequent preservation as a natural sequence.* Now nature is not a power, but a process. *Preservation is positively a constant creation.* And so, as truly as if it were done sensibly and immediately, God gives us a new sun every morning, and hangs new stars every night in the firmament; and gives us, by an Almighty act, put forth every moment, each process of a new life, and each adaptation and blessedness of a new home and world. In other words, we think only of *the added*, and not of the *preserved* mercy — looking upon the continued possession of old blessings as resulting from the stability of the sequences of nature, and only upon the new and superadded blessing, as the positive and directed gift of God. And what we want, is that true philosophic faith, which sees God putting forth creative power in every hour's preservation; so that when we go into life's tabernacle, and see how carefully it has been builded, and how exquisitely furnished, — till it looks like the dwelling in the wilderness of a heavenly monarch's children, — it shall seem to us an immediate gift of God, as if just at the present moment, with all its goodful and joyous things, it has — like the Apocalyptic vision of the New Jerusalem — descended, by a great miracle, out of the very depths of heaven.

Now, although I have but just entered upon a consideration of these obstacles of thankfulness, yet the remainder of our subject compels me to leave other things unsaid, and go on to consider—

Secondly —*The Helps to Thankfulness.* Of course, the first thing is to get rid of these obstacles. But having considered this already in passing, let us advance to some practical and general rules for strengthening our thankfulness. And—

First. —*We just entertain just and philosophic views of life's nature and mission.* We are here in this world only as in a pupilage; —or transition state —for states higher and better, and must learn to judge things and value them only for their uses. A man, crossing an ocean on shipboard, is not discontented because he cannot carry with him his sumptuous furniture and equipage; and grumbles not that his stateroom hath not the breadth and brilliancy of his palatial pavilions. His very gladness is, that he is in a structure so modeled and circumscribed, that it can have speed upon the waters. And just so it is with a man in progress to Immortality. What he wants is rather, a tent, that can be pitched, and struck at pleasure; and provisions of a style and kind that can be carried in journeys; than a splendid palace, and ponderous luxuries, incapable of transportation. And so a true appreciation of the real uses of things, will go far to render us thankful for the peculiar size and shape of the blessings God gives us. Then, as before intimated,

Secondly — We must dwell much in thought upon these Divine mercies, present and actual. We are too much given to daydreams and reveries amid things possible and future. We lift the glass of imagination to the far hills, that mellowed by distance, and haloed with the purple and gold of the setting sun, look like lands of fairy, and grow impatient and dissatisfied with the present and possessed. And yet, there is no one in whose present experience there is not mingled very much — enough at least for constant thankfulness—of comfort and blessedness. And what we want, is a disposition to sit down and count and acknowledge our mercies.

Perhaps you do not all know the origin on this continent of these annual Thanksgiving Days. It was on this wise, and on the point under review is altogether instructive. When the New England colonies were first planted, the settlers endured many privations and difficulties. Being piously disposed, they laid their distresses before God in frequent days of fasting and prayer. Constant meditation on such topics kept their minds gloomy and discontented, and made them disposed even to return to their fatherland, with all its persecutions. At length, when it was again proposed to appoint a day of fasting and prayer, a plain common-sense old colonist rose in the meeting, and remarked, that he thought they had brooded long enough over their misfortunes; and that it seemed high time they should consider some of their mercies. That the colony was growing strong — the fields increasing in harvests — the rivers full of fish, and the woods of game — the air sweet — the climate salubrious — their wives obedient — and their children dutiful. Above all that they possessed, what they came for, full civil and religious liberty. And therefore, on the whole, he would amend their resolutions for a Fast, and propose, in its stead, a day of Thanksgiving. His advice was taken, and from that day to this, whatever may have been the disastrous experience of New England, the old stock of the Puritans have even found enough of good in their cup, to warrant them in appointing this great annual Festival. Passing this we observe,

Thirdly —That in order to be thankful, we must make the best of our misfortunes. What the Germans tell as a parable, we have, all of us — who have gone afield with nature in observant moods — witnessed not unfrequently. Standing by some autumnal, and over-matured flower, we have seen the laborious bee come hurrying and humming, and plunging into the flower's cup, where there was not a particle of honey. But what does the bee do? Why, after sucking and sucking, and finding no nectar, it comes up from the flower's heart with a disappointed air, as if departing to some other field of labor? But no. If there be no sweets at the flower's red core, yet its stamens are full of golden farina, and out of the farina the bee builds its cells; and os it rolls its little legs against these stamens, till they look large and loaded as golden hose, and thanking the flower as sweetly as if it had been full of honey, gladly and singing it flies home with its wax. Yes, and herein lies God's moral — *If our flowers have no honey, let us be glad of the wax!*

And this reminds me of another incident connected with the appointment of Thanksgiving days. When our national Independence had been triumphantly achieved, the Colonies, of course, held great general jubilee. And good King George, who had been sadly worsted in the conflict, thinking himself quite as pious as his disloyal subjects — and not to be outdone in Godliness by such rebels against the Divine right — appointed also a day of Thanksgiving for the restoration of peace to his long disturbed Empire. In the vicinity of the monarch's residence, then Windsor Castle, dwelt a most estimable minister of the Church, who shared his sovereign's intimacy, and conversed with him freely. On this occasion the worthy divine ventured to say:

'Your majesty has sent out a proclamation for a day of thanksgiving. For what are we to give thanks? Is it because your majesty has lost thirteen of the fairest jewels from your crown?"

"No, no," replied the monarch, "not for that!"

"Well, then, shall we give thanks because so many millions of treasure have been spent in this war, and so many millions added to the public debt?"

"No, no," again replied the king, "not for that!"

"Shall we, then, give thanks that so many thousands of our fellow men have poured out their life-blood in this unhappy and unnatural struggle, between those of the same race and religion?"

"No, no," exclaimed George, for the third time; "not that!"

"For what then, may it please your majesty, are we to give thanks?" asked again the pious divine.

"THANK GOD!" cried the king most energetically; "THANK GOD THAT IT IS NOT ANY WORSE!"

Yes, and here is a reason for thankfulness in all circumstances, since it is never so bad with us as it might be. And even if God be pouring out the vials of His anger, yet blessed be His name! He never empties them to the uttermost.

But then this making the best of trials and disappointments involves much more than simply enduring them, in view of their accompanying mercies. —And we observe,

Fourthly —That we must, meanwhile, learn to look upon these very evils as God's disguised blessings. To every true Christian they are so, positively, and beyond controversy. As part of the special Providence of a wise and loving Father, they cannot be otherwise. It is God that determines the bounds of our habitation; the stations we are to fill; the comforts we are to enjoy; and the trials we are to suffer. And if we have not much of the present world, it is not because our Heavenly Father is not able to give us more. It is all to be resolved into the wisdom and kindness of the Divine Administration — God's wisdom discerning how much is best for us — and His love determining Him to allow us no more. As a truth, alike of experience and revelation, these present afflictions are salutary. They produce in the soul, by a most philosophic process, the peaceable fruits of righteousness. And a grace is the measure, and very element, of glory; so, by enlarging heavenly exercises in the soul, *"do these light afflictions which are for a moment, work out for us a far more exceeding and eternal weight of glory."* They are but the storms on the water driving the bark toward the haven! But the darkness of the midnight making glorious heaven's stars! And therefore as real, though disguised, mercies, are afflictions to be regarded as they relate to God's true children. And this leads us, as a direction including all others, to remark,

Fifthly —That to become truly thankful, we must become Christians —And Christians growing in grace and advancing in knowledge. —We have no limits for an enlarged consideration of the philosophic tendency of earnest piety to produce gratitude and gladness —but must confine ourselves to a few points of its illustration.

Religion makes a man humble. —And humility, as a grace, lies at the foundation of contentment. If the Christian's lot be low, he thinks more meanly of himself than others can think of him, and is in no way disquieted at other men's opinions. If his daily mercies seem small, he feels, that, being unworthy of anything, by every elevation of his condition above death and hell, he fares better than he deserves, and gives thanks for that elevation, with true love and rejoicing. And, contrasting his condition at its worst with that of his Savior, feels that a universe would cry, "Shame!" if he should not be thankful, while faring better than the Master, he has "a place to lay his head!"

Meanwhile, *Religion gives him just views of present things, and of the true relation he sustains to them, in this earthly economy.*— They never seem to him ends, but only *means unto ends.* He understands how his present life is a sojourn; an Exodus. And, as a true-hearted traveler, he expects not home-comforts, on a journey; but is content with rude fare, and humble hostelries, and can thank God even for rough roads, and foul weather, if they hinder not his progress.

Moreover: *Religion, as it is essentially a principle of self-denial, moderates a man's wishes, and so creates happiness.* —Diogenes was happier in his tub, than Alexander on the throne of his empire. And for a good reason —because the tub held the wishes of the philosopher; but the world was too small for those of the conqueror. The real necessities of our nature are few and simple and easily satisfied. And all beyond this is the tyranny of fancy. The water drank by the beggar, from the wayside spring, is as sweet as when lifted to a king's lip in a golden chalice. The true want is relieved by the draught, but the fancied want not even by the goblet. And so the grand secret of contentment is found, not in increasing our supplies, — but in diminishing our necessities. Not in revealing new worlds to satisfy Alexander; but in transforming Alexander into Diogenes satisfied with his tub.

Meanwhile: *Religion produces trustfulness, and so brings contentment.* — After all, the great secret of discontent, is born of anticipation. These reveries and daydreams are full of tormenting phantoms. Even if we are hoping for better things in the future; this very expectation begets dissatisfaction with the present. It places the heart in attitudes as unfavorable to present enjoyment, as that of a racer, for observing the beautiful landscapes he is crossing. The butterfly we pursue is grasped at last, all bruised and shattered, just because we pursued it, —whereas, to him that sits contentedly down, there comes one flitting to his very hand, in all its wonderful and unmarred beauty.

But then, the staple of our anticipations is fear and foreboding; we are always conjuring evil for the morrow. In the present, things may be well enough. But not satisfied to enjoy the present, we are always, and at awful rates of interest, borrowing trouble form the future. Climbing mountains that are yet in the distance! Crossing bridges before we come to them. And so this whole habit of living in the future is fatal to all thankfulness, both for the past and the present; and this religion overcomes by making the man trustful. It makes him trustful for *the present*. With his sins forgiven, and his conscience at peace, he carries the celestial elements within his own bosom. And with wings of love and faith is ever soaring, eagle-like, in the sunshine of God's smile; and abiding far above the serpent of discontent, that stings the dwellers in the dust, and the clouds of despair, that fling shadows on the tents of the ungodly. But more than all, religion makes the man *trustful of the future*. Even the earthly and mortal future he trusts gladly in God's hand. There may come to him trials, but he is sure of heavenly strength and consolation. With every cloud in the sky, God's rainbows to span it! With every storm on the sea, the Divine Redeemer to still it! And the more steep and rugged the pathway, only the straighter and nearer it lies toward his home!

Meanwhile, in regard of the immortal and heavenly future, does religion make the man trustful and thankful? His faith is the veritable substance of things unseen and hoped for; and he is mounting ever on its strong wings above all these poor clouds of the mortal, until he can catch through the lustrous gates of the Eternal City, its songs of gladness — its shapes of glory. He stands with John in his blessed exile; he beholds those radiant trains go by — from their palms; their plumes; their robes; their diadems, flinging light that bathes the poor Patmos in a sea of heavenly splendor. He mounts with Paul in his strange rapture, higher and higher, till this poor world fades away in the distance, and those loftier firmaments are ablaze with the ineffable lustres of the city of God! Yes, he enters in! — he walks by the river of life! —he numbers "the hundred and forty-and-four thousand!" —he takes in that overwhelming perspective, rising tower above tower! Pinnacle above pinnacle! Throne above throne! Higher! Higher! Higher! *"Things to come?" "Things to come!"* He catches glimpses of those transcendent and unrevealed realities with whose unutterable magnificence Paul labored vainly when he cried, *"The far more exceeding and eternal weight of glory!"* And though the immensity of the beatitude overwhelms him, as he thinks of his own insignificance and unworthiness — and it seems too much to believe that such things can lie along the future of his experience — yet, he remembers the faith-strengthening argument, that *"He who hath given His Son, will with Him freely give us all things."* And in wondering and adoring love, grasps the great promise of *"All things!" "Paul, and Apollos, and Cephas, and the world, and life, and death, and things present, and things to come."* "ALL THINGS!" —absolutely, "ALL THINGS!" And a wise and sensible man, as he is, he says— "This is enough for me, —Surely this is enough for me." And so, contented with the present, and trustful for the future, he becomes, as he ought, a happy man, and a thankful.

And now, leaving this point, as the first, most imperfectly illustrated, let us pass to consider—

Thirdly. —*The Reasons of Thankfulness, or why we ought to be thankful?*

Of course, the first reason is, *that our circumstances demand it.* We have positively, every one of us, very much to be thankful for. Methinks it were enough to shame any man out of his miserable mood of grumbling, just to sit honestly down for an hour, and count over his blessings. Just contrast your own condition this day, with that of the exulting pilgrims, when they kept their first Thanksgiving festival. See them, amid the solitudes of that great wilderness — the cry of the wild beast, and the roar of the strong wind rising around them — the loved homes of their childhood, and the precious temples of their fathers, far away over the waters — a barren soil beneath their feet; and above, the cold and cheerless azure of a stranger-heaven! And yet, singing triumphantly unto God their Thanksgiving Anthem!—

> "The breaking waves dashed high
>   On a stern and rock-bound coast,
> And the woods, against a stormy sky,
>   Their giant branches tost;
>
> "And the heavy night hung dark
>   The hills and waters oer,
> When a band of exiles moved their bark
>   On the wild New England shore.
>
> "The ocean-eagle soared
>   From his nest by the white wave's foam,
> And the rocking pines of the forest roared—
>   This was their welcome home!
>
> "There were men with hoary hair,
>   Amidst that pilgrim-band—
> Who had come as exiles to wither there
>   Away from their childhood's land!"
>
> "There was a woman's fearless eye,
>   Lit by her deep love's truth;
> There was manhood's brow serenely high,
>   And the fiery heart of youth.
>
> "Yet not as the sorrowing come,
>   In silence and in fear—
> They shook the depths of the desert's gloom,
>   With their hymns of lofty cheer.
>
> "Amidst the storms they sang,
>   And the stars heard, and the sea!
> And the sounding aisles of the dim wood rang
>   To the anthem of the free!"

Thus—thus, did our forefathers make manifest their thankfulness to God for his mercies! And shall we be less thankful? Why, you will keep this festival in homes, and amid luxuries such as old monarchs never dreamed of! Upon your boards will be viands and spicery from all Earth's islands and continents. In your wardrobes, the wools of Saxony, the linens of Ireland, the silks of Italy, and the furs of the frozen zones. And crowding your chambers, furniture and bijoutry, wrought of woods from the forests of Ceylon and Domingo; and of metals from the mines of Potosi and the Ural; and of gems from Brazilian caverns and Indian streams; and of costly stuffs from the looms of Manchester and Lyons; and of plumes from the groves of Araby the blest; and of the magnificent marbles of Egypt and Italy. And if, in such homes, you cannot be thankful, it must be as the sated Sybarite, pained with his displaced rose-leaf. Meanwhile, in your homes, are better things than these. Those beloved forms that sit by its board. Those gentle voices, sweeter to your soul than the voices of angles, that make blessed its chambers. Yes, and more. That precious Bible that shines there as a Heavenly Lamp. That family Altar, at whose side there lifts a new Ladder, from Bethel to the skies, with its descending Seraphim. And then, all these unnumbered, social and civil, and national, and religious beatitudes which surround that mortal tabernacle, as Shechinah-lustres round the tents of the Exodus. All these means of grace! All these hopes of glory!

Living here in America — in this nineteenth century — free men — free Christians — so that your lot seems the veritable realization of the golden dreams of the old Hebrew prophets — those gleaning and distant millennial glories, that colored the page of Isaiah, and made lustrous the clouds of the Apocalypse! Verily, you have cause for gratitude. Verily, in view of what God has done for you, you ought to be thankful! But passing this, I remark,

Secondly —That for your own sake, for the sake of your own souls, you ought to be thankful. We tell you again, and again, that this exercise of fault-finding and grumbling is altogether unprofitable. If some great affliction befalls you — why, give it one grand outburst of relieving tears, and have done with it. Bury the blessing God takes from you with befitting rites of lamentation, but do not embalm the dead thing as a memorial-mummy, and keep it, as an everlasting spectre of misery, in the midst of your dwelling. This habit of mournful sadness destroys alike, happiness and influence, and usefulness and character. I am disposed to believe — though naturalists will differ from me — that the Owls were, originally, as clear-sighted and joyous creatures as the Eagles. But, getting into a bad habit of living in caves, and going abroad only to mourn over the night-side of nature, they, by the great law of adaptations, have degenerated into the wretched and blind of God's winged and plumed creation. And the habit works as disastrously in human experience. It blinds the eye, and dwarfs the pinions of the soul; renders the heart a nervous and neuralgic thing; eats out a man's piety; weakens every Christian grace; and makes the creature a torture to himself, and a curse to his neighborhood. And this leads me to remark,

Thirdly—That as Christians, we ought, for the sake of others, to manifest this abiding spirit of joy and thanksgiving. I speak now to professing Christians. And, as exemplified in the lives of such, this Religion of Christ ought to appear the loveliest and most attractive of all things. But how does it appear as exhibited in the life of a sad-faced and sad-hearted professor! The man walks abroad with his sighs, like the wind in a cedar bush; his step, as the grinding of a hearse over unbroken gravel stones; and the impenitent man looks on with a recoil, and says, "Well, if that man is walking to glory, it must be a hard road to travel!" "If that is Religion, it is a poor thing, make the best of it!" Suppose an Angel should come down from the skies, and walk up and down among men, with his brow wrinkled with sadness, and his eyes dim with tears! Why, then — even if God's Fire-Car, with its flaming coursers, stood all lustrous at your threshold — where is the man among you that would mount it gladly, and with a loosened rein, and a bounding heart, spring exultingly toward a heaven, whose very angels seem wretched! And therefore we remark—

Finally — That for your Heavenly Father's sake, you ought to cherish, and display this spirit of thanksgiving. —I do not mean merely that He deserves your praises; — this I have already insisted on. Nor do I mean merely that He commands you to be thankful. — Although coming, as my text does, as the precept of a Divine Law; I might say, that the man, ever grumbling, does as expressly disobey God, as the man ever uttering false-witness, or blasphemy. But I do mean, in this connexion, that, by this exhibition of sorrowful unthankfulness, you *positively* and *powerfully dishonor*

Jehovah! A monarch, whose subjects are always complaining of their lot, is set down by the world as a hard and selfish tyrant. A father, whose children walk abroad ever in sadness and tears, is anathematized by all people, as a heartless and cruel parent. And so the world judges of your Eternal Sovereign, and your Heavenly Father, when you, his professed subjects and children, go murmuring and complaining about the earth, as if Christian life

> "Were but a cloud
> Brooding in nameless sorrow on the soul,
> A sadness — a sick-heartedness — a tear!"

No — no — no. Shame on us, if surrounded by such blessings — and hastening onward to such revelations of glory — we go over with the bowed head, and the mournful footsteps, saying to the world by our pitiful complainings — "See how the Eternal God is maltreating his loyal subjects!" "See how our Heavenly Father is torturing his children!"

And now, if you gather into one, all these reasons for cherished, and expressed gratitude, you will perceive the wisdom and excellence of the text's great law, "BE THANKFUL!" — "BE THANKFUL!"

And, therefore, as individuals, and as a people, let us see if we cannot keep this great national festival in the true spirit of the requirement. If we will not obey the governor, let us at least obey God, and, leaving all our dead sorrows in the grave, and all our complainings at home, come up with bright eyes, and happy hearts to God's temple, and with voices of praise, wherein is blent no undertone of sadness — sing to our Heavenly Father, some such anthems as this:

> "Come thou fount of every blessing,
>   Tune my heart to sing thy grace;
> Streams of mercy never ceasing,
>   Call for songs of loudest praise;
> Teach me some melodious sonnet,
>   Sung by flaming tongues above.
> Praise the Mount — O, fix me on it,
>   Mount of God's unchanging love.

"Here I raise my Ebenezer,
　Hither by thy help I'm come;
And I hope, by thy good pleasure,
　Safely to arrive at home.
Jesus sought me when a stranger,
　Wandering from the fold of God;
He to rescue me from danger,
　Interpose with precious blood.

"O to grace how great a debtor;
　Daily I'm content to be!
Let that grace, Lord, like a fetter,
　Bind my wandering heart to thee.
Prone to wander, Lord, I feel it;
　Prone to leave the God I love;
Here's my heart, Lord, take and seal it,
　Seal it for thy courts above."

6

CHARACTER

A SERMON PREACHED ON THANKSGIVING DAY, NOVEMBER 20, 1856.

"And who knowest whether thou art come to the kingdom for such a time as this?"

ESTHER 4:14.

In discoursing from these words in our last Thanksgiving service, we applied them to our Nation, as the Divinely appointed instrument for the world's political and evangelical redemption. We propose now to pursue the same thought in a more detailed and special application. Here, as everywhere, truth is weakened by too broad generalization. The duty, and the destiny of a nation, can never become a practical and profitable speculation, if you regard national life, as transcendental, and distinct from, the Individual life that makes up its aggregate, — and so personify States — as Existences, possessing certain powers and prerogatives; and working out influences, and issues; and governed by Divine laws, and judged by Divine standards — all differing from those pertaining to the individual men who compose them.

We are all prepared to admit the truth of the text in its former application. We confess readily that America has been raised up by God for some grand purpose. That it is a great nation, and ought to be a good nation. But then we are at fault in our analysis of nationality. For what is America, and where? — Go to our metropolitan capitol; to the palace of the president; to the halls of our representatives; to the seats of our judges; to the navies on our seas; to the encampment of our armies; and have you yet found America? Does America walk abroad on the hills? Or repose in the valleys? Does she abide in great cities? Or voyage in great ships? The simple fact is, that each American is America. You, and I, and all of us, are the American nation. Let every American die, and America is dead; let every American become good, and America is holy; let every American become profligate, and America is vile. There is no such thing as national character and duty, apart from individual character and duty. And the sooner we abandon these rhetorical personifications of national life, and go down in thought to that individual and personal life, whose aggregate is a nation, the wiser for our philosophy, and the better for our morals.

In dwelling, therefore, upon God's great design in raising up this nation, we dwelt really upon his design in raising up ourselves. And passing now from the general, to the more discriminative, and individual application, of the text's principles, let us consider, what God expects of us personally, in having *"brought us to the kingdom in such a time as this."* We are here to offer unto Jehovah our annual sacrifices of thanksgiving. (*i.e.*) We are here to offer ourselves, as living sacrifices to God, in reasonable service, ready to act our appropriate parts, and work out our respective appointments, in the grand Divine purpose, which has brought our nation, (*i.e.*) *ourselves,* to the kingdom for such a time as this. The simple question, therefore, into which the whole matter resolves itself, and which, at this time, we propose somewhat in detail to consider is,

What ought to be the character of an American Citizen in times like the present?

Before, however, proceeding to an analysis of its elements, I must be allowed to remark a few things of character in general. I suppose I need hardly observe — that in all this discussion — *we shall speak strictly of character* — and not what so often passes for it — (*i.e.*) *reputation.* Character is something within the man's self. Reputation something altogether without him. Reputation is not, as we are often told, even the shadow of character. For then the shadow were ofttimes, not merely the caricature, but the very opposite of tie substance — and always, as the shape and shell of a house, indicates in no case certainly its internal arrangements, and appointments; so reputation indicates in no case necessarily the elements of the character.

Even in regard of truthful and deserved reputation; you will observe, that it depends always on the faculties most used, and the attributes most operative, and obtruded; whereas character, on the contrary, depends mainly on those stronger, and so less facile, attributes, and faculties, which, for the most part, hidden and unobserved, color and control the whole being. Reputation is but the contour of a house's shadow; character is the inner economy of its complicate architecture. So a man may lose reputation — as a building its shadow — when the sun of popular favor is eclipsed above him. But he can never lose character, so long as household light and love make pure and sweet its familiar chambers.

Observe, therefore, again, *That character is to be judged of from the mass, or predominant qualities of the aggregate.* No man is *all* evil; and yet, many a man's character is evil. As copper, with a small admixture of gold, is called copper; and gold, with a trifling alloy of cooper, is called gold, so a good man, with a little evil, is yet good; and a bad man, with little goodness, is yet evil.

Observe, moreover — *That character, to be good, must be complete in its elements, and symmetrical in their developments.* A principle, virtuous in itself, becomes monstrous, and so, vicious, by excessive manifestation; and thus a man may have some great excellencies, yet lacking others as necessary to well-regulated and beneficent influence; may have the while a character which is bad, and bad only. Character is, then, not a conglomerate of a few distinct excellencies, held together by some personal cement; but is, rather, a vital union of all the cardinal virtues, meeting and modifying each other, and essentially mingled in one homogeneous composite.

Observe meanwhile, *That character is not to be judged of abstractly,* but RELATIVELY. Not indeed so much an *absolute thing,* as an *adaptation,* to be considered in connection with times and circumstances. We are not, indeed, thinking to question the essential and immutable distinctions between *right* and *wrong;* or the principles of virtue and vice, which lie at the foundation of all moral character. Nevertheless, quite manifest it is, that all the practical value of character, results from its adaptation to its possessor's circumstances. All the essential elements of a good character are, of course, always good, and always in place; and yet, certain generations, and certain social positions in those generations, may demand particular virtues, or classes of virtues, in extraordinary development. As well in morals as in physics; for everything there is a place and occasion. Courage, and patience, are co-equal and co-ordinate excellences in a well-modeled character. And yet, in man's history, there are certain crises when, on the one hand, high courage seems rashness; and when, on the other, meek patience seems pusillanimity. An engine is a good thing in a steamship — and so is an anchor. But the anchor works disastrously, when it keeps in harbor the ship that should sail; and the engine is a curse when it drives the ship abroad to the seas, that should be still at its moorings. And just so in morals; there are certain periods in human history, when amid popular clamors for progress and reform, the world is at red-heat of most uncomfortable excitement, and then, calm patience does its perfect work. But anon, there are periods when the tides of life are all stagnant as Asphaltites; and then the fire of an earnest zeal is the true inspiration.

And so, too, of character, in its *constructive combinations.* In different zones we build houses differently. Granite bulwarks against polar storms; airy verandahs against tropic sunshine. And he that builds a character, must build with his eye open to the distinguishing peculiarities of his day and generation; cultivating more the heroic graces, if he live in the martyr times; and more the gentle if he live in Millennial. Promising this, let us go on to consider more particularly the style of character demanded by this age and nation. And we remark, as suggested by our introduction.

First of all—*That a deep sense of individual power and responsibility* — must lie, in times like these, at the very foundation of all efficient and available character. In a want of this lay the error of earlier social systems. The *individual* was then hardly known as a power in the State. In the old classic Republics, the lower classes do not even appear as potential social elements. All the old governments of the world have been annihilative of popular individualism. Whether you regard the caste systems of India — the martial despotism of Persia — the rule of craft and wealth in Phoenicia — or the class divisions of Greece, and Rome, and Judea: one obvious characteristic will be found pervading all ancient nations — building everywhere the social system on the same assumption — of *the natural inequality of men – the necessary, because Divinely appointed, inferiority of races and castes.* And herein you find sufficient reason for the imperfect freedom, and consequent decline, of the great Empires of antiquity. To the philosophic eye, history is but a roll of defunct nations, all essentially alike in career and destiny. Unto Chaldea, Tyre, Greece, Rome, unto all, as if by an inevitable law, there came, after the day of civilization and empire, the deep night of barbarism and slavery. This has been repeated again and again, till the world has come to accept it as its established course. To look only, that States, emerging from infancy and weakness, and slowly and laboriously becoming rich, enlightened, powerful, shall, the moment they have consolidated their strength, and perfected their civilization, begin to decline. That the race in its struggling progress, can be successful only up to a certain point, which having reached, all the fruits of a past labor, all the accumulations of legislators, philosophers, statesmen, warriors, must be swept away, and the race begin again the laborious process, — upward from the same gulf, to be overtaken by the same disaster. Alas, History, find it where you will — sculptured on the Etruscan tombs; or hieroglyphed, in the mounds of Nineveh; or written in the glorious records of Greece and Rome; has been but a series of ever-recurring cycles — eras of civilization and power ending in barbarism.

And why is this? We ask anxiously and sadly! Has the Creator set limits to the life of kingdoms, as surely as of men? Must the great laws of physical progress be ever reversed, in the moral and national? The oak, going backward to the acorn; the man, becoming a child again; the star, dissolving from its glorious perfection again into the nucleus of nebulous life? Men tell us so indeed. They philosophize upon the process, as inevitable in nature — power, begetting wealth — and wealth, luxury — and luxury, feebleness. So that to complete civilization, is only to develop the germ of destruction. And to perfect a State, is just to shoot into blossom a glorious Ale, gathering unto one stately flower the accumulated life of a century. Alas! only to be admired for a moment, and then wither and die.

But surely in all this philosophy, they give us only the statement of a fact, and not its solution. There is no sound reasoning in it. It is manifestly the design of Providence, that nations, no less than individuals, shall accumulate and enjoy all things beautiful and good; and unless God has ordained laws necessarily resulting in disaster, there can be no logical connection between national abundance, and national decay. The true philosophic connexion of cause and effect is far different. In past historic progress, power has begotten wealth — wealth, luxury, — and wealth and luxury have precipitated the combined social salt into crusts of distinctive caste: all destructive of the consideration, and culture, and development, of *Individual Man*. What those old nations wanted — What all nations want — What especially this nation wants, to perpetuate its greatness — is a full sense of that sublime prerogative, *individual personality*. The singling the man out from the multitude, and the pressing upon his conscience the truth, so forgotten by the race, that, having that within him which separates him from all beside, he stands one, alone, in the responsibilities of his being. — And thus training its every citizen, man by man, into the sense and exercise of his individual powers, and prerogatives. As the old temples built of conglomerate — clay and adamant in disastrous mixture — the one part decaying, while the other arose — so much be every social system built upon classes and castes.

A careful culture of the individual, is the only foundation of national perpetuity. Not more is this planet needed, to complete the harmony of the celestial choir; than every solitary man is needed, to the perfect song of a well-regulated society. And so every man who would make stable and glorious his nation, must begin with himself. He must find within his own spirit, the first and grand work he is to do for his day and generation. This is God's law in the physical. The fountain must be full, ere it well its waters abroad. The flower must be sweet to its very core, ere it open its bud to be the bee, and make fragrant the breezes. The man must take a torch, and go into his own heart, and cast out all the dark things that abide there, before he think to march abroad as torch-bearer to a progressive generation. Says someone, "He must make himself a good man, and then be sure, there is one unsafe and irresponsible rascal the less in the universe." He must feel, each man for himself, that God has raised him up for some great and special purpose, ere he will set himself earnestly to discern his particular mission, from his own peculiar gifts, and circumstances, and so toil laboriously in the perfection of that personal character, which his Times require.

Meanwhile, this sense of self-hood, is to be cautiously restrained from advance into selfishness. Of every virtue, there is danger of becoming, by extravagance, its counterfeit vice. And so it has happened in all times of social progress, that the very effort to reform, affects disastrously in this direction, the character of the reformer. Passing from that UNDERvaluation of the individual, to which we have objected ,the very momentum of transition is apt to carry the man forward into an overwhelming self-estimate. And then, not content with taking his place as a real and important part of the social system, the poor man looks so closely and continuously at himself, that the atomic individual grows into the magnitude of the whole social system. "No doubt," he says, "we are the people, and wisdom will die with us." "He knows more than the ancients." The accumulated wisdom of antiquity is ignored forever. The grandeurs of *the Present* absorb him, and he is by special calling the high priest of the Present. So his wisdom seems to himself inspiration — his utterances oracular, — he wears a prophet's mantle, credentialed as embassador-extraordinary from the high places of the universe. Reform! Reform! Is his mission. And the spirit of his reform is a headlong and frenzied fanaticism. Feeling himself wiser than all the statesmen, philosophers, theologians, philanthropists of old time, he cuts loose from all established principles; projecting new parties in politics; new systems of philosophy; new schools of theology; new schemes of philanthropy; new theories of society; new measures and machinery of reform. And being at once visionary in thought and headlong in propensity, he swells, and sparkles, and rises in the air, till the over-inflated bubble bursts, the gases vanish, and the amused world laughs at the residuum — a poor, falling raindrop. So far from being perfective of civilization, there is in this intense and egotistical individualism, at once an element, and exhibition of barbarism. Between the extremes of self-negation, and self-sufficiency, lies the golden means of self-respect and reliance. The individual must feel that he is a real part, yet meanwhile, only a very small part, of the grand social system. And while revolving resolutely in his own path of duty, as a planet round the sun, not rush away as a self-consuming comet, thinking that all the stars in the sky will break from their courses, adoring, and following.

This leads me to remark: That this true estimate of the place and value of the Individual in the Social System, will lead the man to the next necessary demand in this desirable character — *A full development, and culture of all his powers of useful influence.* An American in these times ought to be emphatically an *educated man*. All the faculties of his complex being, should be educed in their harmonious proportion, and strengthened for their mightiest performance.

His *physical* nature should be educated. It is a mistake of these times to undervalue the body. What need, say men, of stalwart bone and muscle, when steam, as a blind Samson, grinds the corn of the generation? And I answer, more need now than ever, of the physical health of staunch nerve and muscle. The very fact that the intellect today does the work of the species, is the promise of our argument. The mind cannot work out well life's great physical and social problems, without healthful bodily developments and secretions. Valetudinarianism, with its lily fingers and diseased structure, may spin impracticable theories, and weave romantic fictions. May project Platonic Republics — and sentimental Utopias — improvise Fourier's Phalansteries — and Coleridge's Pantisocracies. Induct women into pulpits, and ministers into politics. Soar or wallow, as it may be, in all impracticable and unintelligible schemes of bedrid and bedrugged sentiment. But the world's practical and philanthropic benefactors, the men who discover new continents in a real world, and ameliorate the condition of old social systems. The Columbuses — the Washingtons — the Franklins — the Howards — of all time, have been men of hale physical developments and healthy secretions, whose bodies were not poor wind-rocked cradles for the soul to sleep in. But strong and well-geared systems of machinery, mighty to endure and out-work the inspirations of the spirit. What an American wants now is a strong body, fitted for physical work, and in love with the vocation; a head that can stand a ruffian's blow, and a hand that can take a ruffian by the beard. Without this, he may be a weathercock, indicating the mind — but never.a sail helping on the great bark of humanity.

Meanwhile, and especially his INTELLECT must be educated. I do not mean that he must of necessity be a learned man; for this were to set forth an element of character, impossible to be widely realized in ordinary life. Learning — a good thing as it is — yet in its profound acquirements is not necessary to our present idea. True intellectual education is, as the term denotes, not an element of erudition, infused into the soul — a mechanical process like that of wood-dying — whereby amid books, and academic halls, and under strong outward pressure, the mind is colored blue with science, or green with poetry. It is *education* — *i.e. eduction* — *a drawing forth*, or development; a mind led forth to think; educed into practical and profitable activity. And such an education is possible and needful to every American citizen. To perform well his functions, he must have studied God's world as it is; and man's nature as it is. The histories of the past, and the processes of the present, — possessing not ponderous erudition, but practical information. Well read in the workings of human nature; the operations of human government; and the philosophy of human society.

And meanwhile, this practical education as needed by this modern American, must be eminently *Political*. Every American should be in the true sense of the word a *statesman*. I use the word of course popularly, not in so absolutely a sense as to be ridiculous in idea, as a thing to be realized only by a lifetime of diplomacy. I do not mean that every man should aim at the grand Websterian standard; a comprehension in its every detail, of the whole theory and practice of our organic, and administrative politics, foreign and domestic. Such a stature of statesmanship demands studies, experiences, natural gifts of genius, qualities of pure and sheer intellect, intrinsic texture and absolute volume of brain; great moral sentiments; uniform and masterly sagacity and good sense — in a word, such powers of steadfast, grasping, comprehensive investigation; and of high speculative, imperial, intellect — as perhaps I may be pardoned for doubting, whether this boy Young America, is in every instance equipped with.

But, if I do not mean this, even less do I mean, that every man should aim at that other, lower and more ignoble standard, which, speaking of a statesman, means only a *politician*. God forbid! For, if there be any character doubly abhorrent to a true patriot, this is that character. Its elements are simply selfishness and sheer dishonesty. Its sagacity is low cunning; an adroit appeal to false prejudices and foul passions. Its patriotism, an ambition of place. Its philanthropy, self-worship. Its emblem, the serpent scaling the Pyramid with slimy sinuosities; and not the eagle, touching it as with a stoop of an imperial pinion. And its whole manifestation, only lifting it into the loathing and scorn of all honest men made in God's image.

But when I say that every American should be a statesman, I do mean, that being a true part of the government of the nation — one indeed of its positive rulers — individually conserving its present — and projecting its future — he is, as such, bound by every law of life to be prepared for his high ministry. He should study our Federal Constitution, till he understands all its great truths and principles, in their philosophy and application. He should know enough of our great complex political system; its adjustment of wheels, and springs, and balances, and many moving, and minute parts into one grand and matchless mechanism. Its large, and delicate, and most difficult questions, of concessions, and compromises, and mutual and large hearted forbearance which — securing the interest of each separate State; and seeking the loftiest destiny for the whole confederacy — tasked in their comprehension the wisdom of our forefathers, and will task as well to the end, the comprehension of their children. Enough of these things — and things like these — should he know; to walk amid the moving machinery of this American system, preserving with all the power that is in him, the harmony of each part, with the grand whole of the system.

Meanwhile, he should understand enough of the principles of political economy, as they have to do with domestic industry, and foreign commerce, to judge for himself, of the ever varying and conflicting theories of our great parties in politics. Enough, moreover, of the general history of mankind, — the progress of the race, in the rise and fall of successive peoples and empires — of men's present dangers, and consequent duties, and perspective and possible destiny. Enough of all this, at least, to enable him to select for himself representatives and rulers, whose theories are philanthropic, whose plans salutary, and in whose hands he can hopefully place the helm of state, outward bound over the ever-stormy and untried seas of all national progress. These republican franchises are tremendously fearful prerogatives. The principle — so essential to our whole national life — of representative instruction — yea of representative responsibility — should be ignored altogether, unless every constituency be so far, at least, educated, as to be able to instruct their representatives wisely, and hold them to account discerningly and justly — understanding well the grand principles of our complicate polity, and knowing how we ought to be governed, and who ought to govern us.

But, discoursing as we are of character — it is education as it has to do with the moral man we are mainly concerned with. Physical and Intellectual powers alike, are but the instruments whereby character works out its high purpose. And descending more particularly to the moral elements of character — we observe again,

That COMPREHENSIVENESS is especially required in the man of this generation.

I use the word here in its very widest sense, both *subjectively* and *objectively*.

By *subjective* comprehensiveness, I mean, that the man's character itself should be made up of all fine moral qualities — and that these qualities, all individually developed, should yet so modify and mutually restrain each other — patience so mingling with zeal — and love so evangelizing courage — and energy so quickening philanthropy — and dignity so ennobling labor — and prudence so directing passion, — and a religious conscience so modifying and moulding the whole into a symmetrical composite — that the spiritual man, according to the Apostolic model of the physical, — "the whole body fitly joined together, and compacted by that which every joint supplieth, according to the effectual working in the measure of every part," — may grow up in all things — not a moral monster with a few gigantic virtues; but a perfect man, in the harmony of all vital graces.

Meanwhile, by *objective* comprehensiveness, I mean, that the objects of these graces should be universal and limitless — that the man should have large views, and broad sympathies — a head too big for half an idea

— a heart too enlarged for half a humanity. It is an age of multiform and most complex relations. The railroad, the printing press, the magnetic telegraph, the world-encircling commerce, all the marvels of this day, have carried the social system, whereunto every man belongs, forward to broader scope and power than our fathers ever dreamed of. They are making all nations, only virtually sister states in a great imperial confederacy — making humanity one, and the world one. And the man of these times must understand, that as he is not of the world — so his city is not the world — nor his state — nor his country — nor his continent. He must come up form the small landscapes in the valleys of self — and standing on the highest Pisgah of faith, take in all the spreadings of earth's teeming population. He must have a patriotism that can overleap a state-line — a religion that intones no sectarian shibboleth — a morality that has heard of more than one cardinal virtue — a philanthropy that reaches more than one caste and color — a loving faith, that sees in every creature of our race, a child of the same Father — and in every tribe, and tongue, and people under heaven, a kindred family of the same great world — alike precious, as redeemed by Divine blood — and borne resistlessly on to the same glorious regeneration.

And this leads me to remark — as that without which all this comprehensiveness, will prove only an indolent, and so, useless erudition — that the man of the present generation should be preeminently PRACTICAL. The days of dreamy speculation, and sentimental and ghostly unrealities, are gone forever — whether in literature, or politics, or the arts, or religion, the man of subtle theories, and metaphysical philosophies is a dead fossil — useful only as a milestone in the path of true progress. Even imagination hath become practical. The poetic afflatus of genius, hath been pressed into the actual work of the generation. And this is true poetry — the very poetry of the Divine Intellect. The great God poetizes in material forms and phenomenon. Niagara and Mt. Blanc are Divine lyrics. The history of the race a Divine drama. The universe itself but a glorious epic of the Infinite imagination. And so it is a progress, real and God-ward, which calls human genius — the race's Samson — from the songs of Delilah, to grind corn for food, and bear away, poet and bar, the gates of the Philistines. The steam-engine — the telegraph — the printing press — these are the grand poems of this practical generation. And to meet the wants of such an age, the man must be practical. His whole character practical. I mean that all those distinct virtues of which it consists, — and which we have not limits largely to enumerate, — must all be preeminently common sense, and practical.

Courage must be practical; our calling today is not to battle with fabulous dragons — nor to break lances with Quixotic windmills — nor to wrest venerated tombs from the power of the infidel. And so the courage we need for our work, vapors not in chivalrous plumes, and mail-of-proof — but wears good honest clothing, like a good honest gentleman. It is a plain, practical, downright, common-sense principle. Courage, not for great crises, but everyday courage. Courage to brave a fool's ridicule, and to let alone a fool's challenge. To stand by an old custom, or a patriarchal opinion, if we know it to be good, — and to resist a popular reform, if we believe it to be tending to evil. To obey conscience against a world's violence — and to change custom and opinion under honest conviction. To speak the mind boldly when needful — and to hold the peace when silence is profitable. To stand by a friend in adversity, though his coat be threadbare — and to turn the back on villainy, in purple and fine linen. Courage to confess poverty, when one is poor — to discharge a just debt at any sacrifice of personal comfort — to wear an old coat till able to pay for a new one — and to prefer honest and homely comfort to fashion in all things. Courage to do right — and stand by the right — as an oak by its rooted rock — yet the while politic: conceding; forbearing, in all tenderness and loving truth — as the same oak resisting the tornado, yet yielding to the zephyr. Courage, — like the princely Greek, stopping the ear, and chaining himself to the mast against the song of the Sirens in the blue Italian seas — so, voyaging in the true course, to stand deaf to all the noisy repetitions of "philanthropy," and "humanity," and "brotherhood," and "progress," wherewith a selfish ambition disguises its heresies, and to tear the religious vizor from the face of a false reform and judge calmly for itself, whether the livery of Heaven be not worn by a demon. Courage, in a word, that in an economy necessarily blending multiform good and evil — understanding what is best for the individual, and the country, and the race, will break with any party, or sect, that withstands its seeking. Careful only of character itself — and leaving Almighty God to look after the reputation.

And like courage, so, too, must *Philanthropy* be practical. The earth is full of men who would take the world by storm, rather than work steadily and efficiently in a good cause; in whom ambition without common sense, and benevolence without logic, have excited enthusiasm in some dream of fancied goodwill to the species. And so ever aiming at the unattainable, and leaving unreached the possible; they utter great, swelling words about human equality — and abstract rights — universal liberty — and Utopian fraternity — the perfection of the man — and the grand destiny of the species — leaving, meanwhile, the useful beggar to starve at their own door, and the seven devils of the Magdalen to rage in their own bosoms; discharging their heavy artillery at distant strongholds of sin, altogether out of range, and lifting no challenge at the ambushes of iniquity lying close to their wayside.

And in fine contrast with all this, what the world wants now is a common-sense benevolence — which talks less and does more — asking not so much, what ought to be done in general? As what good thing can I do in detail and particular? Beginning with the man's own sins, and the sins of his family, and neighborhood, and city, and staggering not abroad like a blind giant, feeling for the mote in another's eye, with a great beam in his own.

And as of courage and philanthropy, so of all other essential graces of character, the demand of the age is, that they be common-sense and practical, not vaporing and windy sentiments, carrying the man up like a balloon; but good, honest, working, principles, making a true flesh-and-blood man of him.

But while in all these respects, the man of this age should *"walk by sight,"* (*i.e.*) should have practical fitness for the positive and present realities of life — he should be meanwhile and especially *a man of strong* FAITH. The age is an age of skepticism — the world is in a ferment — old systems are ignored, and present systems questioned. We are doubtful of all things. Politics, philosophies, religions, are bent irreverently on the wheel and rack as suspected impostors. As a race, we have reached the highest pinnacle of all historic attainment. And with an eye on the past ever recurring cycles, — eras of powerful civilization, ending in barbarism, — we are fearful that we, as well, must experience the retrograde — that our philosophy may recede from induction to metaphysics, from metaphysics to myth. Our government, from freedom to oligarchy, from oligarchy to despotism. Our religion, from faith to superstition, from superstition to Atheism. We question and tremble, as if the whole present were unsafe, volcanic strata, under the feet of giant progress.

What we most want in times like these, is *earnest and steadfast* FAITH. Faith partly *in man* — a philanthropic recognition of the true nobility of the race, through a race in ruins, — as a species fully capable of endless progression, whose past disasters have not been, because the seas were not open beyond for his most adventurous voyaging; but because ignorance sat at the helm, and wild passion filled the sails; and so the bark was turned from the true course, and dashed into shipwreck. Man, notwithstanding all his shortcomings, is a creature by nature, of noble faculties, grand impulses, generous and glorious instincts; and spite of all historic disasters, is yet a creature fully capable of free thought; self-government; the largest and loftiest liberty; And the misanthrope, who will have him to be essentially selfish and villainous — a thing of mean motives and selfish impulses — a brute mechanism, moved only by the low instincts of selfishness — the huckster only and chapman, calculating profit and loss of a dead virtue put in traffic in the marketplace. I say this poor disciple of Paley and Bentham, only approves HIMSELF *knavish* and villainous; and so, out of all true sympathy with his race, and with no power to benefit it. What the age wants, is a noble confidence in humanity, which, rebuking from its presence this infidel misanthropy, sees in man, a creature noble in impulses, immortal in destiny; whom God made in his own image, and regards as worthy of redemption, and has so linked unto His own nature, to be kingly and priestly unto God forever and ever.

Meanwhile, most of all, should this *faith* be in GOD. In His Being — His Providence — His Purposes of benevolence — His Promises — written, not merely in His word of Revelation, but written as well in all His historic dealings with our race — that He is steadily and surely bringing man up from a tumultuous past to a glorious future — and slowly and in circles of immense sweep, out of this tribulated and disorganized universe, educing a new Heaven, and a new Earth, wherein dwelleth righteousness. Faith, that Jehovah, is not a myth, but a living and true God, — never retrograding, — never standing still, — always progressing, always perfecting, not resolving gems into gases, stars into nebulae — and so not about to leave half finished, His grandest work of earthly redemption, casting the race back to the cradle when halfway to manhood; but as surely as He is God, steadily bearing it, as on eagle's wings, in a long exodus, from the low tasks of the Nile to the *grand cities* of Canaan. Yes, a noble confidence in man and his Maker is the great want of thy generation. Meanwhile, in the character fitted for these times, with all this strong Faith, there should be blent as strong a PATIENCE. We live in a progressive and a headlong age, and have grown trustless, and so impatient, of aught save a headlong progress. In the accumulation of wealth; in the diffusion of knowledge; in the processes of locomotion; yea, in the whole march and movement of human life; the old standards of slow and steady advance satisfy no one. "Progress!" "Progress!" is the age's watchword. Progress, on the seas, though already the masts bend in the overstraining storm, and the billows are white with the tremendous momentum. Progress on the land, though the winds are distanced in headlong speed, and the causeway shows white as a charnel, with the bones of the slaughtered Progress! Progress! No matter with what dangers, or in what directions. And what we most want is a calm patience, that will dare to lift the escape-valve, and take in sail; yea, even cast anchor and lie by, when great interests are in jeopardy.

We must have patience with MAN. If human nature be noble, it is the nobility of a ruin. It is a nature stamped with infirmities, full of imperfections. Swerved form the right path by prejudice; and hurried on in the wrong by tremendous passions. If a nature, surely uprising to majestic manhood; — yet a nature jest now, cradled and infantile, and so, justly claiming a forbearing rod and a soothing lullaby. It must be tenderly borne with in all its infirmities; its hypocrisies; its insincerities; its low impulses; its very extravagances of fanaticism and folly. Old men must be patient with the young, and the young with the old. Philosophers with fools, and fools with philosophers. The sanguine with the melancholic, and the melancholic with the sanguine. Northern men with Southern men, and Southern men with Northern men. The Saxon with the Celt, and the Celt with the Saxon. Patience is a soft oil for the jarring machinery, everywhere and ever, and in times like these there is intense friction in the social system. And so to fit an individual for the times, he must not only be a man, but a *patient* man, *(i.e.)* a *gentleman*. A living and lovely composite of manliness and gentleness. I do not mean a mere creature of gentle blood, and broadcloth, and fine linen, and fine sentiment; for such a creature may be a gentleman with *only* THE MAN *left out of it*. Nevertheless, even manliness is not enough if unmodified. A *man* may be only a ragged plateau of rock, — a *gentleman* is that same rock beautified into rich landscape; he is a patient man; a gentle man; he is courteous and forbearing, and pitiful; he does not bluster, nor blaspheme, nor carry weapons, nor practice pistol-shooting; nor talk loudly of his honor. This Young America, (pardon me if there seem treason in the boldness of the personality,) this Young America was baptized with a misnomer. We are partial to boyhood; its flashing eye; its hot blood; its fresh senses; its high impulses; we are enamored of all of them. But then this Young America is not a boy at all. It is old, hoary ruffianism, gone back to toys and sweetmeats, and flaunting swaddling clothes, in imbecility and dotage. A true gentleman is neither imbecile nor infantile. A gentleman governs himself; conquers his passions and prejudices; is modest, generous, genial, charitable, long-suffering, patient. Patient with the men of his day and generation. Self-reliant in the possession of his own spirit, he bides his time in hope; — confident, that, though for a season, stormy passions may drive the bark from her true bearings, yet in due time, will conscience and common-sense, like the trade winds, bring her back to her own glorious courses. And, that a nature cannot be wrong at the last, that with the impress of the Divine Image, was cradled in Paradise, and redeemed on Calvary.

But more than all, must a man of this generation be *patient with God*. Under the Divine Government, the world does not leap from change to change with the startling show of a kaleidoscope; but he rather slowly, and cautiously, steps through long processes of transition, with the silent chemistries of the lingering spring upon ice-wreathed mountains. Jehovah's law of working is no wild and headlong progress. He operates slowly, and steadily, and in circles of immense sweep. Man is ever hurried and impatient, because his working years are but fourscore. But the majestic quietude, wherewith Jehovah evolves His great purposes, is GOD-LIKE, in its manifestation of Infinite Existence, and Power, and Wisdom, and Changelessness. Nevertheless, if He work slowly, He works as well surely. His are no half-accomplished designs, no misconceived, and so abortive and abandoned purposes. If He has made this man-child in His own Image, and rocked its infancy in such a star-hung cradle; then, just so sure as He is God, He will yet give the youth mighty bone and muscle, and bring him abroad to reign on the earth in the full grandeur of manhood. And be it ours — imitative of His great majestic patience — hopefully to trust Him. Seeing in the convulsions of the present, only processes of integration, and transition, whereby the cradle-economy is giving place to the imperial enterprises of heirship and maturity. Patience — patience alike with men, and with God, is the great want in a character for times like the present.

But then, be it ever remembered, patience is no idle and indolent principle of our nature. And this leads me to remark again: That *real, true-hearted* EARNESTNESS *should characterize the man of this generation.*

In what we have already discoursed of patience, we have more than intimated our entire approval of moderation and conservation. Nevertheless, true moderation and conservation are in themselves, and essentially, manifestations of earnestness. If they do the work of obstacles, it is only unto evil. They are exercised in holding the bark to her true course; never in abating her beneficent velocity. There is indeed in these latter days a miserable counterfeit and mongrel moderation, made up of craven timidity, and calculating selfishness — which is ever exercised in *restraining the virtues* — extinguishing inquiry, high impulses, impassioned zeal for man's good, and God's glory; floating the man down into the warm seas of life, like a polar iceberg, chilling its airs, and obstructing its navigation. And, as the brakes ought most to be used on a backing train; and the anchor cast when the vessel has lost headway, and drives stern-foremost on breakers; so most of all things among men, does this false conservation need to be conserved; and this lazy moderation used to be moderated. No wise man fears zeal, if it be according to knowledge. The Apostle's moderation, which he sought to make known until all men, was no slumberous, and Sphynx-like conservation; but the rather, a flaming ministry unto man, which drove him froth, through "stripes," and "shipwrecks," and "imprisonments," and "deaths;" seemingly "beside himself," under the tremendous impulse of the "constraining love of Jesus."

And quite sure we are, that in times like these, intense energy is the true inspiration. Enthusiastic excitement is the law of the generation. In trade, what rage of competition and speculation! In literature, what a flitting of the Muses from the crystal springs of Helicon, to drink fiery inspiration from the lava-jets of Vesuvius! In politics, what a crimson baptism from the French Revolution, into the spirit of convulsions! In pleasure, what a quickening of sentimental taste into a fierce appetite, clamorous, and craving! Alike, in little things, and great things, mean things, and mighty; from the weaving of a shoe-tie, to the conquest of an empire; the whole race is in a furor; and the tides of life are boisterous and white as an advancing deluge. And the man who would be the minister of this age must be baptized with its baptism. We may not affection the law, but we are born under it, and must abide it.

The want of the times is, good men that will march in the very van of the rushing race, guiding it to true courses. Champions that will beat Satan with his own weapons; carrying his strong fortresses by storm; and not satisfied with spiking his guns; but turning them point blank on his routed forces. Men more earnest for good, than the fiend is for evil. Earlier afield with the wheat, than lie with the tares. Men calmly trusting God to do His work — but armed, meanwhile, and eager to do their own work. Who see in the mighty energies around us, indications that the race is only in the fiery infancy of its life, and feel that there is a high calling of God, to watch by the cradle, and ward the playground of the untutored youth, that the might of the manhood be not a blind Samson's; shaking the world's pillars into dust; to die and be buried a poor suicide beneath them.

Now it were to weary you out of all grateful and thankful frames beseeming our festival, were I to enlarge further. Let me, therefore, only add, in conclusion, as a comprehensive resumé of our desultory discourse — and as a point to be especially insisted on in this religious service — that the American of these times ought to be personally, and practically, and emphatically, a CHRISTIAN.

I say this as a *resumé*. For, manifestly, in this one point is involved all that precedes it. Very easy were it to show, that all these aforementioned qualities of character, are only the true developments of personal piety. They are in fact, and quite obviously, all of the, the very essentials of Christian character, everywhere inculcated in Gospel ethics, and everywhere exemplified in Gospel biography. A Christian is a man just fitted in all graces for the wants of his age. He must be *impressed with a sense of his own individuality and its tremendous prerogatives,* as a redeemed man in Christ Jesus. He must be, in the largest sense of the word, *educated for usefulness* – his body strong for its toil — his mind aflame, as a light of his generation — his moral graces all vigorous, in proportion and beauty. He must be a *comprehensive* man — his character a composite of all virtuous elements — his philanthropy overleaping all selfish bounds, grasping the whole round world in the range of its active charities. He must be a practical man — alike in courage and philanthropy, and all kindred virtues — not a monumental pillar by a dead Asphaltates, but a living salt in the tides of a living generation.e He must be preeminently a man of *Patience* — and emphatically a man of *Faith* – alike toward man and toward God – patient and trustful. And above all, he must be *earnest and active* in the work of his generation. Personal Christianity, as revealed in the Gospel, essentially involves all these graces of character. It is not an indolent and sentimental faith, fitting a man only for the elaboration of church creeds and forms, and the elocution of church psalmody. It is rather God's regenerating grace, fully developing man's noble faculties, in their primeval energy, and so equipping him for his brave and great work, on this theatre of his being. And, therefore, self-considered, a Christian is only the highest style of a man. And the very elements of the character needed in these times, are precisely those graces which Gospel ethics enjoins, and Gospel biography illustrates.

 Yes, and had we the limits, we should like to enlarge on another line of argument for this American Christianity. We might show you how nations, like individuals, have a persona, moral life, of which Christianity is the grand conservative element. We do not say that a nation cannot exist without Christianity — we might say that no nation has existed without religion. With the old Greek, we might declare, "That there never has been a state of *Atheists* — for while there have been cities without walls, without kings, without exchanges, without civilization;

yet never cities without sacrifices, and prayers, and oracles, and gods." And we do say, that when, in theory, you deny moral character to a state, and degrade it into a mere system of police — a vast, brute, Atheistic power, conserving only animal life, and the rights of property; then you have divested it, by felony, of all gifts of personality and life, and left nothing but a dead form, without hopes, or joys, or great and glorious impulses — passing upon it a degradation as intense as the reduction to a brute beast, of a singing, soaring spirit. And, instead of John Milton's grand old commonwealth — an organism instinct with genial life. "Like one huge Christian, personating one mighty growth, and stature of an honest man, as big and compact in virtue as in body." Instead of this, you leave us for a state, nothing but a structure of dead masonry, reared with no foundation in the constitution of the race; and so surely, if slowly, crumbling back to the original anarchy of chaos and night. In no form of government, regarded merely as such a police, is there any vital law of self-support and conservation. And, there is no shape of human society, that will not crumble and dissolve, unless a power — that is not in it as a temporal influence, descend upon it Divinely from on high. And therefore, Christianity embodying — as the very consummation of Divine Wisdom — the mightiest and most practical of all moral forces, is approving itself, and shall approve itself more and more to the end, the grand conservator of the inner, and intense life, individual, and social, of the whole human race.

And, from both these lines of argument alike.

From the necessity of Christianity to the perfect development of this personality of society. And from tis power to implant, and strengthen, those vital graces, which make up the character needed by the man of these times. Are we brought to the same conclusion; that above all else — as embracing all else, *the American of this day should be emphatically,* CHRISTIAN.

Now, I may not pursue this thought further. This is but a rude and most imperfect sketch of the qualities essential to the true American character. My purpose will have been accomplished, if you complete the picture for yourselves, and strive practically to grow up into the model's strength and proportion. As American men, and American Christians — *"For times like these you have come to the kingdom."* And what times they are! Who shall read their signs aright, or achieve their subtle analysis, or comprehend their mighty forces, or speak of them fittingly? Times mingling all strengthful and terrible things in their tides of exuberant and intense life. Times of *disintegration* and *transition*, like the eosns, when new and loftier economies emerge from the conditions of geologic chaos! Times of tremendous *moral influences*, when the old brute social forces are ignored as effete mechanism; and the giant THOUGHT, free, vital, electric, imperial, moves and governs the nations! Times of trembling *Fear*, born of the extravagance, the insincerities, the fanaticisms, the social heresies, the hot and fierce impulses, the impatience of restraint, the thirst for change, for agitation, for experiment, of this headlong and restless generation. Fear, dwelling in the truest and bravest spirits; felt ever; confessed at times. Fear so intense in weaker and inferior souls, that the faint heart, faithless of the reality of virtue, of patriotism, of man's progress and destiny, recoils almost despairingly from the rushing of tempests that make white the waters! Times of *Philosophic doubt*; of earnest and deep questionings, whether these agitations, mysterious and profound, of the great moral deep, are breaking up and engulfing man's foundering bark, or bearing it bravely on, to the Ararat! Whether these chills, these shadows, these mists along the mountains, these finally showing stars, are the hopeful twilight of morning, brightening into dawn, — or a mournful vesper twilight, deepening unto night! Times, meanwhile, of overswaying and triumphal *Hope*. When the eye of faith, unscaled by heavenly love and trust, sees God's giant man-child, breaking its baubles, casting off its swaddling bands, springing from its cradled dreams, to its glorious tasks of manhood, an unappalled by the convulsions that stir the nations, perceives in these clouds bedarkening heaven, and these surges breaking on the shores of life, only the mingling of elements in grand geologic antagonisms, whence shall emerge, as a fitting theatre for the last act of the majestic Human Drama, "the New Heavens and the New Earth, wherein dwelleth righteousness."

For such times as these we have come to the kingdom! To read these times aright; to discover their dangers; to perceive their directions; to mingle in their antagonism; to develop their resources; to shape their great paths; to meet their emergencies; to meet them, not timidly, shrinkingly, recreantly, but bravely, hopefully, triumphantly. This is our calling.

As *American* MEN, conscious of our land's young strength, and trustful of its dazzling and limitless future, helping to bear the National Ark onward, through these troublous times; through changing sympathies and tastes; with mingling races; with enlarging numbers; athwart enlarging territories; through sharp antagonisms of sectional and selfish passions; through all agitations, civil or religious, endangering the nation's grand integrity; against the bigot's intolerance; the fool's frenzy; the traitor's lie – yet patiently, trustfully, earnestly; bearing it onward, still onward, till the radiant vision be fulfilled of a nation — countless in its millions, matchless in its wealth and strength; free, glorious, Godly; knowing no North, no South, no East, no West; no jealousies, no strifes; one in immortal brotherhood, genial, generous, loving; filling with its busy life this broad continent; nestling in its valleys, towering on its hills; its morning suns gilding those old ancestral and Atlantic waves; its starry eves glassing their purple glories in the far Pacific seas; — standing complete, consolidate, imperial — the glorious Aloe of man's centuries. The grand Ararat for a race's tossing barks. The embodied majesty and strength of righteous law, and Christian faith. The living, breathing, triumphing, everlasting illustration of God's true oracle, *"That righteousness exalteth a nation." "That blessed is that people whose God is the Lord."*

This, all this, as American MEN. Meanwhile, and more, as *American* CHRISTIANS, - our higher calling — to stand in times like these on Faith's Pisgah top, with a love for man that knows no land, no tribe, no clime — beholding a *world* — living for a *world*. Seeing already the uncoiling of electric wires that shall bind all kindreds, all people, all tongues, and tribes of men, into one *great confederacy of nations* — no longer rival islands, and empires, and continents, and hemispheres, but all, all, rounded as this star-encircled orb itself, *into one great composite world*. One last, grand, glorious, universal empire — *whose subjects are all freemen, - whose only monarch God!* And standing thus — seeing all this — believing all this — yea, knowing, that as possessors of the Gospel, we are equipped with weapons of Heavenly armor, to accomplish all this — then to go forth reading the dream aright — interpreting the vision — realizing the prophecy — our one great life-work, *to redeem the race to God; to evangelize the kingdoms; to conquer the world for the crucified Christ!*

Oh, this — this is our high calling. *"For times like these we have come to the kingdom."* To walk this grand theatre of life, as actors in such a drama, with such a spectatorship! To stand up on this redeemed world — this earth where the cross once stood! And make manifest unto all the wondering ranks of heaven, what a creature MAN is, when he asserts his birthright, as an heir of God, and a purchase of Redemption! This — this is our mission in these times! *"This our high calling of God in Christ Jesus."* And we are here, this sacred hour, in our beloved sanctuary, to respond to such a call heartily, thankfully — exultingly, to give back the old patriarchal answer — *"Here am I," - "Here am I."* To lay such offerings of grateful love at the feet of Jehovah! For a consecration like this, — a consecration so entire, so ennobling, so glorious. A consecration so demanded by our privileges, our great personal and social and national and religious gifts from God. A consecration so worthy our faculties as redeemed men — our immortal rewards of toil — our ineffable destinies in that *"far more exceeding and eternal weight of glory!"* For consecration like this - of such powers as these — to such a work as this — have we come up as a people to this Divine Presence. To stand here in this kingly, Christian priesthood, in the gaze of all the crowned creatures of eternity — *God's great universe the temple! This world a mighty altar! - and such a style of man a living sacrifice of thanksgiving!*

7

THE FEAST OF HARVEST

A THANKSGIVING SERMON; PREACHED IN THE ARCH STREET PRESBYTERIAN CHURCH, ON THURSDAY, NOVEMBER 18, 1858.

"The Feast of Harvest."

EXODUS 23:16.

We have assembled again in God's house upon, what may be called, the great religious festival of the American year. These *"Thanksgivings"* of the separate States are taking more and more the character, and, but for a pitiful perversity characteristic of certain Chief Magistrates, would to-day have taken the character altogether, of a grand National Jubilee. Originally Puritanical institutions, they have become a part of one common and ceremonial law, until, all the families of the land look for and enjoy them.

We have selected for this occasion a text, which, to the Executive proclamation calling us together, adds the solemnity of a Divine sanction. It is historic of the existence, and character, of festivals not dissimilar among God's ancient covenant people. Perhaps we have been accustomed to regard the Hebrew religion as especially wanting in the joyous element; doubting almost the possibility of religious gladness, amid its sternly sacrificial rites, and its august doctrinal Theism. But, if so, we have erred widely. Under every Dispensation alike has religion, as set forth by God, been essentially joyous. *"The ways of wisdom,"* whether trodden by the old patriarchs pitching tents; or by the Levites bearing the Tabernacle; or by the Tribes established in Canaan and going up to the worship of

Zion; or by Christians under the fuller light of the Gospel ascending to glory, have been always and altogether *"ways of pleasantness."*

The pervading spirit of the Hebrew economy was jubilant. Its ritual solemnity was hopeful and triumphant. The later Pharisaism, with its face disfigured, was a monstrous degeneration from the exulting faith of those earlier and palmier days of old Israel, when the harp and the viol, the tabret and cymbal, stringed instruments and organs, were their accessories of worship. Over and above the solemn joy of the daily Temple service, there were several great occasions every year, when the whole Jewish people kept religious festival by Divine appointment.

The design of these anniversaries is apparent. They served as perpetual memorials of grand historic events in their national experience; they counteracted the unsocial tendencies of their peculiar tribal divisions, and, by bringing the males of the people periodically together in their great central City, repressed local and sectional jealousies, and consolidated different Tribes into one composite nation; they moreover afforded the whole people stated seasons of recreation, so necessary to the development of man's physical and moral nature.

With such evident purposes of good did God appoint them, and the old Jews kept them fittingly. Probably the world has never witnessed the parallel of these Hebrew anniversaries. At their approach, the whole nation woke to holiday: every heart bounded, every eye flashed. From valley to mountain top, the land broke forth into singing, and cottage, and palace, and hamlet, and city, with harp and song and festal procession, were joyous before God. Jerusalem, then the glory of the whole earth, the City of the great King, was thronged with exulting thousands. Not only the chiefs and nobles of the Tribes, but the mighty men of the whole earth, philosophers, and sages, and conquerors, and kings — proselytes from furthest lands — came up in their pomp and power, to keep exulting festival before God in the grand central City of their glorious faith.

Now of one of these national holidays, we have record in the text — "THE FEAST OF HARVEST." — This was their Pentecost. So called from a Greek word signifying *"fifty"* — because it occurred on the fiftieth day from the feast of unleavened bread. It was properly a Harvest festival, in which the Jew offered thanksgiving unto God for having kindly brought unto fulness the ripened fruits of the earth.

To understand the peculiar interest the Jew took in this holiday, you must remember that the Israelites, after their establishment in Canaan, were almost entirely a nation of farmers. The peasant and the noble, in their respective spheres, were alike husbandmen. While a small portion of the tribes on the eastern side of Jordan led a purely pastoral life, the great body of the people were engaged mainly in the cultivation of the soil. And they were encouraged in agriculture, as no other people have ever been, by their peculiar civil economy. By Divine direction, not only did every tribe have the ownership of its particular province, but each family in the tribe had as well its specified inheritance, which could never be wholly alienated. No great landholding aristocracy could therefore arise among them. The poorest Jew was by law a full proprietor of the soil. His homestead was a freehold by irrevocable title. If for a time alienated by debt or misfortune, it returned to him again unencumbered at the year of Jubilee. Every husbandman felt, therefore, that all improvements in his freehold were for the benefit of himself, and his children. And, under this encouragement to labor, the whole land of Israel was in the highest state of cultivation. Probably, in this respect, no country on earth ever equalled it. Naturally a land of rare productiveness, it was well described as *"a good land of brooks, of water, of fountains and depths that spring out of the valleys and hills; a land of wheat and barley and vines, and fig trees, and pomegranates; a land of oil-olive and honey; wherein they should eat bread without scarceness, and should not lack any good thing"* — a land, in a word, altogether unrivaled in its exuberant and exhaustless productiveness. And possessed of such a freehold, encouraged to its culture and improvement by such immunities, it is not wonderful that the Land of Promise becomes the garden of the world.

The peculiar productions of all zones were native to its widely diversified soil and climate. Grains of all species grew richly on the plains ; plantations of olives covered its sandy hills; its low clay soils nourished groves of stately palms; its sharp mountain sides were hung with the ripe clusters of vineyards. Even the rocks in precipitous places were made fertile by artificial embankments; so that in the autumn time, corn fields, and vineyards, and orange groves, and orchards, and forests, rose in ascending circles from valley to hill top, covering the whole landscape with lavish beauty, till the old Canaan seemed fittingly a very emblem of heaven.

Now, we say, that unto such a people, inhabiting such a country, this Feast of Harvest was necessarily a grand and glorious festival. Its annual return could not but wake the nation to gladness. Fair and befitting were the exulting rites of that old holiday, when from every hamlet and home, from glens of the vine and olive, and from valleys golden with corn, the thousands of Israel went up to appear before God in Zion, filling the land, as they passed, with those old choral harmonies: "Praise the Lord, O Jerusalem; praise thy God, O Zion. For he hath strengthened the bars of thy gates; he hath blessed thy children within thee. He maketh peace in thy borders, and filleth thee with the finest of the wheat. He hath not dealt so with any nation. Praise ye the Lord. Praise God in his sanctuary; praise him in the firmament of his power. Praise him with the sound of the trumpet. Praise him with the timbrel and dance. Kings of the earth, and all people: princes and all judges of the earth: both young men and maidens, old men and children. Let every thing that hath breath praise the Lord. Praise ye the Lord."

Such was the Harvest-feast of God's covenant people. And herein have we warrant for such feasts among ourselves. Without pressing again the analogy between this American people and the old Hebrew nation, we find in our circumstances this day, precisely the things which rendered these festivals personally, and politically, and religiously, a necessity in their history.

We, too, want great national and religious holidays, *to keep in mind great national providences.* Our history as a people has been as manifestly distinguished as theirs by Divine interposals of mercy; and we, too, should have great annual gatherings, to make grateful acknowledgment of God's wonderful deliverances; thus setting up in the hearts even of children's children, grand memorial-pillars — our Ehenezers of Divine help unto all generations.

We need them, moreover, as verily as the Jews, *for their conservative political influence* — to counteract the sectional and unsocial tendencies of our great tribal divisions. As the old memories of Moses and Joshua, and the triumph at the Red Sea, and the mighty victories of the Exodus — revived and perpetuated by their yearly festivals — bound the several tribes together in loving brotherhood; so would it be with us. And if we could have, like them, a grand national Pentecost — something like our Fourth of July, as it lay in the thought of old John Adams and George Washington — as it ought to be, and would be, without its gas and gunpowder — a sublime national tribe-gathering! — reviving strongly in the great American heart the memories of Plymouth Rock, and Jamestown, and Bunker Hill, and Mount Vernon — memories of our old deliverances and triumphs — deepening, as with the chisel of an old Mortality, the inscriptions which the lapse of time and the ruthless storms of party and fanaticism are so sadly defacing on our old monuments of a common and glorious Past — hanging new garlands, woven by loving hands and fragrant with the dew of old memories, upon the tombs of men, that, like Israel's champions, led us in our Exodus, and established us in our Canaan. I say, if we could come up nationally to such Pentecosts, then no living man would ever again dare breathe of *discord* and *disunion* — for chords, tender as our loves and stronger than our lives, woven of religion and holy with old memories, as the memorial festivals uniting Judah and Ephraim, would bind us together and bind us to God!

Meanwhile we need such Pentecostal holidays for those *personal* advantages which they brought to the Hebrews. They furnish that harmless relaxation so constitutionally necessary to our highest well-being. Real pleasure, as well physical as moral, is always the true law of life. Even "at God's right hand," "fullness of joy" is the proposed end of our being. Not indeed lawless and frivolous gratifications, but pleasures of that serene and celestial quality, which invigorates the body and ennobles the soul. And such pleasures demand for their exercise seasonable relaxations.

Now if there is any thing the American people need it is *recreation*. Perhaps we have enough of an enervating dissipation. But true pleasure *re-creates* and we need re-creating. We want great, noble, national, holidays. Such as God appointed to the Jews in their annual festivals.

Our *physical* nature needs them. We do not live out half our days because the bo^v is ever bent — the sinew ever strained — the brain ever scheming. Men that ought to be young at sixty, are superannuate at thirty. Boyhood is bald-headed, and middle age hobbles on crutches. Our life chords are broken by over-tension: there is no break upon the car, no escape-valve for the vapor, and the physical man is shattered by the very speed of its flight.

Our *moral* nature needs them. Human virtues are like flowers that thrive best in the sunshine. Plato, the philosophic moralist, encouraged in his disciples moods of exuberant gayety, checking their joyous impulses only at the approach of some grave formalist; saying: "Silence now, my friends, let us be wise — *there is a fool coming.*" Stupid gravity is not virtue, else the ass and the owl, the most portentously grave of all animals, were our models of manhood. True virtue is genial, and joyous; walking earth in bright raiment, and with bounding footsteps. And the nervous, restless, unreposing, devouring intensity of purpose wherewith our men follow their business, is as disastrous to the nobler moral bloom and aroma of the heart, as a roaring hurricane, to a garden of roses.

Above all, our *religious* nature needs them. The true joy of the Lord is the Christian's strength. Cheerfulness is a very element of godliness. Religion is not the stern heroism of the soul clothed in sack-cloth, and marching to martyrdom. It is rather the perfect harmony of all the soul's faculties moving together in that music of joy and love, in which the whole man marches heavenward. To come to Christ, is not to abide in tombs, cutting ourselves with stones, and terrifying with our self-torturing cries every passing traveller — but it is rather, to come abroad from these Gadarene graves, having the sorrowful devil cast out of us, that we may return to our loving homes, jubilant and exulting. Piety is not a poisonous mushroom, growing best in the night, but a fragrant rose of Sharon, needing the sunshine. True religion asks, and will have recreations, if denied the pure, it will seek the perverted. The old Puritans strove hard to render religion a torment, and, in their dread of recreations, having abandoned all true amusement to Satan, were forced to seek Satanic amusement, hunting Quakers as wild beasts, and making bonfires of witches.

The old Jews did this thing better with their joyous holidays; when with harp and viol, they went up to Zion. Jehovah was not mistaken in the religious regimen of his children. He knew, and provided for, a great want of their natures, when he appointed their festivals. The American church sorely needs a like baptism of gladness, that shall send her to her Zion with bounding feet, and shining garments, making manifest to the world, that the service of God is not a sore bondage, hut that the ways of pleasantness are her pathways to glory.

It is right, therefore, on all these grounds, and on others; it is right, it is fitting, it beseems our higher frames and moods of true piety, that, on occasions like the present, we should dismiss from our minds all sorrowful emotions, and "worship the Lord in the beauty of holiness."

This is our Pentecost — our feast of harvest. And even in its lowest aspect, *as a grateful acknowledgment of God's goodness, in preserving for our use the kindly fruits of the earth,* it is a fitting occasion of thankfulness.

We have come to the close of a year of great plenty; our fields have yielded their increase, and our garners groan with supplies for the famine of a world. And for this we should keep joyous festival before God.

We, indeed, who live in great cities, ofttimes overlook this. In considering the evidences of our national prosperity, we ignore the Agricultural Arts, Manufactures, Commerce, in those we rejoice. Is the stock-market buoyant? Do the banks discount freely? Are our emporiums crowded with stuffs and merchantmen? Is the hum of industry loud in our workshops? Is the canvass of commerce white on our waters? These are the questions wherewith we seek evidences of our national prosperity. But herein we forget the greater interest whereon these things hinge — the interests of Agriculture — the simpler thrift, and surer, if slower, gains of the husbandman. True it is, the princely manufacturer or merchant, sometimes casts a kindly eye over the cheering records of the corn-trade, and says, "Well, bread-stuffs are cheaper, and the poor man should be thankful." As if the fruits of the earth were to the poor man, more than the rich, God's noble benefaction. Alas, foolish reasoner! Let the labor of the husbandman fail — let God shut up the heavens that they rain not, and parch the plough-ground into barrenness, and what becomes of the rich man? Can he grind his gold with millstones? or leaven his bank stock into bread? with all his hoarded wealth will he not starve side by side with the beggar in the midst of the famine? Ah, these ears of ripened corn, are the true germs of life for the great human household!

The wheels of our workshops, the sails of our commerce, the implements of science, the pen of genius, the pencil and chisel of artists, the eloquent tongue of the orator, the scheming brain of the statesman, the equipages of wealth, the banquetings of pleasure, all — all that render earth, in its tides of life, anything but a great sepulchre — move, and have being and power, only because the fields yield their fruits to the patient toil of the husbandman. We might manage to live without merchants, without manufacturers, without mariners, without orators, without politicians, without poets, — perhaps we might possibly survive the loss of demagogues and opera-singers, and prize-fighters and congressmen. To read some of the newspapers, one would think we might live without a President; *but sure I am we could not live without plouwmen!*

Suspend for a single twelvemonth the world's practical agriculture, and death's shadow is over it. Our harvests are our sustenance; and in their prodigal abundance should be gathered joyfully. *Life* for you, and for me, and for all of us, — life, with all its energies and aims and ambitions, its love and hope and joy, — life in the heart, the household, the home; that grand and glorious thing. LIFE, hath ripened for us in these golden sheaves, and gone unto the garner. And our feast of harvest should be kept like the Jews, as a grand religious holiday.

It is scarcely possible to over-estimate the importance of agriculture. It surpasses commerce and manufacture, as a cause is superior to its effects, — as an inner life is of more moment than its various outward functions. We talk of the immense commerce of England, — when, in fact, she pays more annually for fertilizers of her lands than the entire gains of her commerce; and the total value of her year's crop, animal and vegetable, was some time ago reported to Parliament to be three thousand millions of dollars.

Meanwhile, the *reflex* influences of industrial agriculture on our physical and social well-being are as well incalculable. After all, the finest products of our farm-lands are found *in our farm-houses.* Things better than corn and cabbages are grown on plough-ground, — bone, muscle, sinew, nerve, brain, heart; these all thrive and strengthen by agriculture. The specimens of strong, hale, common-sense MANHOOD seen at our annual Fairs are a finer show than all the fat cattle and sheep and noble horses, and the brave array of farm-fruits and implements. Agriculture purifies morals, chastens taste, deepens the religious element, develops the individual man. And it were a giant's stride in human progress if the whole multitude of non-producing drones that swarm in our market-places, (politicians, speculators, fast men, rich idlers,) were driven into the rural districts, to cultivate at the same time cabbages and *themselves.*

Then, too, the genius of American agriculture is politically Democratic, or (if the Solons of our time have discovered a difference to us unintelligible) Republican. It allows no aristocratic monopoly of the soil. The one-man power, or the few-men power, gives place here of necessity to the every-man power in the proprietorship of small freeholds.

Most easy were it to show, had we time, how incalculable are the benefits of agriculture to all classes; and to make manifest the dependence of our modern civilization, social and political, upon the agricultural interest.

No wonder, then, that the Jew kept his Pentecost! No wonder that in brave old Scotland men went afield with sickle and bagpipe, reaping the ripened corn to sounds of sweet music ! No wonder that the fairest of festivals was the sweet old "Harvest home" of merry England! No wonder that, in view of what God has done for us, as Lord of the harvest, we, looking forth upon the wealth of fruitful fields outside our pent-up cities — that grander world, beyond the narrow world of Trade, the shallow world of fashion, that world of dew, and sunshine, and bursting buds, and bending fruits, where every hill breathes a benison, and every valley is odorous with blessing — at the close of a year whose wealth of golden spoil might spread luxuriously the boards of famishing nations; no marvel, I say, that we, a blessed people ill all our borders, should gather in these Temples where our fathers worshipped with our offering of First-fruits to the God of the harvest.

This, then, is the first and lowest aspect of our annual Thanksgiving — *a time of praise to God for the ripened fruits of the earth.* But then it has higher aspects. It had even to the Jews. When first brought forth from Egyptian servitude, they knew little truly of God ; they thought of Him, as of the dead idols of the Nile; and these feasts of harvest taught them to recognize the Divine agency in life's common blessings. But, as they advanced in intellectual Theology, these festivals took a wider, and loftier range and meaning. The feast of the Passover, at first commemorative of the deliverance from Egypt, came to he regarded as prophetic of Christ's coming sacrifice. And the feast of Pentecost, originally a simple expression of thankfulness for Harvests, became successively a memorial. *First*, of the giving of the Law at Sinai, and *Secondly*, of the descent of the Holy Ghost at Jerusalem. So that, in their later history, this feast of harvest, was an occasion of thanksgiving, not merely for annual physical blessings, but for all their distinguishing mercies, both civil and religious.

And so should it be with us. Our Thanksgiving is partly in view of the ripened fruits of the earth; but mainly in view of other and higher blessings. And in this regard, as well, it is properly — *a feast of harvest*. In respect of all things; not merely the natural fruits of the Earth; but all great human interests. Political, Intellectual, Religious. We may be said to live, *in the world's great Harvest-time!* We have reaped, and are reaping, the ripened and ripening fruits of all Earth's past generations. Consider this a little.

First: This is true — *politically.* Philosophically considered the grand end and aim of all civil progress is *human freedom* — the highest development and culture of the individual and free manhood. Monarchy the one-man-power. Oligarchy the few-men-power, are but the successive stages of the growing life, up to the ripened product of the true Democracy — the all-men-power. To this end hath tendered all political progress; and beyond this there is no progress. This is the harvest of Earth's long political husbandry; and we are reaping it. Till the great American development, the world had known no true Democracy. The old Republicans, falsely so called, were not forms of self-government, but things rudimental and embryonic; the mind's abortive and premature struggles to bring forth freedom. And our American Nationality is the "first fruits" of true liberty. It is, indeed, but the *first* fruits. In one respect this Nationality is only a *germ* — the first sowing of a true seed for a great harvest of Republics, which we know not of as yet — a handful of corn on the mountains, that, in its diffusion of enlightened liberty and universal self-government, shall yet wave like Lebanon in the grand harvest of the world. "The world will be either Cossack or Republican," said Napoleon, and we say, not Cossack, for the world in God's husbandry, not for tares but for wheat.

Ours is but the first fruits, but then they are ripe fruits! The great human Aloe hath shot forth one glorious spike, and brought forth one blossom! For centuries the race made its slow progress from the gnarled roots of the elder Despotisms. On the trans-Atlantic continents, Empires rose, and flourished, and fell; Dome, Greece, Persia, Assyria, Egypt, — in each human nature struggled, into great forms and developments of life. There were buds, and green leaves, and early blossoms, amid the mighty branches; but, alas, the unripened fruit was shaken by convulsions, and fell as the fig tree casteth her untimely figs! But at last, in this western world, the fruits of true Liberty seem ripening in the sunshine. No man can read our past history, and not cry out in faith, "this is God's husbandry!" The careful keeping of this virgin soil for a new product — the winnowing, amid wild convulsions, as with fire and flame, of the old humanity, for a new seed to scatter on this glorious plough-ground — the germination, the strong rooting, the slow growth, amid seething rains and whistling storms of our struggling Colonial life. These are the manifestations of a grand Divine husbandry!

Who questions it longer? Verily, it is a story of marvels! That feeble folk, like seed by the wayside, on Plymouth Pock, and the Peninsula of Jamestown — that struggle for existence, as of untimely buds for life, amid the chill blasts and rank growths of the wilderness — but, as the germs rooted and shot upward, that miraculous progress, as the green vine of Nineveh — hamlet after hamlet, city after city, State after State, — the stupendous growth of a virgin world — rising up in their strength; shooting downward strong roots, and upward great branches; and yet, not according to the old vegetable law — each the germ of a separate and independent life — but, rather like the mighty Indian tree, the lengthening branch bending downward to the ground, forming for itself new roots, and becoming a new trunk, till the whole land is covered with the growth of a *single tree*, with the seeming of a forest — so, all these Sovereign States, covering a Continent, and yet all bound by the common law and life of freedom, into one grand Composite Nation! Verily here is Divine working!

Look at America as she stands before you this day. Her agriculture, her arts, her commerce, her happy homes, her great cities, her matchless civil franchises, her institutions of knowledge and charity, her broad boundaries, her vast resources, her magic progress in the inspiration of her youthful and exulting life, her present beatitude, her boundless and magnificent future, as she stands the living embodiment of civil and religious freedom — the shooting of the civil life of all generations into one grand century flower of humanity! Look at all this, I say, and then tell me if this seems not a harvest field in man's golden autumn? And whether your thought be of the struggles of old nations to bring forth freedom: or of our own historic struggles for colonial life; tell me, if the *ripened grain* waves not in the fields around us, and our thanksgiving this day for civil and national blessings be not unto our God — *a great feast of harvests?*

Then passing from the *political*, the same thought is true in regard of the *intellectual*. It is a thought well worthy our pondering, on an occasion like this — *that we live in the harvest time of mind and thought!* Carefully considered, the development of the "Mental," follows the law of material development. "First the blade, then the ear, after that the full corn in the ear." Genius is first poetical; then practical. First the flaunting blossom: then the substantial fruit. From the beginning, man's law of intellectual progress has been, from the abstract to the practical — from Ideas to Facts. The Practical, being the fruit of the Imaginative, as the ripened com is the fruit of the plant's inner life. And, as the plant-germ must experience its successive vegetable transformations before it ripens out fruit, so it would seem necessary for every great thought to pass through a series of embryonic changes, before it can attain to a perfect and practical development. And in this respect we seem to live in man's intellectual harvest-time. The generations a-gone have been times of preparation — the seasons of thought-germ, and thought-blossom, rather than of thought-fruit.

We cannot enlarge here, but must content ourselves with a few illustrations of the truth — that in our time the old speculative and sentimental "Ideas" have become great practical "Facts."

The old *Astrology* which, looking upon the stars as prophetic hieroglyphics, and reading therein the fate of men and empires, burst into radiant but poisonous blossoms of superstition, on the plains of Assyria and beneath the blue Egyptian heavens, hath ripened into a grand practical science, till our *Astronomy* elevated the race into the regions of most useful philosophy and loftiest knowledge of God.

The splendid yet disastrous dreams of the old *Alchemy*, have showered their false blooms and ripened into a grand science, until the wild visions of the philosopher's stone, the universal solvent, the universal medicine, are more than realized in the immeasurable benefits unto agriculture and manufactures and the arts of true practical Chemistry.

The old Magnetism, whose highest aim was to furnish playthings for children, was the toy-blossom which has ripened now into substantial fruit; and, in the mariner's compass, furnished a key to the gates of ocean, and a guide through the mighty paths of the sea, and given unto man the islands and continents of a world.

The idle fancy of the old Hollander, *carving rude letters in beech bark*, for sport, was the thought-germ, whose perfected fruit is the Printing Press — that gigantic power on the earth, before which, the old despotisms and superstitions of the world are passing away as mists from a sunburst — whose earthly results are all the wonders of progressive civilization, and whose heavenly utterances, are the leaves of the Tree of Life, for the healing of the nations!

Steam — that fantastic shape that played aerial, and useless, before the eyes of old dreamers — hath assumed a personality of glory and power. And the thought-germ, that seemed a vanishing vapor, is today, the mightiest reality of life — Man's Titanic Servant everywhere; chained in the dark caverns of the earth; fettered to the wheels of great machinery; harnessed on the thoroughfares of traffic; rushing through the valleys; leaping on the mountains; marching on the seas — God's own winged wind unto man's chariot, bearing him over all the brute forces, and forms of nature, in imperial dominion conquering and to conquer!

Then latest and most wonderful of all — *the Telegraph!* — Thought's most glorious harvest! The Electric element on which it depends had slept latent for centuries in all material forms, too minute for detection, too subtle for analysis. Then, all unsubstantial and shapeless, it knocked for admission into man's palaces of fancy, and the old Philistines of Philosophy made sport with the Sampson — Muschenbroek's Leyden Jar — Franklin's wandering Kite — those were the thought germs of a glorious harvest. The power, that at the close of the last century, by means of a pith-ball electronometer, carried signals for amusement to an adjoining room, now flashes in the real business of life, through more than a hundred thousand miles of Electric Telegraph. Verily the embryonic germ hath ripened into fruit!

Ami the past year has witnessed its most marvelous development. We are indeed told that the Atlantic Telegraph is a failure; that our rejoicings over it were childish; that all this clamorous congratulation was the cock-crowing before morning, that the less we say about that cable the better, — till it speaks for itself Put we answer — *It has spoken for itself!* It has demonstrated the grand *possibility*. And to Anglo-Saxon thought a great possibility is a great *certainty*. And now the splendid dream that seemed fancy, hath become a great fact. Henceforth, we reckon as verities, all possible results of this matchless achievement. I have no limits to enumerate them — they have perhaps been already sufficiently glorified in the American pulpit. The effects upon the breadth of commerce, and the steadfastness of trade; upon the uniformity of stock markets, and prices current, at the Bourse, on the Royal Exchange, in Third street, and Wall street; upon the perfecting of an international police, upon politics, and literature, and news, and the fashions; in a word — upon all the great physical interests of life, have been eloquently expounded. But, great as these are, they are not the greatest. They are indeed only the radiant petals of a seed-infolding flower, whose ripened fruit is in the *moral*.

A great transformation in the conditions of national life — a breaking down of the barriers of national prejudice — a virtual union of all races by the ties of amity and common interest — these, and such as these, are to be the nobler results of this achievement! These magic wires, stretching over all lands, through all waters, are *earth's strong heart-cords!* — making the dead planet a living creature, sensitive through every fibre of its gigantic frame, to a rude touch anywhere — along whose quivering nerves and throbbing pulses, the great human HEART shall beat, and the great human MIND think! And were our congratulations, over an event like this, ill-timed and extravagant? What though the lamps of illumination have burnt out; and the huckstered stock is at a discount; and the "time and space" which our orators and poets so eloquently "annihilated," yet stubbornly remain; and the ocean, which for a short hour seemed man's great whispering gallery, rolls again sullenly voiceless above its hidden secrets — nevertheless we say, it did become the world to exult over this new and magnificent development — *this ripening into fruit of one of God's great thought-flowers!* — this progress from a weak germ into waving harvest, of one of those stupendous purposes whereby God, "dividing the water-courses for a way for His lightnings," is lifting the race from the ancient thralldom, into his own glorious liberty, and setting up, on the ruins of old Empires, the throne of his Son in triumph and forever!

Now we might multiply our illustrations indefinitely, but our limits forbid. The thought is — That, in the historic progress of the race, every great philosophic discovery passes slowly, like the germination and growth of a plant, from the embryonic of speculation, or sentimental thought, to the practical and useful of life's great realities. And that in this regard, it is our high privilege to live in the *harvest-time*. In past generations, intellect has been busy in a rudimental husbandry — felling the great forests; draining the low marshes; subduing the rugged soil; scattering the seed; and watching, and waiting for the increase. The old philosophy; the old civilization; the old polities, civil and ecclesiastical; the old chivalry; the old poetry — these were the thought-germs, the thought-leaves, the thought-blossoms, which have ripened, and are ripening around us into God's glorious fruit!

We live in earth's prodigal and luxuriant autumn — in times when marvelous things are the rule, and mean things the exception — in an economy of prodigies, each one a seeming miracle to men's earlier comprehension, and yet all, only the ripened development of their own thought-germs! — And if the law of all husbandry be — "to sow in tears and reap in joy" — then, our thanksgiving, that we live in these eventful times, should be unto God, this day — *a great feast of Harvest!*

III. Passing this, we observe once more and *finally* — That this same law of development, we have been tracing through the *Political* and *Intellectual*, will be found to rule in the SPIRITUAL — and in this regard should we mainly rejoice, that we live in life's Harvest time.

From the first rude altar at the gate of Paradise to the magnificent Temple in Jerusalem, the religious development under the old dispensation was — like vegetable life — from the shooting germ to the splendid blossom. But even then it was but a blossom! That Levitical economy, even in its perfection, was only preparatory to the evangelical, — a cumbrous scaffolding to an inner spiritual building! — types and shadows, that found antitype and substance in Christ the Redeemer! Nor even with the coming of Christ did the religious progress end. Hope, rather than fruition, was the law even of Apostolic service. From the hour of Christ's ascension to heaven, *the future* — the magnificent future; the unimagined, mysterious, transcendent, latter-day glory — was that for which faithful men waited and labored and prayed. These men lived in the *Gospel's great seed-time.*

True, indeed, there was even from the first a perpetual gathering of scattered bundles on the earth for the heavenly garner. But the great harvest of the race delayed its coming. And yet that harvest must come, — yea, alike from prophecy and the signs of the times, we judge that even now it is ripening around us.

No thoughtful man can have failed to perceive, as a peculiarity of this generation, a grand awakening of the human mind unto what we may call *the Spiritual.* True, indeed, the set thitherward of the popular thought seems ofttimes in false directions. Our Spiritualized Philosophy is aeronautical, losing itself in the clouds, — home heavenward by unsavory and inflammable gases. Our Poetry, under the Spiritual afflatus, has become mystically spasmodic, — uttering transcendental nothings, very wild and *very watery.* Even our popular Spiritualism, as a *religion*, sits at the feet of tipping, rapping, trance-speaking, psychologized imposture; its man-prophets clairvoyant and celestial, with a very weak and unwholesome inspiration, — its woman-prophets strong-minded and seraphic, as witches in Endor.

And yet, all these things, ludicrous and lamentable as they are, self-considered, nevertheless, as indications of the movement of the popular mind, are, to a thoughtful man, full of moment. They are like refuse wood on the waters, indicating the great tide-currents of thought towards a higher Spirituality, — like sere leaves, falling in a forest, signifying with their sad voices that the autumn-time is near, with its grand gathering of harvest.

Nor are these signs false. For, in the midst of these manifestations, *the true Church of Cod hath been wonderfully roused to a new life of Spirituality!* Let us look as suspiciously as we will upon the great Revival of the present year; and make what abatements we may, in view of false elements and accessories. Nevertheless, no man can fail to perceive a movement, unique and universal in the Church, of a power that seems like a new advent of the Comforter. Nor will the true student of history be likely to question its *permanency.*

Since Christ came there have been but three revival seasons comparable with the present; the old Pentecost, in the first century, the Reformation in the sixteenth, and the great Awakening in the eighteenth; and each of these was an epoch of change in the Church, not only general, but permanent. Each lifted the Church to, and left her in, a higher, spiritual condition.

Now, if this be the law of the present, then we seem to be drawing nigh to the great millennial day-spring! Hitherto we have enjoyed partial and periodic revivals; but today the movement seems worldwide. The old religious forces have been Divinely quickened. Through the old channels Divine grace is flowing as a spring-time flood, till the banks are overflowed with the waters of Salvation; and sectarianism, that went forth of old to dig separate rills for its own feeble vine, sits now exulting in the great wave of Salvation that waters into strength the whole glorious vineyard.

A new law of Christian progress has come. The silent power of this revival, its signal permanency, its seemingly universality; the desire, the hope, the fixed purpose, under God, that it shall remain permanent and universal; all these give it the seeming of the dawn of the world's great harvest.

Let a man walk through the husbandry of a land, and find, here and there, a small field, wherein are a few ripened and scattered ears, and he regards them as the premature fruits of a shallow soil, or an untempered sun, and reads therein no sure sign of the golden autumn. But if, on the contrary, as he walks abroad, he finds the whole land roused by a common impulse — if every hamlet is noisy with men who sharpen the sickle and drive the wain afield — if all the sunny mountain-slopes are vocal with the song of the grape-gatherers, and the mower's scythe gleams in every valley, and reapers bind the yellow sheaves in all the great corn-fields — then he feels sure that no inconsiderable and untimely growth is being gathered, but that truly the latter rains have fallen, and autumnal suns have warmed the broad earth, and that this song of girded men is the great hymn of harvest.[1]

---

1   Preached in 1858.

And just so do the signs of the present times — this universal expectancy — this universal preparation — this universal labor — this unwonted activity of earnest men, in every village and hamlet in the land to gather fruit unto salvation — this mingling together in the toil, of all Christian sects in harmonious brotherhood — this opening of new fields of labor; new channels of labor; new agencies of labor — this expectation, in all hearts; sometimes indeed faint; sometimes strong and exultant; yet felt everywhere, that this Revival- state is to become the permanent condition of the Church's life — these arguments, and purposes, and prayers, and humble, yet God-relying and steadfast determinations, that Christianity shall not sink again from this quickened vitality to the old frames of formal and dead Pharisaism — all these things I say seem, must seem, the results of no local and accidental causes, but the direct inspiration of the Divine Spirit, pouring a new life through the old ecclesiastical being — quickening the steady, onward, majestic march of God's redeemed people, to gather into one great garner the harvests of the world!

In respects then, like these, Political, Intellectual, Religious, we live in times of unexampled blessedness. We have come up to Zion from hills purple with vintage, and valleys golden with corn, *in the rapturous Harvest-home of the mortal!* And it becomes us to keep festival before God, as the old Jew kept his Pentecost. As men, as patriots, as philanthropists, as Christians our cup of joy mantles brightly. What more could God have done for us that he hath not done I What people can be happy before God, if we are not happy! The spirit of *unthankfulness* that, in an hour like this, presents itself before the Lord, must have come from wandering up and down in the Earth, like Job's Satan. It is the monstrous Demon of discontent that drove the poor Gadarene from the fair face of nature, and the loving voices of his home, to cut his flesh with stones, and abide in the tombs; and it ought to be cast out into the wandering swine and the roaring waters.

Oh how happy we ought to be before the Lord today! The man who complains now, must be that very Goliath of unrest, whose discontent feeds upon God's mercies — whose eyes are like the owls' pained only by life's brightness — and who grumbles the most grandly, just, and only because *he hath nothing to grumble at?*

We do not say that there may not be troubled hearts here. Oh, no indeed! For we know too well how life's roses have thorns, and life's music its undertones! We know how some of you have come up to God's house, from homes made sad by bereavements. Your stream in the desert hath been embittered like Marah! Your garden of life, darkened like Gethsemane! And yet we know as well, that even unto you, God hath not forgotten to be gracious. There was a sweetening branch by the desert spring; and a strengthening Angel in the garden's shadow! And the pulses of your stricken hearts bound in grateful love unto your sustaining and comforting Redeemer!

Sure I am, there should be no thankless heart today in the assembly of God's people. Unto no creatures out of Heaven, hath there ever been accorded a lot like our lot. Living here, in this Nineteenth century, free men, free Christians — we seem to stand on the very mount of God, flung up in the waste of Ages, for the enthronement of His great MAN-CHILD! We look *backward* and lo! all the past has been working together for our national and individual beatitude.

Patriarchs, prophets, bards, sages, mighty men, conquerors, have all been our servants. Generation after generation, that have lived and died — great Empires that have risen and flourished, and trod imperial paths, and passed away for ever, seem to rise from their old death-dust, and march in vision before us, laying down all their accumulated thoughts, and arts, and honors — all the trophies of their mighty triumphs in homage at our feet! We look *forward* and the eye is dazzled with the vision of the glory about to be accorded to God's kingly creature, MAN! when standing upon this redeemed world, he shall assert his birthright — *a child of God here! an heir of God forever!*

Verily, we have cause for Thanksgiving. *"The Lord hath done great things for us, whereof we are glad."*

Nor is this all. Here, as elsewhere, there is perceivable an exact harmony between God's Providential and His Gracious economies — a beautiful adaptation of outward conditions to inward character. As the shell ever breaks around the young bird's sprouting plumes and strengthening pinions, so the sphere of life, ever enlarging with the life's growing strength!

How strikingly manifest is this in the Church's present experience.

How wonderfully has God widened her fields of labor, in exact proportion to her roused energies for labor! That moving back of the iron gates of China to the march of Christian civilization — that lifting of the black curtain from Africa, which had so long concealed from the Church's gaze her benighted millions — that fearful Sepoy revolt, wherein, amid the agonies of God's martyrs, ancestral heathenism severed the sinew of her own strength, and rocked into dust her own impregnable fastnesses — that wonderful movement in the old northern Sclavonic Despotism of intellectual and moral life, toward that full and free manhood which the truth makes free — that marvelous cooperation in our day, of the great national powers of the earth, arrayed and advancing in companionship for Christianity against the old Pagan Despotisms. Verily, I say, these things, and such as these, look like the widening of fields around and enlargement of energies! Seem like the comprehensive plan and preparation of an Omniscient Husbandman! The fall of the latter rains and the genial summer suns, bringing the corn to its earing; and meanwhile the preparation of implements, and opening of garners, as the roused reapers make haste to gather for God the Great Harvest of the World!

Say not then, oh faithless heart! "Say not there are four months and then cometh harvest, Behold I say unto you, lift up your eyes and look on the fields, for they are already white to harvest." The sounds that in this eventful hour startle us from earth's valleys and hills, are sounds of the great Autumn! The time of the old prophetic vision draweth nigh, when the earth shall be the Lord's and the fullness thereof; when all the energies of the race shall work together for Christianity; and upon all earth's moving wheels, and spreading canvas, and all her power, and progress, and civilization, "Holiness to the Lord" shall be the blessed blazon — That "Time of times," which patriarchs wept for in yearning faith, and prophets beheld afar off in their wrapt visions of God; when the Divine Tabernacle shall be visibly with men, and the New Jerusalem descend bodily to the earth — that time draweth near! Already is the eastern heaven purpling with the great Day-spring. And coming np thus to Zion in life's golden Autumn — when the last trumpet is sounding and angel-reapers are abroad in God's husbandry - tell me, if in contrast with the experience of other generations, our "Thanksgiving" for what our eyes see, and our ears hear, should not be unto God — *a great feast of Harvest!*

Let us give then free course to our grateful emotions! Thankful for the present, trustful for the future; let us rejoice before God "with the joy of Harvest." As the old Hebrew husbandman came with his offering of First-Fruits, forgetting, in his present moods of joy, all past disquietudes — the weary toil of the seed-time, and watching-time — the wild storm; the seething rain; the chilling blight; the devouring insect — forgetting these, or remembering them only to deepen his sense of that Divine Goodness which, in spite of them all, had brought the full corn to the earing. So let us, forgetful of all past trials and disquietudes — all shadows that darkened our sunshine — all storms that troubled our waters — all financial reverses — all political and partizan jealousies — -all ecclesiastical and sectarian strife — forgetting all these, or remembering them only as new reasons for present thankfulness — turning from all shadows of old griefs; from all valleys of sadness, if thitherward have wandered our pilgrim feet; and coming up, this morning, to the serene mountain-top, where the sun shines, and the dews of heaven be fair and sweet; only mindful of, and thankful for, the present hours of joy! Like the mariner, that with his bark anchored for a brief day, goes ashore to his children's cottage on the hills! Like the warrior, that released for an hour from the stern bivouac and battle, unbraces his cumbrous mail and pitches his tent with the husbandman! — thus standing together on earth's high places, let us be strong and rejoice in the loving kindness of God! And when here in our chosen sanctuary, as the Jew on Mount Zion, we have paid our solemn vows, and rendered our First-fruits of love to God in a living consecration — then, as that same Jew returned to his distant heritage, filling the soft airs of Palestine with glad songs, and waking the echoes of its landscapes with bounding feet; so let us get us again to our homes — these earthly dwellings as truly God's gift as those possessions in Canaan — these homes hallowed by Divine goodness; by the voices, the ministries, the gentle looks of love ; by memorials, tenderly sad it may be, but cherished and heavenly, of the beloved dead — to these firesides where children play; these boards where kinsfolk gather; driving out every reptile of discontent, every bird of evil omen from our bowers of peace; hanging the heavenly lamp of Hope from our lowly lintel — our hearts, like the lark that having first soared to the sky to warble its praise around the portals of the Temple of Heaven, sinks again softly and gladly to its nest of love in the dewy grass! So let us go down from our Zion, as the Jew from the Mount of God to his own humbler dwelling, in glens of vine and olive, or valleys golden with corn — peaceful, joyous, thankful for the *present;* and for the *future,* full of faith, of hope; looking forward to that hour — to some of us so near — when, in the great Autumn of Time, gathered by Angel-reapers, borne by God's flaming chariot to such a Harvest-home as no husbandman ever knew! we shall take our joyous way up through these lustrous heavens, along yon starry paths, through those gates of pearl, through those golden streets, through those portals of the Many Mansions — that there — in that Eternal Temple; in those blissful homes where this mortal Love puts on Immortality — there, with the beloved dead; with the countless multitude bearing palms and white robes; with Angel and Archangel before the Throne; we may keep unto God —

A GREAT FEAST OF HARVEST!

8

THE JOY IN HARVEST

A THANKSGIVING SERMON; PREACHED IN THE ARCH STREET PRESBYTERIAN CHURCH, ON THURSDAY, NOVEMBER 24, 1859.

"They joy before Thee, according to the joy in harvest."

ISAIAH 9:3.

WE are not, today, specially concerned with the text's original reference. The prophet here uses a figure illustrative of Christian life. He is describing prospectively the gladness of Gospel times—a joy not profane and sensual, but holy and religious. A joy *"before Thee"* (i. e.) *in the presence of Jehovah,* or in holy exercises and ordinances. And this joy he compares to "the joy of harvest."

The text suggests two simple thoughts, befitting our circumstances: *First—That the season of harvest is a proper occasion of joy;* and *Secondly—That this joy of harvest is a pattern of true Christian gladness.* Let us consider them in their order. *First—*The text teaches *that the season of harvest is a proper occasion for joy.*

Under the old dispensation, such manifestations of gladness were prescribed and ceremonial. On last Thanksgiving morning we described at length that old feast of harvest, and we need not repeat it. It was an occasion of exceeding gladness. The old land of promise woke into rapture as a child to its holiday. Eyes flashed, hearts bounded, lips broke forth into singing, and from valley to mountain top, Judea foamed and sparkled with glad life at this God-appointed festival. And all these festal rites were of Divine appointment. The priest standing before the altar in the solemn Temple-service was no more truly, nor indeed formally, worshiping God, than were these exulting Israelites at this feast of harvest.

Now this feast is our pattern. We have assembled to render grateful acknowledgments to God for this gift of harvest. Nor is the occasion unworthy such religious offering. It would be difficult to exaggerate the importance of agriculture. Without subscribing the French system of political. economy, which regards the produce of land as the only true source of national wealth and revenue, and ranks artificers, manufacturers, and merchants with non-producers; and without adopting Franklin's celebrated saying, "that there are but three ways for a nation to acquire wealth: the first by War, which is robbery; the second by Commerce, which is frequently cheating; the third by Agriculture, which is the only honest way;" still there is alike in the system and the saying no little of truth. For although manufacturers, and merchants, and indeed men of all trades and professions, do add to the value of national property—and a true political economy will therefore classify all true work with productive labor—nevertheless, all such labor requires agriculture as its substantial basis. In cultivating land, labor moves the great mainspring of all physical, national, moral life. The proximate products of the spade and plow may be reaped with sickles and gathered into barns; but their products, remote and yet real, are seen in all the wheels of machinery, all the sails of commerce, all the creations of art, indeed in all the substantial and beneficent realities of civilized life.

A joy for harvest, is therefore a joy for all God's countless benefactions. In praising Jehovah "for preserving to our use the kindly fruits of the earth," we are praising Him for our whole merciful experience. For our *bodily* blessing—the continuance of life, health, strength, in all our organs of speech, and sense, and motion. For our *intellectual* blessings—reason, judgment, memory, imagination, all unimpaired and operative. For our *social* blessings—that the lives of our beloved are spared to us, and our homes are beautiful as ever, with their cheerful hearth-fires and abundant boards. For our *civil* blessings—that our land continues free, prosperous, united, the fairest and noblest heritage of manhood on the face of the earth. For our *spiritual* blessings—a true faith, an open Bible, a free sanctuary, a pure Gospel—all these means of grace, all these hopes of glory. For one and all of these countless and immense blessings, do we rejoice before God in our *"joy of harvest."*

It is fitting, then, that on occasions like this, we should gather in these sacred temples, with songs of Thanksgiving. As a religious service, thanksgiving has its foundation in the very nature of things; for, as we can by no equivalent recompense God for his favors, it is only a better instinct that prompts us to entertain a lively sense of his goodness, and give utterance to our gratitude in appropriate forms. And this instinct religion seizes and sanctifies. As a worshipful service, this gladness in view of personal benefits rises from the low form of a selfish joy for a gift, into a gracious thanksgiving unto the Great Giver. Here the rapt visions of the old prophets of God and the narcotic reveries of infidel philanthropists meet in one grand consummation, when a holy day becomes a "holiday," standing out as a type of millennial and celestial worship, when the sacrifices of the Lord shall not be a broken, but a bounding heart.

We have, then, the sanction both of our better impulses, and of divine precepts for this "joy in harvest." We have no right—it is sinful as well as unseemly—to sit in our sanctuaries today in garments of sackcloth; or to return to our homes moody, sorrowful, despondent, as if the lines had not fallen to us in pleasant places, and ours was not a goodly heritage. We are gathered here as the Hebrew tribes at their Pentecost, to fill the Temple of God with the old choral harmonies, and then, like them, to go down from our Zion with bright eyes, and smiling faces, full of thankfulness for the present and trustfulness for the future; forgetful of life's trials, or mindful of them only as of clouds to the eye of faith haloed with rainbows; thoughtful mainly of our abundant mercies—of life bounding in our veins, and made soft and fair by the hand of the great Father; of homes sheltered by his grace, where dwell angels of love, flinging purer light from their plumes over all our times of gladness, and nerving us with a ministry of strength for each sharp hour of evil and peril; making our return-path jubilant as Israel's along her luxuriant landscapes, and our homes as bright at our coming; with the voice of music, and the glad laugh of children—feeling blessed in the beatitude God accords us today; and blessed more fully in the guarantee, that "tomorrow shall be as this, day, and much more abundant." Demonstrating, by our smiles, our looks and tones of love, our serene and festive frames, that it is a sweet, and a blessed thing to have God for our Father—that wisdom's ways are ways of pleasantness, and that our religious service in God's temple is but a holy *"joy in the harvest."*

This is the text's first lesson—*That we should keep a joyous feast before the Lord at the gathering of harvest.* But this is not its only, nor, indeed, its chief lesson. If it were, the speaker's task today would be easy. We have little fear that on this point any of you will even *"seem* to come short." Infidelity itself will join with us in this service. It shrinks not from our "holy days" when we pronounce them "holidays." Even the stern old Puritans came grandly out in behalf of mirth—*when the Governor so ordered it!* On Sabbath days they may have borne themselves as if their sanctuary dropped ice-water, but on "Thanksgivings" they were anointed with the oil of joy "even above their fellows." Then, heads before bowed down as the bulrush, went up with the rebound of a loosened bow-string! Iron brows relaxed, sad eyes flashed, the merry laugh rang out, and the fire-light sparkled at the old Puritan's hearthstone, and boards were loaded and relieved of luxuries—as if absorption and digestion were the chief end of man And this is one of the few graces of our forefathers we de light to honor. Sure we are, no progressive infidel will sneer at Christians today as "sour-faced evangelicals"; we shall make manifest enough for the most progressive of them all, the spirit and the power of this *"joy in harvest."*

But the text has another and more important lesson, and leads us to consider, *Secondly—that this joy of harvest is a pattern of true Christian joy.*

Speaking of the period of Israel's redemption, the prophet declares, that *"their joy before God"* (i. e.) in his service—shall be, in its common spirit and manifestations, ACCORDING TO *the joy in harvest.* This annual gladness in the season of fruit-gathering is set forth as a *type of the joyful spirit of the latter-day piety.*

The text is therefore intended to teach us, *that gladness is the very essence of advanced Christian life.* And this is the other thought we now propose to consider: *the duty of cultivating and manifesting Christian joy—* making all our days, like this, days of thankful happiness. Of course, we are not thinking to commend sinful pleasure, or the delight which an unholy nature takes in unholiness. Nor have we any fear of being so misunderstood, or misrepresented by any man of ordinary intelligence.

All this casuistry as to *whether professing Christians may or may not join in the popular amusements of the world,* is a useless waste of poor logic. Prove that they *may,* yet they *will* not! Make it plain as with a sunbeam that such amusements are not inconsistent with piety, and nevertheless is your labor lost, for no pious heart will go after them. In the process of regeneration a man's *taste* is regenerated. "That power whereby he receives pleasure or pain from the beauties or deformities of things around him," has itself been made holy, and in all its affinities turned away from the evil and toward the good.

And so the Christian does not merely refrain from worldly pleasures as a matter of conscience, but instinctively recoils from them as a matter of taste. You might convince a butterfly, plumed with azure and gold, and flitting freely through gardens of beauty, that it would be altogether seemly to return occasionally to the groveling life and rank garbage of its caterpillar kinsfolk. Nevertheless, it would say, "No, I thank you, sir; please excuse me. New tastes have sprung up in my heart with these plumes and pinions; your logic is capital, but on the whole I rather prefer to rest on these flowers and float in this sunshine." And so, though you, or Dr. Bellows, or an Archangel, should convince a Christian that the theatre, or the card-table, or a fancy ball, or a racecourse, were quite proper as religious amusements, still you must, moreover, unregenerate the man's taste, enveloping his spiritual wings back again into reptile-hood, ere you can persuade him to rejoice in them. A Christian is not a Frenchman to "follow his logic down Niagara." You can not indeed thus convince him; for he regards a *delight* in sinful pleasure as the greatest of all sins. It is the going forth, not of the hands and feet merely, but of the loving heart, in evil courses. The offering, not merely of the fed beast, but of the sacred incense of the Holy Temple at the shrine of Infernals. I say you cannot thus convince him. But if you could—(if there were wind enough in a thousand Bellowses to blow away his conscience and the laws of his God)—still his renewed tastes will revolt from them. The restored prodigal has found his Father's house so full of exquisite delights, that he casts no longing eyes back to the old husks of the swine field.

Our text speaks of this Christian joy as a *"joy before God,"* (i. e.) a joy in the Divine presence—pleasures wherein we can look for the guidance and the smile of our heavenly Father. And sure I am, no Christian can exercise such trust in scenes of ungodly amusement. He could not ask the Divine blessing over a card-table! He could not hope to see God amid the painted landscapes of a theatre! Nor trust that God would give his angels charge over him to keep his feet from stumbling in the maze of dizzy dances! He will not "look for God" in the devil's old haunts, even though the devil has gone out of them! Oh no! in speaking of Christian joy, our text speaks of such "pleasures as are at God's right hand for evermore."

Nor, in speaking of the culture of such joy, are we in danger of being misunderstood as teaching that such happiness can be cultivated in an unrenewed nature. Real "joy before the Lord" is possible only as a development of the new life of holiness. All philosophic systems of happiness are false here. They deal only with outward semblances, not with inward facts. They are busy with mere phenomena, not with vital principles. They weave pleasure like painted calico out of cotton with machinery; and do not grow it like wheat from an inward, germinant life. We are speaking of joy as a mood and temper of mind to be cultivated by the true Christian. And here, indeed, it seems a strange thing that such exhortation is needful. One would suppose that instinctively all Christians would at least strive to be happy. But, alas for these moral paradoxes of our nature! There are many Christians who will have it, that godliness on earth is essentially sorrowful. That there is some natural connection between acerbity and holiness; some philosophic necessity that the heart of a Seraph should wear the face of a Sphynx. Sure we are they are mistaken. In the unwritten law of our nature, God proclaims pleasure to be good, and pain evil. Every organ of our body, every faculty of our intellect was created for purposes of enjoyment. And so pain is God's warning that the thing causing it is evil; and pleasure is his guarantee that its excitant is good. But even more clearly does he proclaim this in his written law of Revelation. Here we are as frequently and earnestly commanded to be *joyful*, as to be pure, or humble, or beneficent, or honest. In our text, God's very pattern of a high style of piety is this "joy of the harvest." *To be happy* is therefore a great Christian duty.

Now, in order to a successful cultivation of happiness, *we must form right notions of its nature and conditions.* Observe then, First, That *true happiness is not a thing of circumstances, but of character.* Not as the word meant originally, something "happening" to ourselves from without;

but as the word means in the *ennobling* progress of language, something springing up within us.

A man with an inflamed eye cannot delight in fair landscapes—nor with an aching tooth in the pleasures of a banquet. Put an aching heart into a balloon, and send it afloat through the firmament, and it will carry with it its whole burden. Empalace a guilty conscience in imperial pavilions, and remorse will fill all its chambers of imagery with terrible phantoms. True joy is of the soul itself, not of its accessories; a bliss in ourselves, not the beatitude of circumstances.

And here is the fatal error of unregenerate men. They deal with accidents, not elements. And so, though they shift the scenery of the outward life with the brilliant changes of the drama, still they escape not the unrest. For the pursuing tormentor is only their own unblessed shadow; and the brighter the sunshine, so the deeper the gloom! Happiness, we repeat, is a thing to be cultivated in ourselves, and not in our circumstances.

Meanwhile observe, *Secondly,* that, as felt within ourselves—*Happiness is rather an exercise than an element;* depending not on the possession of faculties, but upon their *healthful and rightly-directed functions.*

According to the great English moralist, "Happiness consists in the exercise of all our faculties in some engaging end. If a faculty does not act, it is as if it were not. If it act without appropriate objects, the action is mere yearning, and so results in unhappiness." In order to be happy, therefore, we must keep all our various powers healthful in themselves, and appropriately active.

In this work we must begin with *the body.* Our animal nature lies at the very basis of our being. A man, therefore, neglecting bone and muscle and nerve, and his various organs of sense and digestion, and depending meanwhile upon his higher faculties for happiness, is like a foolish keeper of a vineyard, who should leave his vines to wither at the root and think to grow and gather grapes from the trellises. Our intellectual and spiritual comfort depends much upon physical health and exercise. Much of religious gloom results from bodily ailments. There are devils that encamp in the outposts of man's nature, as their very vantage ground for attacking the inner spiritual citadel. Dyspepsia and disordered bile, and imperfect secretion, are foul fiends all of them, and calomel and quinine have an apostolic calling to the casting out of devils. Medicine is ofttimes a very means of grace—and a wise physician better for the soul than a whole sanhedrim of ministers. Much of the acerbity of the old theological and ecclesiastical controversies, did not indicate a zeal for the faith so much as an imperfect digestion. A more generous diet would have rendered John Calvin a gentler and a holier, and so a happier man. And a hard-trotting horse would have shaken John Knox into a sweeter temper, and more mature piety. Even the inspired Paul advised the beloved Timothy not more earnestly to fight the good fight of God, than to take medicine for his stomach's sake.

Let all Christians, in regard of exercise and aliment, observe wisely the laws of their physical nature, and we shall soon see a braver and more manly spirit pervading our piety, casting off this morbid and sickly sentiment, and going forth in trustful and serene gladness to the service of the Lord. For, in our condition as mortal men, the body and the flesh have their rights—and the moral nature will be diseased, and so suffer till these rights are respected.

Of course the same law must be fulfilled in regard of the *Intellectual*. All our mental faculties must be kept active with wise regulation, and in right directions. Idleness is the corroding rust of the faculties. Causing the mind, like an unshining sun, to be self-consumed by its own self-centering energies. And so mental activity is the first law of life. But then simple activity is not enough—all activity is not action. A wind mill whirls as rapidly as a chariot wheel, but makes no progress. There is much that we regard as intellectual exercise which is at best useless. Men give themselves to day-dreams and reveries—pore over the gaseous issues of the press, which they call *"literature;"* gape and stare in popular lecture rooms, where hucksters of "old nonsense as new truths," astonish the natives with analyses of smoke and illustrations of spider webs; go ballooning through the clouds of liberal and transcendental philosophy—and think themselves in all this cultivating their intellects. As if an ass's body were edified when it snuffs the east wind! Alas, this is the May-game of thought, not its battling with Principalities—a promenade in silk slippers, not a pilgrimage over mountains. A simple up and down see-saw of the mind, productive only of giddiness.

Meanwhile, there is much hard, honest, intellectual labor that tends not to happiness. Samson might as well dream in the enchantments of Delilah as grind corn for the Philistines. Intellect, to fulfill the law of its life, must not only labor but labor rightly. Minds are not all alike. Each hath its strong instincts—one is logical, another is imaginative; and in order to enjoyment in work, we must follow these instincts. And alas for our mistake here! Regarding that only as real labor which is hard labor, we strive to sail not with, but against the strong currents of faculties. Milton writes state-papers, and Johnson grinds out hexameters—elephants strive to fly and eagles to draw in the harness. All profitable mental labor is under the direction of the grand master-faculty—developing the intellect according to its strong germinal instinct—finding out what *the mind delights to do*, and doing that earnestly, so that our activity—not self-restrained, and so working sullenly under task-masters, but springing, spontaneous, free, from its once strong impulses—becomes in itself not a burden but a very blessedness, like the free music of birds in the air, like the free motion of stars through the firmament.

Again: This free play of thought must be in right directions, or toward appropriate objects. A search after the philosopher's stone, or the universal medicine, or the dead God of Pantheism, or the infidel phantoms of social reform—such toil after unattainable objects tends to unhappiness, because to disappointment. To be happy, the mind must exercise itself amid God's great verities—not floundering, like a blinded beast, through pathless fens and tangled forests, but advancing with sure footstep along adamatine pathways of truth, upward bound to those imperial heights where all science centres in the knowledge of God, and all human interests are merged in the grand interest of immortality. And thus obedient to the laws of our intellectual nature, the mind active with right impulses, and in right directions, all our faculties become sources of joy, like the chords of a noble instrument, neither rusted by disuse nor weak with over tension, each responsive to a heavenly touch, giving gloriously out the grand harmony of happiness.

But especially, and above all, must this law be fulfilled in regard to our *moral nature*. Our *affections* must have fitting exercise and in right directions. In what we have already said, it is implied that in order to happiness these affections must be turned heavenward. But what we mean now is, that their exercise in this direction must follow the great law of happiness.

And here, perhaps, is the great Christian mistake. Setting out with the theory that religion has its foundation in a broken heart, we strive to render our very affections. sources of sorrow. Forgetting that happiness is the true law of life, and that all our emotions, no less than our physical organs, were created not for purposes of pain but pleasure, we seek to disquiet ourselves religiously, as if God could possibly be honored by trampling under foot the very laws of our nature.

We treat this harp of the human spirit very much as an Italian artist manipulates his fiddle. There it is, the most perfect of instruments, with its four strings in tune, and at hand the bow with which to make exquisite music. But, as if all soft and fair harmonies were a sin, off goes the fierce horse hair over the tortured cat-gut, rushing wildly up and down the scale, in the search after vagrant and hidden discords; now roaring and grumbling down in lowest bass—now high up over the bridge with the piercing shriek of a lost spirit—now vexing two poor strings at a stroke, as if in the marriage hymn of discords—shrieking and shaking, and crashing, imitative of the cries of all angry cattle, and creeping things, and fowls of the air,—a true execution of poor harmony in those "fashionable agonies" that some men call music. And so, under this false view of religion, some men treat the heaven-strung chords of the human spirit. Worse even than the old fanatics of the cloister and cavern, they will torture, not the body, but the very soul with the knotted scourge and the bloody hair-cloth.

And they do this with a seeming of true piety which sometimes deceives the very elect. *"Whom the Lord loveth he chastens,"* say these men. "Afflictions, tribulations, distresses, these are visitations of God, and so to be kindly cherished." As if God's chastisements were not severe enough without additional self-torture! And so if a trouble comes to them, as if it were not large enough at its birth, they must needs dandle it and nurture it into a mightier stature. But alas for their reasoning. Many of our troubles in life are not divine chastenings, but self-torture. You may have lost money in business, but it was not God that led you into wasteful extravagance or imprudent speculations. God's gravitation did, indeed, break the neck of the foolish aeronaut; but God neither inflated his balloon, nor sent him afloat in it. Your wife may be a termagant, and your children unfilial and disobedient; but it was not God who dashed from your weak hand the golden sceptre of your household, and substituted the phosphorescent glare of decayed wood for the holy fire of your family altar. Your body may be worn out, you overtasked it. Your mind may be enfeebled, you weakened it. The thing that troubles you is not always a disguised angel, and therefore to be welcomed; it is, perhaps, oftenest a very reptile, bred of your own doings, and therefore to be trampled under foot as a deadly serpent.

And even in regard of those trials which seem to come directly as a heavenly visitation; this is the true law of their treatment. They come to the Christian as a means of grace. But our graces grow strong, not when we fondle and cherish them, *but when we rise up and master them.* Thorns and thistles are a Divine punishment! But must a conscientious husbandman therefore give them careful tillage? Diseases are Divine afflictions. But because they strive to remove them, are all doctors devils? Gnats and wasps and scorpions are God's creatures. But must I anoint my head with honey and beguile them to torture me? Oh, no, no! The same Divine power which armed them with stings, armed me too with a strong right hand to crush them! It is God's law, in regard of all afflictions that he sends, that man shall meet them in Divine strength and overcome them—working out in man's soul, as elsewhere, his grandest good through the great law of *Antagonisms.* The direction of this duty is threefold.

I. In regard of evils that are *past.* Yesterday's evil fulfilled yesterday its mission. It may have been a great and sore sorrow—the loss of all your possessions; nay, the loss of that which gave possessions all their value. Parents, brothers, sisters, children, friends—alas, they may have gone from your bosom to the pitiless grave! The sorrow may seem colossal, overmastering! But what then; must you refuse to be comforted? Because the Divine hand has led you into the valley of the shadow of death, must you therefore pitch tent in the ravine and abide in the darkness? Should you not rather take hold on the Divine staff, following the lead of the great Shepherd up from the gloom to the green pastures and still waters that lie beyond it? A great grief falls on a man as a tempest on a cedar. But may not the tree rebound from the stroke, flinging again its remaining branches to the breeze and the sunshine? If I have lost a fortune, shall I sit down in sackcloth amid its ashes, or rise up like a man and go forth to make another? Because one beloved one is dead, shall I refuse to cast the green turf on the dear dust, and keep an embalmed mummy-grief in my household till the cherished ones that are left to me grow pale and spectral as dwellers in a sepulchre?

But say these men—"These afflictions were the punishment of my sins,—to forget the affliction were to forget the offense, and surely you would not have me forget my past sins." Well, we would have you treat your past sins just as God treats them! He says; *"I will forgive their iniquities, and I will remember their sin no more."* Verily, if you have truly repented of past sins, then has he sunk them in the ocean of his infinite love, never more to flit as spectres along the seas whereon you make voyage to eternity. Paul "forgot the things that were behind," not laying again the foundation of repentance, but "going on unto perfection." But we, we alas! often mistake remorse for repentance. Repentance is the patriarch's dove fleeing at once with white wings to the heavenly shelter. But remorse is the black raven ignoring the ark, and forever hovering and screaming and feeding on the carcasses of the dead. The one is a blessed angel diffusing heavenly peace—the other a fierce fiend casting appalling shadows.

II. But this rule applies as well to evils that *are present*. Even when a trouble is at its height, it is our duty to feel it as lightly as possible. While the affliction is recognized as a visitation of God, yet the soul should rest under the bright side of the Shekinah. We should think more of our mercies and less of our trials. If God is afflicting, yet the while is he more fully blessing you. If he has taken away your fortune, he has left you health. If one dear friend has died, a whole hundred are living. And true piety will turn, like the desert pilgrim, from the scorching sun to the sheltering palms and the sweet water. Like the sailor, who fell from the mast-head, our mood should be, not sorrowful that we have broken an arm, but joyous and thankful that we have not broken our neck!

Alas, for our folly in thinking over our *great* troubles! But then we have a greater folly in thinking everlastingly of our *small* troubles. Regarding it as a mark of godliness, and so a matter of conscience to *feel bad*—some men are always on the watch to find something to feel bad about. In the midst of lives full of mercies, they lie in wait for small afflictions, as a spider for flies in a flower's sweet bell. Meet them where you will, they are always complaining. Sometimes it is the wife that is sick, sometimes the eldest son, sometimes the baby! Now they have a pain in the head, and now in the side, and now in the chest or the shoulder, or the great toe. Sometimes it is rheumatism, and then indigestion, and anon neuralgia. Sure we are they are always complaining, and they settle down into a fixed habit of disquiet till their high calling of God seems but a constant nursing of small troubles.

Now, instead of this, it is our duty to rise from these complainings up to higher moods of joyful thanksgiving. Our trials at their worst are as nothing to our mercies. Shame on us for our thanklessness! Providence builds us a palace of Aladdin, full of all rich and fair things, and tempted by the fiend of discontent we rub the mystic lamp, and cry out for the roc's egg from Mount Caucasus to hang as a devouring curse in our halls of glory.

III. Meanwhile this rule applies as well to all *future evils.*

There is a right and a wrong way of looking forward. To anticipate rightly is *to hope*, and Hope is God's angel of content singing in the bosom. The hopeful man sees even in a present evil the germ of a coming good. Evil to him is only imperfect development—the sourness of green fruit becoming savory as it ripens. Pain is only the birth-pang of joy, the sore labor of a travailing soul bringing forth gladness. Hope is a servant of God, bringing back from the future glorious clusters of Eschol. Therefore, a right looking forward tends greatly to happiness.

But there is a *wrong* looking forward, a spying of Canaan only to find its great cities and giants. There are men that scan the future only to torment themselves with imaginary troubles. They watch the sky only for signs of storm; they feel the pulse only for symptoms of fever. Their harvests are always to be blighted, and their ships to founder, and their cattle to die. That bank is sure to break with their deposits, and that steamboat to blow up with their wives and children. Frosts in their corn field, crises in the money market, a pestilence in the city, a dissolution of the Union, a general European war, a comet wrecking the solar system! These things are the demons of disquiet that stalk through their future. Imagination is to them a Witch of Endor, calling up denouncing phantoms, not a true angel of God going before to part the rivers and open the great gates of a glorious Canaan.

Now, without enlarging, we repeat it as a general rule, that it is a great Christian duty *to make the most of our mercies and the least of our troubles.* Walking with God, like Enoch, with a trustful and loving faith, we should cast all our cares upon God, and not like foolish children, strive ever to take them back again from his Almighty hand, that we may go tottering and stumbling and bowed down under them; not torturing our mortal nature into discord, but attuning all its affection into soft, and joyous, and triumphant harmonies.

This is manifestly our duty as Christians, because such joyous harmonies are the necessary result of advanced piety. Every Christian grace is but a distinct development of a new pleasure. A devout disposition is happiness; a benevolent emotion is happiness; a strong faith is happiness; a glowing love is happiness; an aspiring hope is happiness! Christian joy is not, indeed, so much a distinct grace, as the heavenly blossom and fruit of all the graces—the music of all our regenerated faculties moving together in the grand harmony of a well-regulated life! Therefore our religious nature must be developed in symmetry—not one great grace by itself, but all graces in their proportions; each perfect in its play—all nice in their adjustment! Some men are always cultivating special graces. One labors for faith; another for hope; another for charity; another for gratitude. And this is like playing forever with a single stop of the organ, either thundering with the bass or shrieking with the alto. And the result is always a monstrous monotony. Courage, without gentleness, shocks the sense like the roar of a roused lion. On the contrary, gentleness without courage, sickens the sense like an everlasting bee-drone. To the true music of Christian life there is need of the whole range of the grand instrument—the hand of the Divine Player moving along the whole scale and all the octaves, if it would bring forth from the soul, well rounded in its whole sphere of faculties, that complete and magnificent harmony of religion, which is *happiness!*

This, then, is the conclusion of the whole matter. Happiness is but another name for the healthfulness of our whole complex constitution. And when these laws of happiness are effectually worked out, then only do we come fully up to our practical duty as Christians. For religion takes care alike of the body, and the mind, and the heart—adjusting all our varied powers and faculties into the range and play of one harmonious system. And this is happiness. Not a thing of condition, but of character. Not to be sought without us by sore labor, but springing up within us, the very breath and heart-beat of the new life of godliness—piety in its own pure, genial, beneficent, trustful nature, lived freely out man-ward and God-ward. As the harmony of the spheres from the simple and mighty gravitation of matter, so this harmony of our whole spiritual nature, from the higher gravitation of the soul, revolving in the free heavens of faith and love, and tending still and forever onward to fuller revelations of God.

Such is true religion—such has it ever been, a spirit of gladness. The old patriarchal altars were centres of the purest social pleasures. The march of the Tabernacle through the Wilderness was, in contrast with surrounding heathenism, as the passage of a strong and shining angel. So long as Israel remained faithful to God, her national and religious life was one long, pastoral holiday. The ritual service of the temple was triumphal: "Four and twenty thousand Levites ministered by turns—a thousand at a time. Four thousand more performed the lower offices. Four thousand singers and minstrels, with the harp and trumpet, and all the richest instruments of a land whose native genius was music, filled up the pauses of prayer with harmonies that transported the spirit beyond the cares and passions of a troubled world."

Even their Sabbaths were of the character of great festivals, and it was regarded as a manifestation of the severe judgments of God, when those Sabbath-days became sorrowful. They were not, indeed, as men would have us now believe, days of simple, sensual pleasure. True, even the old Hebrews regarded the Sabbath as "made for man." But the Jewish notion of a "man" was a being with a soul as well as a body; and a Sabbath made for such a being must have a mission unto his spiritual as well as his physical nature. The infidel holiday-Sabbath was never made for man at all, but only for *swine!*

Perhaps Moses did not understand the thing. It may be only a mark of his ignorance—a proof in himself of the infidel-development theory, that he was as yet only in the transition state between sea-mucus and manhood—a sort of spiritual chrysalis that had not, as yet, got its wings free nor its eyes open. But certain we are, Moses regarded the seventh day as strictly religious. Joyous indeed, but with a "joy before the Lord," and a joy "in his sanctuary."

We have not been able to find in his Institutes any specific mention made of Sunday excursions into the country, for air and exercise. He did indeed allow every Israelite on the Sabbath to loose his ox, and his ass, from the stall, and lead them away to water. But it strikes us as hardly logical to infer that therefore he must have directed each man to carry his *wife* and *children* into the country, for the sake of *cheap liquor!* It does not seem to have struck him how wonderfully fresh the atmosphere is likely to become in a crowded horse-car; nor how surpassingly invigorating to nerves and muscles is the noble exercise of a ride, three miles an hour, on a city railroad. Had he been more thoroughly developed into the grand stature of our modern Moseses, he would, perhaps, have appointed another course of Levites to open restaurants in the rural districts—and mounted the whole Tabernacle on wheels for the sake of a grand, general, Sabbath ventilation!

But though in no sense a day of profane mirth, yet the Jewish Sabbath was a religious *festival.* They called it "a delight." It was their type of millennial and celestial rest, and every eye flashed and every heart bounded, as with fulness of pleasures at the right hand of God!

Then besides their Sabbaths, their year abounded with religious holidays; and the world hath no such records of gladness as that which filled Judea at those God-appointed festivals. That joyous spirit did indeed pass away when the austere Pharisaism of dust and ashes made a clear sweep over the festal moods of the old Hebrew faith. But upon nothing did prophecy more terribly denounce the fierce judgments of God, than upon that diabolical self-righteousness that bowed down a man's head as a bulrush, and spread sackcloth under him; and when the time of Israel's deliverance was accomplished, and the incarnate One came, and the heavens rang with the angelic harmony of "good-will to men," then religion shone forth again in her primeval loveliness, purified of every speck and stain of human infirmity, gloriously and lovingly transfigured, "her face like the light, and her raiment white and glistening," and enraptured men stood worshiping in her celestial splendor, and cried, "It is good to be here; let us build tabernacles."

Such is religion as a divine revelation! God's angel of peace, and joy, and good-will, smiling and singing in the chambers of the spirit. Such God made her and intended her to be; and methinks it is time that religion were justified from the foul, infidel suspicion that she is the mother of all grief and the enemy of all gladness. It is high time that we tore the Gorgon vizor off her heavenly loveliness, and wiped her eyes of tears, and washed her face of ashes, and arrayed her in Zion's beautiful garments, and put a harp in her hand and a crown upon her head, and sent her forth singing with bounding feet, in the practical demonstration that "her ways are ways of pleasantness, and all her paths are paths of peace."

Embodying as religion does the mightiest influences of gladness—recreating the disordered soul of a man from a chaos of raging passions into a fair and well-rounded sphere of gentle and generous affections—bringing man, as related to Christ, into actual possession of "things present," so that in regard of their manifold uses he is, over all title-deeds and tenure, positive "land-lord"—"sea-lord"—"skylord"—all things working together for good under the gracious smiles of his Eternal Father—and opening before him in the "things to come" an inheritance and enthronement over all the enrapturing realities of the eternal world. Doing this, being this, Religion has only to come forth from the old sepulchres wherein Pharisaism would imprison her as an unblessed spirit, and in all her glorious beauty walk this lower world, wiping away man's tears, unloosing his heavy burdens, binding up his broken heart, singing sweet songs at his death-bed, pouring eternal light through his grave. And then shall the old visions of prophecy be realized in her victories over the nations—the new Jerusalem descending out of heaven, and the tabernacle of God being with men, and the gladness of Zion upon earth become *"a joy before God, like the joy in Harvest!"*

Christian life then should always be joyous. But ours should be true harvest joy, *because we live in the time of harvest.* We have no new theory of the Millennium. Perhaps we have had quite enough of them already. We have, most of us, survived several "final consummations"; and heard more than once the trumpet call to "the great battle of Armageddon." And if the seven angels were compelled to follow our "symbolic interpreters," there would be not a little confusion in blowing the trumpets, and pouring out the vials. "Of that day and that hour knoweth no man, no, not the angels which are in heaven, neither the Son, but the Father."

But of the special prophecy of our text there is no presumption in saying, it is even now being fulfilled before us. A year ago we sought to illustrate the thought, that physically, politically, spiritually, the world is golden with the fruits of its great Autumn. That in the historic progress of the race, all past generations have been busy in a rudimental husbandry, felling forests, draining marshes, subduing a rugged soil, and scattering and watching the precious seed. But that now the time has come for gathering the corn, and treading the wine-press—that the old thought-germs, thought-leaves, thought-flowers, have ripened into practical thought-fruit, and that it is our lot to live in the great time of the harvest.

But what we would now furthermore consider, is: that all this is really but the *harvest of Christianity*. That the things in which, as men, as patriots, as philanthropists we rejoice—a*re the results of Christianity*. The wisdom of man—philosophic, constructive, progressive—has no more produced our grand beatitudes, than the bright blossoms and singing birds of the green wood have produced the summer. Such wisdom is not a cause, but in itself only a consequence. Philosophers, legislators, conquerors—men whose hands have seemingly shaped human destiny—have not been powers, but simply *phenomena*. They have wrought out the higher forms of our civilization, as the bee its geometric cells, and the coral its noble islands, under those laws of instinct which are the inspirations of God. The grand creative controlling force of humanity is the Spiritual—the Religious. The power of a new and inspired life, first germinant in the individual soul—then working outwardly in the development of personal character—then influencing man's social relations—then moulding laws and institutions, and all the organic forms of society.

Many of the grandest movements of the race have resulted manifestly from this pure religious instinct. The Reformation, under Luther, produced as its result our grand civilization. But did Luther, amid his toil, think for a moment, of these new developments of intellectual and social life? Ah, no! He thought only of the truth as it is in Jesus! And in that simple religious impulse, as oaks in an acorn, lay all the philosophy and philanthropy of that industrial civilization which that Reformation has brought forth.

Our Puritan forefathers laid in this western world the foundation of our wondrous nationality. But in all their work, they had no thought of social compacts and forms of government. So little did they project our progressive Democracy, that their avowed and recorded purpose, as to merely worldly things, was "the advancement of his Majesty's dominions." They worked only under the impulse of a purely religious thought, and this grand nationality, with all its marvelous, beneficent developments, came to these shores in the May Flower, enveloped in the simple godliness of the Pilgrims, as the luxuriant harvests of autumn are borne afield in the seed-basket of the toilful husbandman.

Throughout all the broad movements of our race, it is easy to perceive the controlling influence of this religious leaven; and philosophers and legislators and conquerors, working out civilization through wars and convulsions, have been manifestly, though blindly, obedient to a great religious law, producing social systems, as the fire-mists of the nebulæ, stars, under the Divine scope and order of a resistless gravitation.

There is, in truth, no great vital germinal force in the race but its *religious faith*—in itself simple, and one, but manifold in its developments. This alone is power, all else is phenomena. Hence have sprung all pure moralities, all sweet-voiced charities, all that progress of the race away from selfishness in the direction of the beneficent and useful, all those green leaves and fair blossoms and precious fruits of a pure philanthropy which prove the engrafting of a new scion on the old stock of our selfish nature. And so all these things which distinguish us above earlier generations—Steam, Electricity, the Printing Press, the Magnetic Telegraph, Learning, Science, the Arts, Philosophy, Franchises, Nationality, Civilization—things wherein we rejoice and do well to glory, as the ripened fruits of the race's long husbandry—are, in fact, only the practical results of man's religious faith and life. The golden corn on the hills, the purple clusters in the valleys wherein Christianity in earthly developments brings forth and ripens her glorious harvests.

Our broad, comprehensive, industrial, civilization, elevating and blessing, not the titled few, but the whole huge mass of humanity, and so differing from all historic and effete civilizations, as the sun in Heaven, giving light in all the dwellings of the world, differs from the splendid yet straitened lusters that flashed in the pavilions of conquerors and the palaces of kings; this civilization is but the earthly fruit of beneficent, expansive, practical Christianity.

We have heard, indeed—for who has not, in these days when blind men hold up their farthing candles to the sun—we have heard this boastful cry, *"Christianity is a failure!"* Infidels, gazing upon the splendid and beneficent achievements of our Heavenly faith—having their daily life in an economy where every genuine cheering fact is a Christian phenomenon—dwelling in a world, once a wild howling wilderness, through whose deserts this river, which makes glad the city of God, hath flowed in an ever deepening and fertilizing flood, till already the solitary place is glad for it, and the desert buds and blossoms as the rose—sitting indeed, as invited guests, at the great harvest-feast of Christianity, eating her fruits, and drinking of her vintage, and reclining in her pavilions,—even thus, and there, infidels, in the frenzy of overfulness, dare to blaspheme, as a "great failure," that very influence which has loaded the board and issued the invitation. Verily if Christianity has *failed*, it is as a mighty tree fails, when standing up in full strength it shelters beast and bird with its broad shadow, and showers to earth the abundance of its ripened fruit. Christianity is around us this day, in all our social and national beatitudes, garnered in these great store-houses of civilization, just as the principle of vegetable life is around us in these crowded agricultural garners.

Truly, we live in the fair autumn of the world. In these prophetic times, when the heavenly truths, scattered by patriarchs and apostles among the nations, after long watching, and slow progress, amid seething rains, and chilling storms, have budded and blossomed, and brought forth fruit, that today waves around us in the glorious realities of man's last civilization—and our Christian joy before God ought to be—for it is—*"a joy in the Harvest."*

Now we may not detain you longer.

The text's practical application is twofold. First, *that we keep this day fittingly as a great Religious Festival.* What abundant reasons we have for this annual Thanksgiving! Who can number our blessings? Blessings physical, intellectual, social, national, religious! Living here in America, in this Nineteenth century—free men, free Christians! Verily this day is the promise fulfilled in our ears—"He hath made man a little lower than the angels, and crowned him with glory and honor, and put all things under his feet."

Standing on this redeemed earth, looking upward and onward to immortality, a Christian does seem the child of a great King, journeying in a world-chariot, along the star-paths of the firmament, blessed with mercies beseeming an imperial sonship, and homeward-bound to the Palace of the Eternal Father!

Let us be thankful then today. Let us keep the day fittingly. Let us cast out the demon discontent, from heart and household. Be not afraid of overmuch gladness. Hush not the music of your children's song, and merry laugh, and bounding feet. Repress no impulse of a joyous heart, swelling up in thanksgiving. It is your household festival. It is your great State festival. It is your grand National festival. Never before, did so many sister States keep lovingly together this Feast of harvest. We know, today, no North, no South, no West, no East. It is not the going up of the Tribe of Dan and of Benjamin to the old Puritan tabernacle on Plymouth Rock—it is the gathering of the one great household—all the kith and kin of the Anglo-CelticSaxon blood—the hundred and forty and four thousand of all the tribes of the children of Israel, all going up together with offerings of praise to the one common temple—the central Salem of peace—the God of Love in the midst of her, that she shall not be moved!

Thanks be unto God for this American Pentecost! Never were the bonds of our beloved brotherhood so revealed in their strength! Millions upon millions of trustful, loving hearts, from Northern snows to Southern savannahs—from these fair Atlantic daysprings to yon Pacific golden eves—all lifted up in hallelujahs above all old tribal jealousies, all strifes of parties, all "rivalries of regions," till we stand together, brothers all, with common prayers and praises for our great common birthright, in His august presence whose eye slumbers not nor sleeps, keeping watchfully and well the city of his love! And who fears now the cry of the bird of night that builds her nest on the battlements?

These prophets of alarm are false prophets, all of them. Abundant indeed they are—crowding press-rooms and pulpits and platforms—men mighty to dream dreams, to whom every child's rocket is a flaming comet of wrath, and every mosquito-drone in the night is the burst of the last trumpet—who mistake the rapids of the Blue Ridge for another deluge, and poor John Brown for the destroying angel—looking with blood-shot eyes toward the future, and eloquent with great swelling words of vanity and vexation of spirit. As if the bond wherewith an Eternal purpose holds us together, were a spider's web—and our American nationality every fool's football! But believe them not, my brethren. Spite of all this scolding cant of shallowness and fanaticism—the great masses—the bone and sinew and soul of American life—the countless and ever increasing majority of men everywhere—east and west, north and south—are wise men, all of them, and will never cut down a mighty oak tree because it overshadows a gourd—nor sell their grand national birthright for a mess of black pottage.

This great western Nationality—this glorious creation of God, before whose guiding Shekinah great seas have been parted, and the armies of kings fled discomfited—this young Giant of empires and ages, that breasted triumphantly the ocean-surges of old conflicts—*can abide John Brown's raid, and ford Harper's Ferry!*

One of these "wise men of the East," with his "golden mouth" full of curses, wandered hither on a pilgrimage of lamentation over the "lost arts" of the earlier civilization. But sure we are, that amid all our losings, our American civilization hath not lost these two noble old arts—perhaps he would call them—*castrametation and cement;* we call them—*resisting the devil, and sticking together!*

Every year's experience of the working of this American system is strengthening a wise man's faith in its permanency. Such sacrifices of thanksgiving as we offer this day—these mingling and ascending prayers from ten thousand, thousand, thousand hearts, as with chains of adamant are binding us together, and binding us to God! They sanctify this low, selfish, jealous federation of expedients and compromises, into the loftier and immortal brotherhood of Christian adoption! And standing together by these altars in our common Bethel, our selfish earthly glory rises till it is blent and lost in God's own light, and along the ladder of our higher patriotism there are seen the angels of God ascending and descending; and our National Thanksgiving seems but the first outburst of the song of universal praise, that, going forth from our Zion, shall pervade all nations, and we will keep in the length and breadth of our land a Pentecost unto our God *"with the joy of Harvest."*

But our text has a further application. It teaches us that God deserves at our hands not merely an occasional but a constant Thanksgiving, and exhorts us to see to it hereafter—*that the whole spirit of our Christian lives be pervaded with this gladness;* that having devoted this day to sacred pleasures, we be not found tomorrow dark-browed, gloomy, despondent—our joys, like the cold remains of our feast, left to beast and bird again; that we honor a Divine command at least as reverently as an Executive Proclamation; and having obeyed our worthy Governor and rejoiced for a day, we should now obey the everlasting Jehovah and "rejoice in God always."

Alas for our fitful moods of gratitude and thanksgiving! God calls us graciously to a better spirit. "Awake, awake, put on thy strength, oh Zion! put on thy beautiful garments, oh Jerusalem, the Holy City!"

Life, life, the whole life of a redeemed man on earth, should be like that glad Pentecost, when the tribes of Israel, going up to Zion, made that fair old land of the covenant jubilant with praises, and woke glad echoes even in the dark dells and gloomy caverns of the earth that lay along their pathway. For we, too, beloved of the Lord, even on our wearied pilgrim feet, are going up to Zion—to the city of our God—the heavenly Jerusalem! Though our way is still on the earth, yet it lies through "the land of promise"—a goodly land of fig-trees, and fountains of water, and oil-olive, and honey! Even now are our locks soft with the dews of Hermon, and our garments odorous with the breath of the roses of Sharon! This wind that fans the pale cheek, comes fresh from the glorious heights and waving cedars of Lebanon! And this murmur of waters in the ear is the joyous rippling to the shore of the blue waves of Galilee! Just behind us lies Bethel, all lustrous yet with its old vision of Angels! And yonder away, the stars shine fair and soft on the hills of Bethlehem! Presently! *Presently!* For oh how near seem today, through this cloudless air of faith, the eternal hills that are round about Zion! Presently we shall be, "even at the descent of the Mount of Olives," and our feet stand within thy gates, oh Jerusalem, Jerusalem, the Holy City! Awake then, oh awake from these dreams of sadness! Awake psaltery and harp! Oh people of God, break forth into singing! Behold the pinnacles of the Eternal City are crowded with shining forms in white robes, that watch for your coming! They have caught the cadences of your distant songs, and the faint tread of your pilgrim feet, and the lustrous gates stand wide open, and the golden harps are strung, and the glorious temple is all ablaze with its uncreated Light, that you may be welcomed fittingly from the laborer's toil, *and joy before the Lord with the great joy of the Harvest!*

9

IN EVERYTHING GIVE THANKS

A SERMON PREACHED IN THE ARCH STREET PRESBYTERIAN CHURCH, PHILADELPHIA, ON THURSDAY, NOVEMBER 28, 1861.

> "In every thing give thanks: for this is the will of God in Christ Jesus concerning you."
>
> 1 THESSALONIANS 5:18.

THE simple and obvious meaning of the text is, that we have always something to be thankful for; that gratitude is due to God in every earthly condition in which a living man can be placed. And this is a truth appropriate to this occasion, for we are observing our great national festival in circumstances wherein some men judge that the keeping a fast in sackcloth were a more seemly service. It cannot be denied that we are today a deeply distressed people, and that our attempted offerings of thanksgiving will ascend largely from desolate households and sorrowing hearts.

To this occasion, therefore, the usual style of service would be manifestly inapt. We have little of the old exulting spirit; and amid this evident and almost overwhelming despondency, need exhortation even unto the solemn *duty* of thanksgiving.

Such an exhortation is the text; and in view of it the question, which perhaps we have all asked, why should we keep festival when fasting better becomes us? appears ungodly, infidel, blasphemous; for we have here a Divine command, *"To give thanks in everything,"* (i.e.) in every actual or possible earthly condition. And this command is most manifestly both reasonable and righteous; for where is there a living man today that has not abundant reason for gratitude to God? It is never so bad with us as we deserve. It is never so bad with us that it might not be worse. If a man have lost property, he still has friends; if friends have deserted him or died, he has yet health; if health too be wanting, still he lives; if an arm has been broken or palsied, he remains strong in his feet; or if he be halt and lame, he has the use of his eyes; or if sightless, he hears; or if deaf, he yet speaks; or if at once blind and deaf and dumb, he yet feels and thinks; and for this single power of thought, allying him unto God and his angels— this function of a spirit winged and waiting for immortality—he should, were it heaven's only gift, give thanks unto God reverently with a joy unspeakable and full of glory.

But we may go further than this, affirming that, even in our worst estate, we are receiving at God's hand vastly more of good than of evil. In our experience there are always more days of sunshine than of storm, and more senses ministering to delight than to anguish; so that, reckon as we will, God has ever large claims on our thanksgiving. Meanwhile it will appear that very much of our misfortune is the result of perverted dispensations, in their design merciful. Our poverty is a result of abused, or at least neglected, opportunities of accumulation; and our sickness is caused by a willful violation of beneficent physiological laws. Even these sore national troubles, whereof we especially complain, have sprung, at least proximately, from our own evil passions.

We may ascribe the evils we experience to God's special providence, but with manifest injustice. Our Heavenly Father never constrained as to that indolence or imprudence resulting in bankruptcy, nor to the physical intemperance ending in disease.

Nor is it the great and gracious God, that for half a century has excited at the North and the South those extreme and intolerant fanaticisms which have brought this sore distress upon us. On the contrary, it is the very prodigality of His goodness unto us above all peoples of the earth, which, working perversely upon a corrupt nature—like Heaven's sunshine on tropical jungles, developing noxious and deadly growths—has strengthened thus malignantly these principles of evil.

Verily, if our land be doomed to destruction, and this fair fabric which we fondly deemed Liberty's great temple, be now abandoned of God to the destroyer, nevertheless, will its mighty ruins remain through all time monumental of God's marvelous love unto a self-destroyed people, and upon every stone of shattered pillar, and arch, and aisle amid our death-dust will be found inscriptions testimonial of the tender mercies of our God! If the American Nation be today dying on these hills like a strong giant in the very flush of its youth, it is not because God's thunderbolt hath smitten it—*it dies as a suicide.*

But then this nation is not dying! We are afflicted indeed, we are sorely in straits, and the kings of the earth shake the head, and shoot out the lip, and laugh us to scorn, and against us hath the feller lifted the axe as upon a cedar of Lebanon, boasting against this mighty tree that grew and was strong, and whose leaves were fair, and whose fruit much, under whose shadow we had pitched our tents, hopeful that our children's children, yea, and the children of the stranger unto the end of time, would find joyous shelter—against .this goodly tree—this grand growth of God's centuries, proudly boasting—"Behold we will hew it down, and cut off its branches, and shake off its leaves, and scatter its fruit; therefore, let the beasts get away from under it, and the birds from its branches."

Nevertheless, blessed be God, *"there is hope of a tree if it be cut down that it will sprout again."* We are hopeful of our old cedar yet, that *"through the scent of water it will bud and bring forth boughs like a plant."* We have before God an abiding confidence, that our nationality will survive this assault and emerge from the conflict only more radiant and powerful—a confidence, not of doting credulity, but of philosophic reckoning, resting on the goodness of our cause; the greatness of our strength; the whole history of our past as demonstrative in our behalf of Divine purposes of mercy; and all thoughtful prophecy of the future which foresees for us a great mission of civilization and Christianity to a redeemed yet oppressed world. We have indeed as small fear that we are to be permanently dissevered and destroyed, as that this well-rounded world will resolve to the old nebula, or the Copernican system go back again to chaos and night.

On the contrary, we regard the trials we are now enduring as only parts of a great transitional development—a very evolution of that Divine wisdom which, overruling man's iniquitous purpose, delights to bring good out of evil. And in this connection there are considerations very obvious and simple, which should both reconcile us to these trials, and make us grateful in the midst of them. Observe then:

FIRST—That our nationality is and must be a *growth*, or *development*, and therefore, like all growing things, depends for its progress on constant and sharp antagonisms. This is God's ordinance from the beginning. It was the primitive geological law whereby from fiery cataclysms emerged systems fairer than before in their materialism, and with races more numerous and perfect in their form and organization. And this remains manifestly the law of all life. From its lowest type, through manifold gradations, to the highest, it is developed amid, and strengthened by, antagonisms. Even vegetable life is a long and ceaseless conflict. An acorn falls into the ground, and at once the elements of the soil set to work to destroy it. Nevertheless, these destructive agents are seen presently only to have weakened the husk, and quickened the germ of a higher organism —a green blade pierces the hardened earth, and lifts itself heavenward, while vigorous roots shoot abroad in the soil, drawing up and assimilating and so growing strong upon those very elements that seemed armed for its destruction. Meanwhile this natural antagonism goes unceasingly on—gravitation pulling heavily at its growing trunk and branches; and tempests wrestling to cast it down to destruction. And yet the living tree constantly roots itself and rises, not merely in spite, but positively by means of the conflict: its trunk grows in stateliness amid the rough ministry of the storm, and its branches clothe themselves with green garlands—the very spoil it has won from a hundred baffled tempests. And the secret of the oak's great growth is this law of antagonisms.

So, too, of all higher types of life. The sea-polyp floats reposefully yielding to every tide, and the butterfly wages no war with sunbeam and zephyr; but the lion's awful strength is matured in savage wilds, and the eagle's mighty wing is nerved by the hurricane. No man becomes great in any direction of his powers through a gentle ministry—the Columbus of the seas is tempest-tossed into seamanship— the Caesar of Empires is fought into courage.

Nor is this less the law of great, social, and national existences. It is on this very principle of antagonisms that God works out His grandest problems of moral government. Human progress is ever like that of a ship beating to windward, in the very eye of the tempest. Civilization, like the oak, is the result of an assimilation of seemingly destructive elements, and its sheltering branches, as the tree's, are bright with the spoil of a thousand hurricanes. Even Christianity, from its rude cradle, down through all its mighty triumphs in long antiquity, has fulfilled the same law, and grown strong through antagonisms. So that the consummation of God's most stupendous purpose, was achieved, not by the ministry of singing angels, but through human antagonisms, with treachery and a cross.

Now, studied where you will, this will seem the great law of all national life, and most manifestly of our own. American nationality is rather a growth than a production. Not a social edifice, planned by human genius, and realized by man's art and device, but a social organism, growing from a germ, and silently, under God's law of development. The heroic men who planted these colonies, and whose social virtues and sublime Christian faith have shaped and colored our destiny, seem not even to have foreseen, much less projected, this great Republican Commonwealth. But, as the oak in an acorn, unperceived by man, came, in the rough old Puritanism, the national germ, and its development has been through this law of antagonisms.

At first, the colonists were not only a feeble, but a widely scattered, and unsympathizing folk—uncongenial communities, dwelling each in its own sphere, as aliens and strangers, and brought, only by outward pressure, within the power of social attraction. First, the cruelties of a common savage foe kindled friendly sympathies among the scattered hamlets, and then, as they grew into considerable colonies, the intolerance in turn of English, French, and Dutch rule, linked stranger-hearts into a community of suffering, and stranger-hands into a community of resistance. Then came the Revolutionary period—when the attack of insane tyranny upon sacred charters, and the storm of foreign invasion around those homes in the wilderness, brought a scattered race more tenderly into sympathy, overcoming old prejudices of envy, or ignorance, or fear, and through that stormy era of confederacy, ever strengthening those social ties, till they took the seeming of nerve and sinew and vital tissue in a single, common, organic life.

With the adoption of the Federal Constitution, the colonies became, at least in theory, a composite nation. Old leagues and compacts and articles of confederacy, were put away as partition walls—provincial watchwords were forgotten, provincial flags furled forever, and in the form and with the functions of a single organism, the young Republic set forth in her progress, all her sons keeping step to the same music, following the same banner, E Pluribus Unum, their one glorious motto amid, or against, the kingdoms of the world!

And yet, though from the first our theory of a nation was perfect, there was lacking in the reality something of the compactness of a vital organism, whose great strength should be wielded by one imperial will, and wherein a common heart should beat, and a common mind think. There was, as philosophical statesmanship had foreseen, the working within, of powerful unassimilated elements threatening destruction. Sectional interests, State jealousies, personal ambitions, all tending to occasional interruptions—indeed, seemingly to the ultimate destruction of the one common life. There was need of another and a last antagonism, to compact the organism—the burst of another fiery flood over the conglomerate strata, melting and molding them forever into one composite world.

Now, just this thing we are experiencing. And though to short-sighted and timid reason it seem a veritable destruction, yet to masterful faith it is no more than a fulfillment of the law of all social progress, by which a state of conflict, of discomfiture, of seeming overthrow and disintegration, precedes a condition of higher excellence and triumph.

The grand obstacle to our permanent nationality has been, from the first, this heresy of State Sovereignties—the selfishness of the old Colonial and Confederate eras, transmitted as hereditary virus to disorder the functions of constitutional life. But the effect of this war must be to annihilate that pestilent heresy at once and forever. This, indeed, is its grand end and aim. One resistless, controlling, central power—one great, sympathizing, supreme heart, sending the tides of a common healthful life through all the members to the farthest extremities—this is what we want, what we are struggling for, what we are sure to obtain.

For whatsoever else we may lose in this fiery trial, if we come forth with national life at all, it will be with a strong, common, constitutional life—in fact, as in theory, not discordant congeries of States, but a composite nation. If true to ourselves, we may, and God helping us, we will, drive out forever this disquieting demon, and bequeath to the future more than we inherited from the past—a government, not only the freest and fairest, but as well the most immutable and mighty of the governments of the world.

But obviously this could be done only by sore conflicts. There are evil spirits that yield not to gentle exorcisms—"a kind that goeth not forth even by prayer and fasting,"—fiends that "cast into the fire and into the water to destroy," and must needs "tear and rend sore," even unto a seeming of death, ere they depart forever.

With such an one are we wrestling, and the struggle is good in itself, and will be glorious in its influences. With all its terrible evils it seems, as well to the eye of philosophy as to the heart of faith, of the phenomena of development, —a great step in our political progress—an affliction, indeed, in form, but in fact a great blessing, which it becomes us, not merely with patience, to endure, but to receive as from God with true Christian thankfulness.

Observe again—

Secondly. How this thankfulness becomes us in view of some benefits incidental to this great national struggle. Evil as War is self-considered, yet in the experience of a sinful race it is oft times a necessary, always a mitigated evil. And though Peace is always self-considered a blessing, yet in its influences upon human character, it proves, not infrequently, more disastrous than even War itself—like a long calm on a campagna breeding pestilential malaria, until we thank God for the purifying and strengthening ministries of the storm.

There are principles of our nature, developed by long continued industrial and commercial prosperity altogether more fearful and foul than those which inspire and arm men for patriotic battle. One of these, and the most fearful, because the root or ground-form of all evil, is covetousness—the consummation of all iniquities—toward God the idolatry that denies Him the throne—toward men the selfishness that inflicts every injury.

Now, in our enjoyment of unexampled and almost uninterrupted peace, this evil principle has been terribly developed. "We were fast becoming the most mercenary people on the earth. So intensely material had become our civilization, that we were tempted to say, that the old chivalric and sentimental barbarism were better. In the absence of a feudal aristocracy of birth and blood, we were inaugurating that worst of all social castes—an aristocracy of riches. Craft, shrewdness, subtlety, artifice, cunning—anything, everything mighty in money getting, were grounds of claim for our patents of nobility. The men successful in heaping treasures, let them be whatsoever else they might—dexterous cheats, unscrupulous defaulters, adroit stock-gamblers, robbers of public revenues—though uncultured in intellect, unchristian in morals, uncouth in manners—were nevertheless fast becoming the principalities and powers of our social hierarchy.

Esquire Money-Love, Colonel Many-Acres, the Reverend Dr. Make-Gain, the Honorable Mr. Great-Purse—these were the men taking precedence of the great nobles of character at the court-end of the Republic. Gold was becoming our supreme national god. Gold controlled our franchises, elected our rulers, shaped our politics, and colored our religion. For gold our juries rendered verdicts, our rulers reversed sentences, our statesmen endorsed measures, our physicians turned charlatans, and the very ministers of our sanctuaries left God's sheep in the wilderness, to wander vagrant and mountebank through the land, lecturing on — moonshine. Virtue was a thing quoted in prices-current; conscience and character rose and fell with the stock market. "The creed of the multitude was, life is the time to get rich; death is the winding up of a speculation; Heaven is a mart with golden streets; hell a debtor's prison for unsuccessful men; the chief aim of man is to glorify gold and enjoy it forever." The very temples of God were places of money changing, and the priest at the altar an alchemist with a crucible in its holy fire, seeking the philosopher's stone. The public, in a word, were mad for gold, and when gain becomes the grand popular end and aim—the summum botium—the highest and ultimate good—then has avarice become the spreading leprosy of the social state, and all things fair and noble and of good report sicken and die, as in the breath of the pestilence.

I speak not these things invidiously. I but say what we all know.

We were, proverbially to the world, and consciously to ourselves, fast sinking into the unleavened sordidness of avarice. Like the Hebrews at Mount Sinai, we had torn off our ornaments of honor and honesty—the jewels of price which our fathers brought through the flood—and cast them into the raging fires of covetousness and then came forth a golden image, and with songs and dances we worshiped the calf!

Meanwhile this insane greed of gain was naturally and necessarily working out our ruin—for by an immutable law of life, wealth begets luxury, and luxury palsies the strength and digs the graves of nations. There was indeed an hour, only just past, when it seemed that this dire palsy of avarice had already reached the national heart, and we were hopelessly death-struck. That season no American heart can ever forget, and its record shames us more than flight from a hundred battles! Alas what days those were! When with the old flag spurned, torn, trampled under traitorous feet, our nationality reviled, our capital threatened—the derision of enemies—the gazing-stock of a world—we stood yet calmly by, ease-loving, pusillanimous, servile, seemingly troubled only about prices-current and stock markets, careful only of trade and gain. There lay the grand old ship of State, with all her priceless freight of human interests and hopes and fears, and divine purposes of mercy to an oppressed world, yet driven back from her course, dismantled, dismasted, on her beam-ends, rolling a shattered wreck upon the waters, seemingly about to be broken up piecemeal and go down forever; and yet we, not girding ourselves in seamanship to wrestle with the storm, neither tightening a rope, nor standing to the rudder, we only anxious about her lading—the supercargo's invoices—with outstretched hands and quivering lips crying, *"Out with the life-boat, the long boat, the yawl, the pinnace, for Heaven's sake save*—THE DRY GOODS! *To the rescue! Bear a hand every man* —*Oh!* THE COTTON—THE COTTON!"

Verily it did seem that the palsy of avarice had reached the national heart! Columbia the fairest child in the family of nations seemed dying! The old Empires watched for the death and made ready mourning weed and cypress-wreath for the burial! Her disconsolate sisters beyond the sea were quite prepared to administer, not exactly to her relief but—*upon her estate!* —But blessed be the Lord God the young giantess did not die! Presently there gleamed from that glazed eye a flash of the old fire!

There was a re-knitting of wasted sinews! a quickening and deepening of the old vital flood! the stricken one staggered to her feet again; she breathed heaven's pure air and drank the living water, and grew strong, and walked abroad! and her old flag floats again! her old eagle soars! She concluded to defer dying, at least for the present! our disconsolate English cousins cannot have their "wake" yet! Sir Lytton Bulwer writes glorious romances, but rather fails *as a prophet!* And God's hidden meaning of love in these American providences lies a little too deep even for the stupendous plummet of Earl Russell's intellect!

Blessed be God we are saved! But how? By *Wood-letting!*—the good old allopathic, and only infallible remedy for this plethora of avarice! We are saved from this deadly evil of Peace, by the sharp, but smaller evil of War! The thunder of cannon in Charleston harbor broke the lethargy that was fast destroying the national life—and every true heart thanks God this day that the death spell was broken, even by the tramp of armed men and the roar of the battle!

And in emergencies like this surely even war is a blessing. It is the natural antagonist of the sordid lust of gain. It calls into play other and higher social instincts—the craft, the subtlety, the guile of unscrupulous avarice give place to the self-denial, the self-sacrifice, the chivalrous daring of patriotism and soldiership. Evil as it is, it is still the less of two evils. Better a thousand times the wild torrent from the mountains, sweeping away the corn and the vines, wherewith human industry has clothed the fair lowlands, than the stagnant pool breeding deadly malaria! Even these blasts of war have quickened our better impulses. We feel now that life has nobler aims than to build fine houses, to drive fast horses, to beautify large estates, and leave much wealth unto children. That courage, and manliness, and patriotism, and the preservation of a strong national life, and the homage and respect of a world, are of more worth even than a monopoly of the cotton trade.

This war, in a word, is developing an American manhood and womanhood, full of the old noble and heroic impulses, worthy of our glorious ancestry and traditions, in whose reckoning the accumulations of industry, the thrift of trade, the gains of commerce, yea, even the life and blood of the beloved, are all only as the dust of the desert when the stake of the mighty game is a great philanthropic and Christian nationality.

Meanwhile there are other collateral benefits which this conflict will work out for us. If we triumph here—as, if at all true to ourselves we must and shall—we shall have convinced the world of the permanency and strength of free institutions, and indeed so have developed that strength in grand naval and military organizations, that we shall hear no more sneering at "the bubble-bursting Republic of the West."

Sure we are—the more sure from all their malignant manifestations in this, our sore trial—that the old Empires in their essential antagonism to our institutions, and the intense hatred they cannot but cherish toward a social system elevating into self-government the masses of the race, as from the first they have prophesied our destruction, so they stand ready now to aid and exult in it. And it needs this great demonstration, not only of our inalienable right, but of our inherent power of self-government; this bringing forth of old banners; this marshaling of countless men; this lavishing of wealth; this triumph of the old flag, the old patriotism, the old unparalyzed, undivided, indomitable national life over an antagonism within, compared with which all foreign invasion were as nothing; it needs just this, I say, to teach a gazing and gainsaying world that, ordained of God for a great philanthropic mission into all nations, ours is as well the resistless power as the steadfast purpose to achieve it, even should it lead us into conflict with the despotisms of the world.

Meanwhile, beyond all these simply temporal benefits, has this struggle a great spiritual use, in restoring our old primitive and puritan sense of dependence upon God. As already observed, under the united influences of prosperity and covetousness, we were fast becoming an irreverent, and indeed, atheistic nation, and that divine favor, whereon solely our fathers relied, was scarcely reckoned among our sources either of preservation or prosperity. But we are now learning, once for all, and thoroughly, that our national salvation depends neither on political sagacity, nor military strength, but on the protection of that Arm that ruleth in Zion—that, indeed, all those material resources, and social influences, which we counted as strength, are, without the divine blessing, only so many elements of destruction; and that all those bonds of national Union, that we pronounced indissoluble—this broad communism of industrial and commercial interest—this grand geographical unity—this brotherhood of kin, and cast, and race—this proud partnership in blessed memories and glorious hopes—that these, and whatsoever else have seemed bands of triple steel round our beloved confederacy, are yet only as a spider's web when an incensed God, turns away from us the light of his countenance. God is teaching us herein great ethical and theological lessons, and will bring us forth from the trial, as gold purified from the fire, not the old boastful infidel nationality, but a reverent and Christian people, whose God is the Lord.

We may not pursue this point further. Enough has been said to illustrate, and guard from misrepresentation, our simple thoughts. We have attempted no commendation of war; we have not said that self-considered, it is not ever and only a great and sore evil. We have only insisted that, terrible as it is, yet life, may have greater evils—that anarchy is a greater; that the dismemberment and destruction of this fair heritage is a greater; that to live without a country, or a government, or an earthly future for ourselves and our children is a greater; that to be stripped by traitorous hands of all that renders life enjoyable or endurable is a greater; that just here and now to pause in our national progress, and suffer our free institutions to fail, and the American name, with all its traditionary glory, and all its fair promise unto oppressed humanity, to become an offense and a scorn unto a gain-saying, or a disappointed world—that all this is immeasurably worse, than any evils war itself can bring.

We believe, indeed, that just this conflict is a great philosophic necessity in our national progress—sure to occur at some time, best to occur now—that it is only a mysteriously merciful dispensation of Providence working out for us, through much tribulation, the integrity of a strong national life in the present, and in the future an enduring and far more excellent glory.

We, perhaps, may not live to witness the end of the conflict. Indeed there are some men who, in view of our present rate of progress, have little hope that we shall. God seems to be treating us as he treated Israel—because of their unbelief and cowardice, keeping them marching backward and forward forty years in a desert, which a band of Bedouin cavalry would have crossed in a month. It looks like this now. We are surely as yet perplexed in the Exodus; there is a wild howling wilderness around; and the water of our springs runs bitter; and enemies fierce and strong are encamped in our path; and there are among the tribes mean men, like Achan, that would turn back our march for gold; and traitorous men, like Korah, who rejoice in our discomfiture; and timid men, like the spies of evil counsel, who whisper with pale lips of walled cities, and armed giants; and between us and the longed-for rest rolls a dark deep river, and as yet we have not found our Joshua with the rod of God in his hand. And it may be God's purpose of judgment, that not a man of ours as of that old generation, shall pass the Jordan in triumph. But it shall be passed! If not we, yet our children shall go over dry-shod and exulting and in the morning light. And when, in the serene calm of that sure future, the philosophic and Christian historian shall write up the record, and from that Canaan—that fair land of the promises and the covenants and the glory—reached at last way worn and with weary feet, through wild deserts and armed foemen and dark and angry floods, shall review the strangely checkered past—all that weary way which the Lord God led us in the wilderness to humble us and to prove us—then it will, I doubt not, be seen that this our Exodus, like the old, was the very richest in the experience of God's loving wisdom.—a transitional era when a grandly rounded world emerged from a fiery deluge—an epoch of social progress, when a divinely strengthened people, having thoroughly mastered themselves, went up to a place of peerless glory amid the nationalities of the world.

Now we have dwelt thus at length upon this war, because more than all else it tends to disturb our moods of thanksgiving, and we would have you feel that even this is no exception to the divine rule, —"*In everything to give thanks.*"

But as yet we are only on the outskirts of the text's important truth. This war is but a single item of our large personal experience, which, even if it be reckoned only and altogether an evil, should not yet beguile us this day of the grace and joy of thanksgiving. So paramount and absorbing has become our thought of this war that it will at once surprise and benefit you to consider how little, with all its evils, it really lessens your reasons for gratitude to God. Grant that it is an unmitigated evil, it is nevertheless, only one evil in a vast and ever varied experience of good. In spite of it, and in its midst, God has spread His banner of love over your banqueting house, with your table prepared in the midst of your enemies; your head anointed with oil, your cup running over. No less than before has this bright sun shone on you, and healthful breezes fanned you, and ministries of love gladdened your habitations. And yours have been all the ineffable consolations of the Gospel of Christ, and the hopes of a far more exceeding and eternal weight of glory. Count this war only a divine judgment, nevertheless, it is no more than a solitary cloud on a firmament still lustrous with the sun and stars of His infinite loving-kindness, and scarcely weakens the force of the inspired exhortation —*"In everything give thanks."*

Nor this only. This balancing of accounts with God, to feel that He has done us, on the whole, more good than evil, is a very pitiful and unworthy view, to take of the duty of thanksgiving. Our text takes much higher ground. It enjoins thankfulness in all circumstances. Even if they should seem utterly distressing. And teaches us that true thanksgiving is not a selfish emotion gratified by prosperity, but a vital grace in the soul, existing independent of circumstances or condition.

Let us then in our brief remainder of discourse consider: *Thankfulness as a gracious affection of the soul— What it is? and How it is to be strengthened?*

FIRST.—*What is the thankfulness which the text enjoins?* And we answer that it is not a simple, but a composite emotion—consisting of *joy from benefits*. And *love for the benefactor*. Simple joy alone has no determinate moral quality; it may be good, it may be thoroughly evil. Without love it is altogether bad and abominable. Thankless delight belongs to the class of selfish and malevolent emotions, and may be felt in full strength by a beast, or a demon. *Joy sanctified by love* is that heavenly grace which the Bible calls *"Thankfulness."*

SECONDLY—*How is this grace to be developed and strengthened?*

It is implied in the text's very language that true thankfulness does not depend upon our outward condition—because it is enjoined in the midst of, and despite the most calamitous circumstances—"IN EVERYTHING *give thanks."*

And here we are reminded of the nice old distinction of language (now indeed lost) between "Happiness" and "Joy." The word *Happiness*, from the verb *"to hap"* expresses our delight in what *happens* to us—or comes to us from without. But the word *"Joy"*—from a root which means *to spring*—denotes a delight, not produced by outward things, but by the quality and harmony of the soul's inbred emotions. In short—Happiness enters from without— Joy issues from within—the one results from condition: the other from character. In this sense the ground-form of thankfulness is not *happiness* but *joy* —the abiding grace—not the occasional emotion.

The text implies moreover that unthankfulness is not merely a sorrowful mood caused by conditions, but a sinful disposition constituting character. —And a sin it surely is everywhere and always—a fearful distemper of the spiritual man—an insanity of the will—a neuralgia of the affections—rendering the arm nerveless for good—the heart pulse less of gladness—a malignant inspiration, moody and wrathful, thinking evil of God and working evil toward men, unfitting the soul for heaven, and excluding it from its blessedness.

Thankfulness is the effluence of a fine grace of character, which like all graces is to be strengthened by the culture of the various dispositions upon which it depends. Among which are—

1st. *Humility.* —Much of our discontent results from pride—an overweening estimate of our own dessert. But let a man in true humility regard himself, as he is, a wrath-deserving sinner, and by every mercy that lifts him above eternal despair will his heart be filled with joy, and his lips with thanksgiving.

2ndly. *Benevolence.* —A disposition that rejoices even in the superior happiness of others. Augustine calls envy the besetting sin of the devil, who envied Jehovah in heaven and Adam in Paradise, and the essence of whose torment is a thought of happiness which he cannot share. To an envious soul true joy is impossible—if perfect in conditions of manhood, it will writhe at the thought of angelic spheres and pinions—if raised to Gabriel's ministry in the very presence of God, it will be in anguish at the sight of that higher throne and the loftier One that sitteth on it. Now in a universe like this we must all have superiors—spirits of loftier spheres, even fellowmen of finer gifts and positions. And to be thankful in our lowlier estate, we must have that benevolence which finds joy in the happiness of others.

3dly. *A Good Conscience.* —A sense of ill dessert gives to real good the seeming of evil. To a murderer the gentle footstep and voice of ministering love seem, sometimes the fierce tread and cry of the blood avenger. It was an accusing conscience that made that lustrous handwriting terrible unto Belshazzar as words of doom; and unto Herod arrayed the miracle-working and most merciful Savior in the terrors of an avenging phantom risen from the dead. And so it is ever. A troubled conscience makes our good seem evil—like the Gadarene demon driving the man, whose lot God had cast under the glorious skies, and by the blue lake of Galilee, to torture himself in the mountains, and make his home in the tombs. While a peaceful conscience builds for itself a palace even in the wilderness, gathering joy from all circumstances, prosperous, or adverse, adjusting the heart's chords, like an Æolian's, to give forth pleasant harmonies, whether touched by the zephyr, or swept by the hurricane.

4thly. *A Sound Judgment.* —Our discomfort with things as they are, springs often from a misconception as to how things ought to be. Setting out with the notion that present comfort is our chief good, we will be sure to misjudge God's dispensations. For, in that case, the kindest thing he can do for us, is to sink our rational powers into mere animal instincts. An immortal spirit, within the limits of time, and the conditions of probation, must necessarily be restless. The bird-of-paradise will never sing in a cage like a pet linnet. But zoophytes are proverbially uncomplaining, and periwinkles float with the tide in a very sea of comfort, and well-fed oxen and geese and swine are, in their own sphere, and after their kind, as contented as the angels. But then present pleasure is not the supreme earthly good. Man's life here is not terminal, but a transition, not a May-game, but an earnest work—a battle in heavy armor with Principalities and Powers—an Exodus through a desert where angels encamp round us under burning suns, and the fiery serpent hisses even in the shade of the Shekinah. And the true heart prefers the pilgrimage to the playground, accepting and exulting in its condition of discipline, and, wise to value blessings according to their spiritual uses, thanks God more for the crown of thorns than the May-queen's garland, and counts the star-fire of the firmament of greater price than all the colored lamps of an imperial pavilion.

5thly. *Patience.* —In considering our obligations to God, we are to remember, that He works for our good, as elsewhere, slowly and in circles of immense sweep. His buildings are not Aladdin's palaces, nor his oaks

Jonah's gourds. His mercies come to us often *in the germ*, and sometimes the kernel has a rough shell, which yields only to acrid chemistries and sharp frosts. And we must perceive the oak in the acorn, and the perfected temple in its slowly wrought walls and pillars, and, patiently awaiting the consummation of God's gracious purposes, be thankful for undeveloped blessings, even though their rind be rough, and their bud bitter.

6thly. And above all, as indeed the strength and life of all else, will thankfulness depend upon the cultivation of *Faith*—or a firm persuasion of and trust in God's loving kindness. This, in its connections, the text especially teaches—*"In everything give thanks; for this is the will of God in Christ Jesus concerning you."* Whatever be the precise force of the words—"in Christ Jesus"—they certainly connect thanksgiving with Gospel faith. If we are in Christ Jesus—or instructed by Christ Jesus, we shall reckon all that comes to us from God as truly and only beneficent. If our cup be bitter, yet trustful in the great Physician, we judge that our true need is of medicine, and take it, as more richly a "cup of thanksgiving," than a crystal chalice of the water of life from the hand of an angel. If our way be in the dark valley, where overhanging cliffs shut out sun and stars, and the air is chill, and the path flinty to the bleeding feet, yet we know that through it the Great Shepherd leads his flock in love to richer and greener pastures and fairer landscapes beyond, and so walk it with joyous footsteps and thankful songs.

Faith.—Faith resting on the Gospel of "God in Christ Jesus," and strengthened by livelong experience of God, unfailing loving-kindness—this is what we most want to quicken our thankfulness. *Faith in the present*—not considering with Job, *"the parts of God's ways"* (i.e.,)—the lower parts, or endings, of His wonderful workings—not looking solely at the one wheel moving on the dust of the great car of Providence, but lifting the eye heavenward to take in the whole pageant, until it seem, not merely a revolving wheel but a careering chariot—"a fire unfolding itself and a brightness, round about it," and above it, "a crystal firmament and the likeness of a sapphire Throne," and upon it, the Eternal One triumphantly marching in His great purposes of love. And *Faith in the future*—looking even beyond the careering chariot to the Eternal borne whither it is bearing us—that celestial city with its golden palaces—that immortal kingdom of peace and righteousness and rapture, where God's germ of love bursts into magnificent blossom, and 'these light afflictions' bear fruit in "that far more exceeding and eternal weight of glory." Such a *faith* we need, until every part of our present experience, whether joyous or grievous shall seem a necessary step in a triumphal progress, and instead of balancing the evil against the good in our reckoning with Providence, we feel that there is no evil about it—that it is good only and good altogether, so that we can not do otherwise than—*"in every thing give thanks."*

Such are some of the dispositions to be cherished if we would live in obedience to the exhortation of the text. Such is the nature of the grace of thanksgiving— and such is the ground of the apostolic exhortation—*'In everything give thanks."*

It is sad to think that such an exhortation should be needed—that thankfulness should ever he enjoined as *a duty*. An unspeakable privilege, an irrepressible and joyous instinct of a loving heart, it should be rather! What living man can be unthankful? What place in a heart here for the demon—Discontent! What could have been done for God's vineyard that He hath not done? Go, compute, if you can, heaven's constant and marvelous benefactions! Creation, preservation, redemption—who shall ascribe values to such things? *Life!* what a gift it is in contrast with non-existence! Life, even the lowest —a flower's life—a bird's! How the lily and the lark praise God, till the air seems odorous and musical with their thanksgivings!

And yet the winged bird is a poor soulless wanderer and the brightest flower dies with the summer! How then with your life can you be thankless! An immortal life, bearing God's own image! With a power of thought and love to soar over the grave and wander through eternity! A life springing from the depths of the Heavenly Father's love, and preserved at the price of the eternal Son's redemption! A life so conditioned for development, awaiting such a destiny—watched by angels in a star-hung world— approaching spheres for whose glory, thought has no image, and language no name!

Oh, men! Immortal men! Sons of God! Princes of endless empires, borne in this world-chariot to palaces and thrones! How can you be thankless! How can you sit in God's house in sackcloth, or return to your homes disconsolate! You, who might have been fading flowers—dead stones—nothing! Nay, who, but for God's amazing and infinite grace, would be this hour *lost spirits*—the eternal gulf between you and the heavenly mansions—the immortal wing outward-bound unto the blackness of darkness! You, whose afflictions, even at their worst, are no more than a stain of dust on a conqueror's chariot wheel—a plume gone from the wing of a soaring eagle! What mean you, thus thanklessly to count your losses and trials and sorrows in a reckoning with God? Oh, awake to better thoughts! Lift your eye from the low path you are treading to the brighter things before and around you—the divine love that watches over you; the shining angels that wait on you; the eternal city that opens its glorious gates to welcome you!

Awake! Awake from those frames of thankless sadness! Awake, psaltery and harp! Oh, sons and daughters of God, break forth into singing. Praise ye the Lord. Sing unto the Lord a new song. Let Israel rejoice in Him that made him. Let the children of Zion be joyful in their King; both young men and maidens, old men and children. Sing unto the Lord with thanksgiving. Praise God in His sanctuary; praise Him in the firmament of His power. Praise Him for His mighty acts; praise according to His excellent greatness. Praise the Lord, oh my soul, and all that is within me bless His holy name!

10

WAR A DISCIPLINE

A SERMON PREACHED IN CALVARY CHURCH, SAN FRANCISCO, ON THANKSGIVING DAY, NOVEMBER 24, 1864.

> "Every Branch that beareth Fruit, He purgeth it that it may bring forth more Fruit."
>
> JOHN 15:2.

The text is metaphorical of husbandry. It describes the process whereby the fruit of a vineyard is improved and increased. It is appropriate to this occasion, because these annual thanksgivings were originally designed, and should always serve, to quicken our gratitude to Almighty God for the ripened fruits of the earth. They answer, in our religious life, to the Feast of Harvest, under the old dispensation. And such festivals are befitting and beautiful. They were so, preeminently, in regard of the Jews, because, as a nation, they were farmers. Peasant and prince, in their respective spheres, were alike husbandmen. While a small portion of the tribes on the eastern side of the Jordan led a purely pastoral life, the great body of the people were emphatically tillers of the soil. Their peculiar civil polity was intended to make them such. Not only did each tribe possess a particular province, but each family had, as well, a specific inheritance which could never be wholly alienated. No great land holding aristocracy, therefore, could obtain permanently among them. The poorest Jew held his freehold by irrevocable title. If, for a time, haply or willfully alienated, it reverted unencumbered to him or his at the year of Jubilee; and every husbandman felt that all improvement of the estate was for the benefit of himself and his children.

Under this peculiar encouragement to labor, the whole land attained the highest agricultural condition. Naturally exceedingly fertile, it became, through culture, the garden of the world. The peculiar productions of all zones were found in its widely diversified soil and climate ; grains of all species grew on its sunny plains; plantations of olives covered its sandy hills; its low, clay soils nourished groves of stately palm ; its sharp mountain ridges were purple with rich clusters of the vine ; even its precipitous rocks were made fertile by means of artificial embankments, so that, in the autumn time, corn-fields and vineyards and orange groves and forests rose, in ascending circles, from valley to hilltop, covering the whole landscape with a lavish beauty, until the old Canaan, in its loveliness, seemed a fitting type of heaven. And to such a people the Feast of Harvest was, of course, a glorious festival. Its annual return woke the whole laud into gladness. Fair and befitting were the exulting rites of that old holiday, when, from every hamlet and home, from glens of the vine and the olive, and valleys golden with corn, the thousands of Israel went up to appear before God in Zion, filling the land, as they passed, with those old choral harmonies: — *"Praise the Lord, Jerusalem; Praise thy God, O Zion. For He hath strengthened the bars of thy gates; He hath blessed thy children within thee. He maketh peace m thy borders, and filleth thee with the finest of the wheat ; He hath not dealt so with any nation. Praise ye the Lord. Praise God in His sanctuary. Praise Him in the firmament of His power. Praise Him with the sound of the trumpet. Praise Him with the timbrel and dance; kings of the earth and all people, princes and all judges of the earth; both young men and maidens, old men and children. Let every thing that hath breath praise the Lord. Praise ye the Lord."*

Nor even in this aspect, as simple harvest festivals, do these annual Thanksgivings beseem us less than the Jews. We that live in cities sometimes forget this. We think of agricultural fairs and harvest-homes as things especially appropriate in rural districts; while in the progress of the arts, and manufactures, and commerce, we feel a deeper interest. But we should remember that even these have their springs in, and depend upon, husbandry. Suspend, for a single twelve-month, the world's practical agriculture and it would become a great sepulchre. Therefore, the sailor on the sea, the artisan in his shop, the merchant on exchange, the orator on the platform, the statesman in the cabinet, the noble in the palace, the king upon the throne arc all as deeply and personally interested in husbandry, and should be as thankful for its success, as the humblest tiller of the soil.

Such feasts of harvest, therefore, become all men; and not least of all, Californians. First, manifestly, among our occasions of praise are our agricultural blessings. California has a thousand things to be thankful for. In regard of manifold interests, a bright and boundless future lies before her.

Her mines are inexhaustible. The whole land shows like a cabinet which the great Father has stored for the delight of his children. Yea, like a treasure vault, whose riches might suffice for the traffic of the world. Verily, in comparison with other lands, is the old prophecy fulfilled: — *"For brass God hath given us gold; and for iron, silver; and for wood, brass; and for stones, iron."* California may well be thankful for her treasures of the earth.

She may be thankful, too, for her commerce. Already, she is the most important commercial State of the North Pacific; and this relative position she must maintain, for she can have no rival. So that, in that hastening time, when her population shall have marvelously increased; and, the cost of labor being cheapened, her canons and cities shall hum with the wheels and spindles of her own manufactures, and her vast mineral wealth be economically and thoroughly developed; and more than all, when the immense products of the East shall flow through her Golden Gate, as the navies of the Pacific pour their treasures at her feet, and a thousand rushing chariots, along pathways of iron, bear through her Sierran passes all this measureless traffic; then the commerce of California will be the grandest in the world. Over her mineral and her commercial resources, may our fair State well keep thanksgiving.

And yet, second to nothing, should be her glory in her agricultural promise. Her harvest will, in the end, be of more value than her mines. Soil, atmosphere, climate — each a marvel in itself — combine, in this behalf, almost unto miracle. They have already rendered her vegetation the wonder of the world — for here are clusters heavier than Eschol's, and fruits more abundant than Arcadia's, and flowers more wonderfully fair than Paistum's or Sharon's. And when, in her swift progress, she shall have come to that period of repose and culture, when wealth sinks from its importance as an end, to be reckoned only for its uses, and her merchant princes shall delight to beautify her glorious scenery — building amid gardens like Eden, palaces to enshrine her new types of art, and embosom her new social life — then, in that long, fair, pastoral holiday, will her simple landscape scenery, and agricultural wealth render her, most of all, the world's envy. And it shall come to pass, if not in your day, yet in the days of your children, that the grand old harvest feast of Judea will be fully rivaled here, and your loudest songs, like her's, be these autumnal thanksgivings for the divine love that crowns the year with radiant blossoms and ripened fruits of the earth. It is eminently proper, then, to observe these anniversaries in the spirit which originated them — public gratitude unto God at the ingathering of the land's ripened harvests.

Meanwhile, in each succeeding year, these Thanksgiving Days have, by common consent, assumed, more and more, the character of national thanksgivings for great national blessings — seasons in which the preacher in the sanctuary is expected to discourse especially on our civil and national reasons for praise. And as appropriate in both respects we have chosen our text. It befits a simple harvest festival, for it is metaphorical of husbandry. It befits our civil and national condition, as a stricken and suffering nation; because, under this figure of a pruning-knife, it presents even national sufferings in merciful aspects, and reveals God's hidden meaning of love in these phenomena of disturbance.

Now, we need not say that to the world this day, our country presents almost only aspects of disaster. The vision is just that upon which the great statesman of New England prayed that his eyes might never look: — "A sun shining on the broken fragments of our once glorious Union — States dissevered, discordant, belligerent — a land rent with civil feuds and drenched with fratricidal blood." We are observing our National Festival in conditions which, some men think, call for a national fast, as a more seemly service; and our praises will ascend largely from desolate households and sorrowing hearts. Nevertheless, a thoughtful christian will find, even in our present circumstances, abundant occasion of praise. Though suffering many things, yet many blessings remain to us. Our national aspects might be much worse than they are. Surely it is a matter of praise before God, that, through the length and breadth of our land, the cities are not smouldering ruins, and the fields red with blood! Even this thought were enough to inspire our thanksgivings. But my text gives us another and a better ; for it teaches us to regard even our disasters as merciful, and to find occasion of praise, even, in the seeming judgments of God.

The text speaks of the benefits of a pruning-kmfe! — of processes of cutting, with a purpose of good! And such, it is the privilege of faith to believe, are the afflictions we are experiencing; we are to regard this sword of war as but the divine pruning-knife, purging unto greater faithfulness a grand vine of God's planting. Of course, we are not thinking to speak of war as, self-considered, a blessing. Oh no! God forbid! For according to all the teachings of His word it is evil, and evil only. Nevertheless, in all the histories of God's dealings with nations, war is the very evil by which He hath wrought out their good.

Sure we are, God permits it, overrules it, manages it for His own glory. We may find fault with it, abhor it, anathematize it, pray against it ; yet, as believers in a divine Providence, we must accept it as a divine dispensation toward us — either purely a judgment — or a judgment meant mercifully — i.e. — either *an axe at the root of an evil tree to be cut down* — or a *pruning-knife amid overgrown branches, that there may be increase of the fruit.*

But there is no man here prepared to regard these disasters as positively destructive. Surely, God hath not yet laid his devouring axe at the root of the tree ! We are afflicted indeed; we are in straits; and the nations of the earth laugh us to scorn; as if the divine Feller had gone forth against our glorious tree, whose leaves were fair, and whose fruit much, and whose branches gave promise unto children's children, and unto the children of strangers, of a blessed shelter to the end of time; of this goodly tree, declaring: — *"Behold I will hew it down, and cut off its branches, and shake off its leaves, and scatter its fruit; therefore, let the beasts get away from under it, and the birds from its branches."*

But *we* do not believe this. This American tree — this grand growth of God's mountains of love — is not yet to be cut down. No great nation ever perished in its youth, or on the threshold of its progress. And we shall not thus perish. Indeed this tree is not evil that God's axe should fell it. We are sick of this priestly and pharisaic cant about the supreme wickedness of this nation. The history of the American people, up to the hour of this fearful visitation, was the purest national history the world ever read. No pages, elsewhere, are so illustrated with the great popular virtues of benevolence, patriotism, philanthropy, and practical godliness! Surely we are not especially obnoxious to divine wrath; if God has borne so long with earth's old monstrous despotisms, He will bear yet a little with us! And therefore, we judge confidently that our emblem this day is not a great tree, which, having been long cultured, and bringing forth no fruit, or fruit only evil, is reserved for the destroying axe; but is, rather, a fruitful vine that, in the very lustiness of its growth, needs the pruning-knife, which cuts, not for destruction, but for the sake of the fruit.

Now, this thought we will pursue through the remainder of our discourse — that these afflictions are designed for our good — *that this war is not God's destroying axe, but His beneficial pruning-knife.* For surely this is conceivable. We all understand how, in the workings of divine providence, there is often a great blessing even in a curse — as from the primitive curse of *labor* sprang the great blessing *industry* — and through *death*, the great evil, did Christ accomplish *redemption*, our infinite good! And thus, in regard of this scourge — war. There are principles of human nature, developed by long continued material and commercial prosperity, more to be feared than those which arm and inspire men for patriotic battle; and as we look carefully to our national character, we shall discover many great and growing evils which this sore chastisement will destroy or modify — overgrown branches of the American vine that needed God's pruning-knife. Let us consider a few of them. And

FIRST — *Covetousness* — that foul lust of Mammon which even Jehovah ranks with the master-sin, idolatry. Verily, here was an evil thing in the midst of us. Up to the time of this visitation, we were fast becoming the most mercenary people on earth. So intensely material had become our civilization that we were tempted to say that even the old chivalrous and sentimental barbarism were better. In the absence of a feudal aristocracy of birth and blood, we were inaugurating that worst of all social castes — an aristocracy of riches. Craft, shrewdness, subtlety, cunning, anything, everything, might in money making, had become grounds of claim for patents of nobility. Gold was fast becoming our great national idol. Gold controlled our franchises, elected our rulers, shaped our politics, colored our religion. Proverbially unto the world, and consciously unto ourselves, we were fast sinking into the unleavened sordidness of avarice; and this insane greed of gain was working our ruin; for by an immutable law of life, wealth begets luxury, and luxury palsies the strength and digs the grave of nations.

Now I need not pause to show philosophically and historically how war is naturally, and hath ever practically proved itself, the antagonist of covetousness. Not only does it destroy the idol, by consuming its substance, but it destroys the idolatry, by calling into play higher social instincts — the craft, the subtlety, the sordidness of unscrupulous avarice giving place to the self-denial, the self-sacrifice, the chivalrous daring of patriotism and soldiership; and thus, evil as it is, it is yet the smaller of two evils. Better a thousand times the wild torrent from the mountains, sweeping away the corn and vines of the thrifty husbandman, than the stagnant morass breeding deadly malaria! Even these blasts of war quicken some of our better impulses. We feel now that life has nobler aims than to build fine houses, and drive fast horses, and beautify large estates, and leave much wealth unto children — that courage, and manliness, and patriotism, and the preservation of a strong national life, and the compelled respect and homage of the world are of more worth than all the prizes grasped by the withered hand of avarice! The result, at least, is certain. Our golden god is being fast crushed under the iron chariot of conflict — the dust of our molten calf is making life's waters bitter. Our vine was wasting its vigor in an overgrown branch of covetousness; and Jehovah is pruning it with His terrible knife — WAR!

SECONDLY — *Lawlessness* — a widespread, popular independence of, or restlessness under, wholesome restraint, was another of our fast growing evils. Our liberty, through its very greatness, was fast becoming license. Many of our laws lay dead letters in the statute book. Property and life, in our midst, were fearfully insecure. Even family government — the great source of all civil restraint — was fast disappearing, under the practical working of the Young-American theory of exclusive self-government. To the philosophic statesmen of Europe our free institutions seemed tending to anarchy. There appeared in our body-politic no resistless central power, to control and conserve. Hence arose, not unnaturally, in our midst this grand heresy of State sovereignties — the lawlessness of the individual man becoming the lawlessness of the masses — the selfish individualism of the old colonial and confederate eras, transmitted as hereditary virus, to disorder the functions of the new constitutional life. It has disordered it from the first. This war is to be regarded scarcely as a new thing. We were not at peace before. For the last fifty years the condition of these States has been a mighty composite antagonism — a seething caldron wherein mingled all elements of hot strife. Witness our national legislature; our national elections! What scenes like the barbaric conflict of armed champions in our national capitol? What excitements like the mingling tides of armed battle in the exercise of our franchises! What tearful questionings of our political future at home! What exulting prophecies abroad of our hastening destruction! And do you think to call all this a condition of peace? Alas, no! It was at best but an armistice — the peace only of a millennium wherein the lamb's heart was chill with terror, and the recumbent lion was but crouching for his spring! This war is not the creation of our day nor of our generation. It is but the development of latent elements, mighty from the first. It was, even then, a war of hot breath, of angry words, of wrestling opinions — the strife of fierce and untamed spirits! — the scattering, in our fair heritage, of the fabled dragon's teeth, of which these bristling bayonets of armed men are but the natural harvest.

I repeat it. *Impatience of restraint* has been our great national evil. It grew with our ever-growing idolatry of popular sovereignty, and culminated in this inevitable heresy of State sovereignty. For a heresy it is; its absurdity is apparent in its simple statement. The very word "Constitution" implies the vital connexion of parts in the same body — the condition or laws of one individual, indivisible, organic life. If therefore, our Federal Union be no more than a conglomerate of States, rounded by outward pressure and cemented by selfish interests, then it never had a constitution, nor has it anything to glory in; for the "Six Nations of

Indians" confederated for purposes of mutual defense, and roaming in lawless savageness their native wilds, were as truly and nobly a "North American Republic," three hundred years ago.

Surely this theory of government was false; and its inevitable result was sharp sectional antagonism. For what, as thus considered, was our nationality? A *constellation* of States, held omnipotently together by a supreme central law, and revolving in beneficent harmony through the firmament of heaven? No, indeed. It was only a KENNEL of States, hunting their prey together through a wild jungle of compromises, ready to part at a moment, if their paths separated, or to spring madly at each other's throats, if those paths crossed! And why should not our national legislature be a scene of barbaric strife, and the exercise of our national franchises convulse the whole land!

This unconstitutional lawlessness was a terrible evil; and the natural result — yea, the positive and grand design of this war is forever to remove it. In its origin in the popular American mind and heart it had no meaner, no other end. It was not a war for pride, for passion, for gain, for conquest, for selfish interests, for personal ambition, for the jealousies of States, or the rivalries of regions. Oh no! It was a war simply for constitutional life — constitutional government — for the enthronement of national law — one resistless, controlling, central power — one great, sympathizing, supreme popular heart, sending through the whole body-politic the tides of a common healthful life! This was at least its aim, and if it accomplish anything, this must be its end. For, whatever else we may lose in this fiery trial, if we come forth with a national life at all, it will be with a common, mighty, constitutional life — a government not only the freest and fairest, but the most immutable and irresistible the world ever saw. Thereafter forever, will Law, as a tremendous and inexorable power, be enthroned in the midst of us ; and we shall be law-abiding and blest. Our vine of Liberty was shooting forth a monstrous branch of license, and Jehovah is pruning it with his fearful knife — WAR!

THIRDLY — *Political Atheism* was another, and the most terrible of our fast growing evils. Under the specious plea of separating Church and State, we were attempting a practical divorce of God and our Government. We were not merely irreligious; we had become infidel; we were fast becoming atheist. The divine law was not recognized in our high places of authority; the divine favor was scarcely regarded among our elements of prosperity. Nay, so positively idolatrous had become our trust in our wonderful nationality that we regarded it not only independent of divine purposes, but indispensable to them: — "Where" cried the infidel, "shall God raise up an instrument to destroy us?" — "How" cried the believer, "shall God evangelize the nations without us?"

And this political atheism which has destroyed so many nations, and will destroy any nation, was growing on our fair national vine like a monstrous fungus ; it was eating out its strength and destroying all its fruit. And by this war God is pruning it. We are learning, we have learned, once for all, and thoroughly, that our national salvation depends neither upon political sagacity, nor military strength, but solely on the protection of that great Arm that ruleth in Zion; that, indeed, all those material resources and social influences, we regarded as our strength, are, without the divine blessing, only so many elements of disaster; that all these bonds of national union, we had pronounced indissoluble, this grand geographical unity, this intimate association of our broad industrial and commercial interests, this prouder partnership in our land's blessed memories and glorious hopes; yea, even that tenderer brotherhood of kith and kin, rocked in the same cradle, nourished in the some household; that all these, and whatsoever else had seemed as bands of triple steel round our beloved confederacy are but as a spider's web, when an incensed God turns away from us the light of His countenance. God is teaching us, not merely lessons of political wisdom, but, as well, great ethical and theological lessons, and he will bring us forth from the trial, as gold purified by the fire; not the old, boastful unbelieving nationality, but a reverent and christian people whose God is the Lord! Our vine was shooting forth rank branches of atheism and Jehovah is pruning it with his sharp knife — WAR!

Now, time would fail me to pursue this thought further. There are manifold other evils from which this war will deliver us; but, inasmuch as they are either smaller or sectional, and obvious to every thoughtful man, we need not consider them. Indeed, we have brief space left for the remainder of our subject. Thus far, we have considered only the text's *negative* aspects — *the evil growths of which the divine Husbandman is pruning us.* But the text has a *positive,* and not less important aspect — *the improved fruit which, with pruning, the great vine will produce.* Of these overgrown branches "He purgeth it, *that it may bring forth more fruit."*

Glancing, then, hastily at some of the positive results this fearful war promises, we mention,

FIRST — *A nobler style and type of manhood.*

This is indeed implied in what we have said of the qualities of character this conflict is developing. In this regard, the American vine bore precious fruit from the first. History has no nobler page than our old colonial record — no story of truer heroism, of character better fitted by lofty qualities to do man's noblest work. Verily, God gathered out of Christendom the choicest specimens of the race to plant in this western husbandry. Yet it was but the old manhood after all. Every colonist remained still a part of his ancestral nationality. We were still distinct races; each with its own father-land of grand hopes and memories. Wo were a conglomerate of all peoples and not composite Americans. But even this we are now becoming. Fighting together for the same great ends, bearing each other's burdens, binding up each other's wounds, struggling and suffering together unto death, mingling tears and blood in one common conflict for a common home and heritage unto children's children, we are fast becoming one people, with all our noblest affections rooted in the same common land of precious memories and glorious hopes. Through this sore fellowship of suffering we shall be hereafter a composite. And a priceless composite it will be — like the celebrated Corinthian brass, an amalgam of all metals — when the best qualities of the iron Saxon, the volatile Frenchman, the grave Spaniard, the reflective German, the effervescing Italian, and the warm-hearted Irishman shall be harmoniously blended in one type of American manhood.

And doing this, as this fierce conflict is, and meanwhile, as we have seen, calling into play all our higher social instincts — instead of the greed, the craft, the sordid selfishness of avarice, substituting the self-denial, the self-sacrifice, the lofty aims and ambition, the chivalrous daring of patriotism and soldiership — doing all this and more — it is evidently developing a style and strength of American manhood, full of all noble and heroic impulses, worthy of our ancestry and traditions, in whose reckonings the accumulations of industry, the gains of commerce, the ends and aims of mean and selfish ambition; yea, all life's smaller and lowlier things, yea, life itself, our own life, our children's life, will seem only as the dust of the desert, when the stake of the mighty game is a great imperial and christian nationality. Surely, in this respect, will God's primed vine bring forth nobler fruit!

SECONDLY — *It will bring forth a new style and type of civil freedom.*

It is a popular mistake to regard liberty as one absolute and immutable thing. There are as many ideas and forms of liberty as of religion. There was the old patriarchal liberty and the old theocratic liberty, and the fierce old Grecian and the stern old feudal liberty. There is to-day, the old English liberty, and the French liberty, and the Swiss liberty, and the Central and South American liberty. And in this direction there has ever been progress. After centuries of struggling with imperial despotisms, the race achieved for itself the grand old feudal liberty — a noble composite of historic growth — the equilibrium of immense and antagonistic social forces — the harmony of compromise and counterpoise amid the mingling and mighty elements of state — a limited monarchy, a limited oligarchy, a limited democracy, all mutually modifying and moulding each other into grand forms of free social life. And this perhaps, till now, has philosophic statesmanship regarded as the freest possible social system consistent with strong government; and therefore as the last and best form of popular civil liberty. The fair old Grecian dream of true equality and fraternity, a condition of liberty without feudal antagonisms, a government truly representative, republican — i. e. — *absolute self-government* — seemed in theory beautiful, but practically absurd. It might obtain for a time. It might work wonders for a brief season, and upon a narrow field, and amid serene pastoral holidays, but would surely be resolved into anarchy by the first wild ministry of conflict and storm. And therefore, in the opinions of wise men this new form of American liberty seemed destined to perish. European Sanballets mocked it with the old sneer: — "Wherefore do these men build? Verily if a fox go up he will break down their stone wall." Nor had our American Nehemiahs much of the old prophetic hopefulness. From the last days of Washington, unto the days remembered by our children did that noble race of statesmen (alas they have passed away and left no succession!) lift up voices in solemn warning, enduring unto the end the taunt of being "alarmists," and "union savers," just because they perceived that the very greatness of our liberty was its most terrible attribute, and believed that such storms of civil strife as the old staunch, kingly ships of state could weather, would drive our fairer but frailer bark hopelessly into shipwreck. Yes, and they died, every one of them, though in the fulness of their fame, yet with eyes dim and souls darkened in the shadow of evil things seemingly coming on their children.

Indeed, for half a century, the great American heart has beaten intermittently and convulsed under this dread incubus of Disunion. Men have felt, if they did not confess, the fear that the holy and beautiful house of our fathers, wherein are treasured all our blessed memories, and cradled all our glorious hopes, was built of brick piled without mortar, which the first throe of civil strife would rock hopelessly into ruin; that though this self-government might serve our purpose in times of peace, and even lead us in triumph against all foreign aggression, yet it would bo blown hopelessly into anarchy by the first fierce breath of a great civil convulsion.

But how seems this thing now? Why, we are this very hour governing ourselves even better than before, positively more scrupulously law-abiding, more observant of all ordinances guarding property and life ; and this over a breadth of territory which no feudal despotism could control; and in the face, yea, amid the very throes of the most terrible civil convulsion the world ever saw. Verily, the exhibition we have just made of our matchless franchises — calmly electing our Chief Magistrate amid the excitements of a war like this — with all our cabals and factions, and unprincipled appeals and malignant attacks upon character, and the selfish ambition of leaders, and the roused passions of the masses, with our great cities filled with a reckless populace, and the land swarming with armed men ; and yet, the whole agitated nation, as quietly as before appealing and submitting to the decision of the ballot-box — this, I say, proves that an intelligent self-government is possible in any and all popular conditions, and is positively the strongest and most steadfast of all governments; that men born and bred with the most extravagant notions of civil freedom, are not driven into anarchy, but only compacted and consolidated by great civil pressure; that they will restrain themselves, tax themselves, conscript themselves, yea, to the last farthing and drop of blood sacrifice themselves, yielding implicitly to that invisible thing — Law, moving, each in his own sphere, and achieving his own task, scrupulously observing all civil ordinances and social customs, amid elements of convulsion that would have shaken into fragments the mightiest feudal despotism on the face of the earth!

We say then, this war is developing the last grand type of free government. It is dispelling all doubts as to its possibility and permanence. It is proving that the fair old Grecian liberty was not a distempered dream, but a divine type, yea, prophecy of the popular, civil perfection to which, in the latter day glory, christian manhood shall attain. Surely then, in this regard also, will God's war-pruned vine bring forth precious fruit.

THIRDLY — *It will bring forth a new style of Christianity.*

After what has been already said you will not misunderstand me to speak of war as, self-considered, favorable to Christianity. On the contrary, we hold it to be a thing, evil, barbarous, brutal, infernal, between which, and the spirit of the Gospel of Christ, there can be only antagonism. Nevertheless, it is under this self-same law of antagonisms that God works out often His grandest purposes. And in this way only, do I speak of this war as developing christianity. At first, indeed, this seemed impossible. We all heard, and felt, and blushed at the infidel clamor, that, if the nation on earth most thoroughly christianized, could thus be convulsed with civil strife, henceforth, the gospel must be reckoned a failure. Yes, and the gloomiest fear, at first, of the christian patriot was, like Eli's not for his country, nor for his kindred, but for the ark of his God. Nevertheless, we can now perceive how even Christianity will be shorn of no glory, but rather illustrated and magnified as it passes through this conflict. This illustration is manifold,

1st — *In the christian character so frequently displayed in a patriotic soldiery.*

From the wars of Abraham, and Moses, and David, history has nothing to match with it; and we venture to predict that, when this conflict is ended, the biographies of these Christian men dying for their country will furnish the richest and most wonderful religious literature the church ever possessed. My limits forbid an enlarged illustration of this thought. I can only read, in this connexion, some paragraphs of a letter written on the eve of a great battle, as a specimen of thousands which God's grace inspired, and will not suffer to perish. It was addressed by Major Sullivan Ballou, of the Second Rhode Island Regiment, to his wife, the night before his departure for Manassas, where, on the following week he was killed.

"CAMP CLARK, WASHINGTON, Jul 14, 1861.

"MY VERY DEAR SARAH: — The indications are that we shall move very soon, perhaps tomorrow. Lest I should not be able to write to you again, I feel impelled now to write a few lines that may fall under your eyes when I shall be no more. Our movement may be one of a few days duration and full of pleasure, and it may be one of sorrow, conflict and death to me. "Lord not my will but thine be done." If it is necessary that I should fall on the battlefield for my country, I am ready. I have no misgivings about, or lack of confidence in the cause in which I am engaged, and my courage does not halt or falter. I know how strongly American civilization now leans on the triumph of the Government, and how great a debt we owe to those who went before us, through the blood and suffering of the Revolution, and I am willing — perfectly willing — to lay down all my joys in this life to help to maintain this Government and pay that debt. But, my dear wife, when I know that with my own joys I lay down nearly all of yours, and replace them in this life with cares and sorrows; when, after having eaten, for long years, the bitter fruits of orphanage myself, I must offer it as the only sustenance to my dear little children, is it weak or dishonorable that, while the banner of my purpose floats calmly and proudly in the breeze, underneath my unbounded love for you, my darling wife and children, should struggle in fierce though useless contest with my love of country? I cannot describe to you my feelings on this calm, summer, sabbath night, when thousands of men are sleeping around me, many of them no doubt enjoying the last sleep before that of death, while I am awed by the feeling that death is creeping around me with his fatal dart, as I sit communing with my God, my country and thee. I have sought, most closely and diligently and often, in my heart for a wrong motive in thus hazarding the happiness of all those I love, and I could find none. A pure love of country, and of those principles which I have so often advocated before the people, — another name of honor that I love more than I fear death, has called upon me, and I have obeyed.

"Sarah, my love for you is deathless; it seems to bind me with mighty cables, that nothing but omnipotence could break; and yet my love of country comes over me like a strong wind, and bears me irresistibly on, with all those claims, to the battlefield. The memory of all the blissful moments I have spent with you come creeping over me, and I feel most grateful to God and to you that I have enjoyed them so long. And how hard it is for me to give them up, and burn to ashes the hopes of future years, when, God willing, we might still have lived and loved together, and seen our sons grow up to honorable manhood around us. I have, I know, but few and small claims upon Divine Providence, but something whispers to me — perhaps it is the wafted prayer of my little Edgar — that I shall return to my loved ones unharmed. If I do not. my dear Sarah, never forget how much I loved you; and when my last breath escapes me on the battlefield, it will whisper your name. Forgive my many faults and the many pains I have caused you. How foolish, how thoughtless, I have oftentimes been.

How gladly would I wash out with my tears every little spot upon your happiness, and struggle with all the misfortunes of this world to shield you and our children from harm, but I cannot. I must watch you from the spirit land, and hover near you while you buffet the storms with your precious freight, and wait with patience till we meet to part no more. But, oh! Sarah, if the dead can come back to this earth, and flit unseen around those they love, I shall always be near you; in the gladdest day, in the darkest night; amidst your happiest scenes and your gloomiest hours, *always — always;* and if there be a soft breeze upon your cheek, it shall be my breath; or if the cool air fans your throbbing temples, it shall be my spirit passing by. Sarah, do not mourn me dead, but think I am gone and waiting for thee — for we shall meet again. As for my little boys, they will grow up as I have done, and never know a father's love or care. Little Willie is too young to remember me long; and my blue-eyed Edgar will keep my frolics with him among the dim memories of his childhood. Sarah, I have unlimited confidence in your maternal care, and your development of their characters, and I feel that God will bless you in your holy work. Tell my two mothers that I call God's blessing upon them. Oh, Sarah, come to me, and lead thither my two children.

My wife, farewell,

SULLIVAN."

I will not trust myself to read more of these letters. The whole land is full of them. They are preserved as precious memorials, not of human love merely, but of love sanctified by God's grace; and when the christian soldiership they illustrate shall be embalmed in the richest biographies of earth, then will the history of this conflict be glorified by them, and the very gospel of peace and love bo magnified in them 1 Surely the dying song of old martyrdom went up to heaven from dungeon and stake no more triumphantly eloquent of that gospel's blessed power than the farewell and dying words of such christian patriots! Meanwhile the gospel is magnified,

2ndly — *In the christian spirit which this war is developing, in new agencies of benevolence!*

Here too, my limits forbid more than a single illustration. Take this "Christian Commission," in whose behalf you are asked this day to contribute — a miraculous creation surely of practical christianity! — a grand evangelical and philanthropic organization at once catholic and national — the whole church of Christ of every name united in behalf of the soldiery of every State and section, embracing in its charities, navies of hundreds of vessels, and armies of a million of men, and extending its operations along a war line of three thousand miles, and all this mighty christian machinery working voluntarily — its officers and offices and store-rooms, and the regulated freedom of 20,000 miles of railway, and 20,000 miles of telegraph, and all government vessels, and the service of more than 1,500 christian ministers and laymen, and the immense supplies distributed, freely received, freely given! Verily, here is a grand catholic and national christian development in a sphere and on a scale which is a new thing upon the earth.

Behold these christian men and women in camps, and hospitals, and battle fields, ministering, with all a brother's, a sister's, a mother's love, alike to body and soul not only of friends, but enemies — going forth to the very men who, perhaps an hour before, stood armed against themselves, their beloved ones, their country, lifting them tenderly, bearing them gently to sheltered places, wiping away their tears, their blood, binding up their wounds, assuaging their agony; receiving, in behalf of the living, their last messages of affection, and pointing their departing spirits to the great and gracious Redeemer! Yea, behold those glorious prayer-meetings! Observe those precious religious books and tracts, taking the place of the vile old literature of the camp! Hearken to those earnest gospel sermons, those resounding hymns of praise to God, superseding the old bacchanal songs of battle — and all upon fields torn with shot and shell, and hi the very face of advancing squadrons! Behold, in a word, all this softening of the horrors of war, in ways and with a power, of which philanthropy never dreamed — this positive carrying of the gospel of peace, in all its celestial loveliness into the wildest tides of the battle, and then tell me if here be not truly a new development of Christianity, and if that gospel which hath hitherto achieved such triumphs in scenes of blessed peace, is not now gathering trophies of more wonderful beauty and power, in the dark and deadly sphere of war's frenzied antagonisms!

And thus, and otherwise is christianity shewing itself, even now, in new forms and power in this strange field of its ministries — like an angel from heaven revealed in fairer splendor and strength, because of the wild night and devouring tempest that surround it. And when, in that surely coming hour, so longed for and besought, these great armies humanized, evangelized by this heavenly ministry, shall return from this strife — not, as of old armies came, profane, dissolute, insubordinate, to fill the land with violence, and pollute the airs of heaven with songs, ribald and blasphemous — but armies of self-governing, self-denying, God-fearing, law-abiding men, making the earth fairer with their peaceful ministries, and heaven's air pure and sweet with the breath of praise in these old songs of Zion — bearing back that old banner borne in triumph through a hundred fights, and never lowered to a foe, yet with all its unfaded, undivided, constellated stars, to be cast down in humble acknowledgment of God's sovereignty, as a glorious trophy at the foot of the cross — returning with sword and spear, not to be suspended, as blood-stained trophies of old conflict, in emblazoned halls, but to be transformed, even by the warrior's mighty hand, into implements of peaceful life — beaten into ploughshare and pruning-hook for the blessed uses of piety — then, surely then, it will appear that Christianity, which before had dwelt in spheres of peace, holding its serene way beside bright waters which no tempest stirred, did walk at last a nobler path, and win braver spoils, as it lifted a heavenly voice amid the thunders of war, and poured light as from angel wings along the black surges of battle! Surely in this respect, as well, will God's war-pruned vine bring forth more and better fruit.

But we must pause here with our illustrations. We have been considering some of the more obvious ways in which divine love seems overruling this awful conflict for our ultimate national good — some simple reasons why we are not to regard this war as God's axe at the root of our national life, but rather as God's pruning-knife among the overgrown branches, in illustration and fulfillment of that great law of husbandry: — *"Every branch that beareth fruit, He purgeth it, that it may bring forth more fruit."*

And let these simple thoughts serve to lighten our load of apprehension and deepen the cadencies of our songs of thanksgiving! Surely our grand national life is not ended; nay, it is as yet scarcely begun, and all these sharp conflicts it is enduring arc only the necessary antagonisms in the development of strength for its higher walk and work! Hitherto, our young land hath been, like Jesse's youthful son, delighting, with shepherd's crook to keep sweet pastoral holiday; but destined too, like David, to move in loftier spheres and wield imperial influences, it must, like him, endure, in the face of the Philistine host, the stem discipline of battle!

We judge, alike from divine providences in the past, and divine prophecies of the future, that we have been raised up as a nation, as the great instrument of the world's civil and spiritual regeneration, and therefore believe that through this terrible military discipline God is fitting us for the last great conflict of liberty and Christianity against the despotisms of the world. Sure we are that, if we do not perish hopelessly in the struggle, we shall come forth from it in possession of a power, and with a record of achievement which the monarchs of the world will not dare to despise. And verily it needed just this great demonstration, of our inalienable right not only, but of our inherent power of self-government — this stern wakening from long, sweet, pastoral dreams — this girding on of armor — this marshaling of countless men — this triumph of the old flag, the old patriotism, the old undivided, unparalysed, indomitable national life over an antagonism, compared with which, all foreign aggression were as nothing. It needed just this, I say, to teach a gazing and gainsaying world, that, ordained of God unto a grand philanthropic mission unto all people, ours is as well the resistless power as the fixed purpose to accomplish it in the face of, or if need be, against all the antagonisms of earth! And when, in God's own time, chastened into purer life and storm-beaten into vaster strength by this sharp and sore discipline, with a navy imperial on the water, and an army whose measured tread shakes the land, and, floating over all upon land and sea, that old banner in its place of pride, not a star gone from its field of unstained azure this mighty nation shall set forth afresh on its triumphal progress; then shall we and a wondering world understand the hidden meaning of divine love in this terrible discipline, and perceive and acknowledge that God's blows arc in mercy, that He chastens for profit, that *"He purgeth the vine only that it may bring forth more fruit."*

So at least, would we fondly hope, on this day consecrated to the sweeter and fairer moods of thanksgiving. And in befitting frames would we rest here this hallowed hour, not forlorn as under the prophet's withering gourd, but exulting as under God's great vine of the centuries — thankful for the present — hopeful for the future — rejoicing before God with "the joy of harvest." And when here in our sanctuary, as the Jew on Mount Zion, we have paid our vows to the Most High in loving consecration, then, as he returned to his distant home, filling the soft airs of Palestine with glad songs, and waking all its echoes with bounding feet, so let us go forth again to our pleasant homes — dwellings hallowed by divine goodness, by the words and ministries of love, by memorials tenderly sad, it may be, but cherished and heavenly of the beloved dead — to those firesides where children play — to those boards where kinsfolk gather, and happy voices blend — dismissing from our souls all anxious cares, driving out every reptile of discontent, every bird of evil omen from our bowers of peace, untroubled, restful, loving, joyous; for the present, thankful, because it is our own: for the future, trustful, because it is God's!

11

A CALL TO PRAISE

A SERMON DELIVERED ON THANKSGIVING DAY, NOVEMBER 26, 1868 (SAN FRANCISCO)

"Bless the Lord, O my soul."

PSALM 103:22.

We have come into our sanctuary at the summons of the Chief Magistrates of our State and Nation, to render public thanksgiving unto God for his manifold mercies. Our text is appropriate to the occasion, in its connections suggestive, and as a climax remarkable. This beautiful psalm is a call upon all creatures to praise Jehovah. In the preceding verse David had exhorted the whole angelic hierarchy unitedly to praise Him. In the first clause of this verse, as if impatient of further special precept, he summons the whole universe at once to join in the anthem: "Bless the Lord, all his works, in all places of his dominion;" and yet, in the next sentence, as if there were something not included in that comprehensive category, he adds: "Bless the Lord, O my soul."

Now this strange climax is suggestive of important truth. There is a possibility, yea, there is a positive danger, of overlooking the individual in the universal. There are few evils more common than this ignorance of ourselves in our scrutiny of others. As Solomon expresses it: "A keeping of vineyards while neglecting our own;" as Paul puts it: "A preacher unto others while himself a castaway." And this is especially manifest in our public thanksgivings. We dwell in thought too much on universals, too little on particulars. In the matter of our praises, we think too little of our own special blessings amid God's general benefactions; and in the manner of our praises, we bless God too exclusively "by proxy" — by the utterances at the two ends of the sanctuary — the preacher's in the pulpit, the choir's in the orchestra — while the whole body of the congregation, silent and meditative, indulges in repose. And this our text rebukes. It breaks in upon this call to universal praise, with an exhortation to individual praise. It insists, as the Bible does everywhere, on thankfulness; not as a jet of emotion, but a practical Christian grace; and bids us close all our broad public exhortations unto "all angels," "all creatures in all places of his dominions," with this particular injunction: "Praise the Lord O my soul."

Meanwhile, as the text specifies the *subject* of thanksgiving, i.e., the human soul that exercises it, so it designates the object of thanksgivings, i.e., the glorious Spirit that accepts it — the infinite Jehovah. Thankfulness is not simple joy for a gift, but as well gratitude unto the giver. The absorbing thought in a truly thankful heart is God, the great Benefactor. So let it be today. Let our first thought be of God — turning, as it were, away from his benefactions to himself; rejoicing, above all else, that we have such a God to approach in our sacrifices of thanksgiving — a personal, omnipotent, omnipresent, Spirit, from whose hand of love come all our mercies, and who, in unerring wisdom, as he has created, so controls all the universe.

In the world's catholic theology "there are Lords many and Gods many." The truth of a Supreme Being lies at the foundation of all religion; but the practical value of the truth depends upon the notion formed of Him, or the qualities ascribed to him; for, by a law of our nature, "we become like what we worship." The gods of the old Northmen, such as Odin and Thor, were simply hero-kings, and their worship transformed the adoring man into a bloodthirsty monster. The deities of classic mythology were personified passions, and, in their adoration, Greek and Roman virtues are only beautified lusts. In the grand Egyptian temples were enshrined beasts, birds, creeping things, and, as a result of such idol-worship, the morality of that early civilization became simply brutal. I need not enlarge on this. It is an aphorism even of the Chinese priesthood: "Worship Buddha, and you will be transformed into Buddha." And you have but to study the moral character of this modern infidelity, which, instead of a personal God, glorifies an impersonal Nature, to perceive therein a reflex of the indolent, limited, practically unrighteous THING they ignorantly honor.

Now, in contrast with all this, how transcendent is the Object of our worship! How glorious, if we would adore! How goodful, if we would imitate! Our God, our Jehovah, is a Being of all immaculate attributes — all pervading, controlling, sustaining energies. Not the infidel's deity, reposing in indolent majesty, but the omnioperative Spirit, whose energy is manifest in all natural phenomena; without whose cognizance — nay, without whose control — nothing happens unto his children — our Creator, our Benefactor, our Redeemer, our Father. And it should be our chief joy and thanksgiving today, that our sacrifices are rendered to such an object of worship; that we and our children are now assembled, neither by yonder Chinese altars, nor in yonder unbelievers' clubroom; that we bow in dread adoration neither before the stuffed wolf-skin of the California Indian, nor the soulless, unsympathizing phantom of the California infidel; that we think not of all our numerous mercies today as the simple productions of nature — prodigal growth of our orchards and cornfields — but as the loving gifts of our Heavenly Father; and that our language of adoration in this Presence is not a song of foul license, nor the wail of despairing spirits rushing to annihilation, but an anthem of joyous thanksgiving, in unison with "all his angels," "all creatures of his in all places of his dominion:" "Bless the Lord, bless Jehovah, bless the living God, O my soul."

Thus our first thought should be of God, the great Giver; passing onward to consider, secondly, his wonderful gifts; and here rising at once to the height of the Psalmist's argument, and gathering all these gifts, as it were, into one. Let us—

First — *Praise the Lord because he has prepared for us this wonderful world;* for a goodly and glorious world it is. Some men complain of it; infidels deride it as a clumsy malformation of chance, and some morose believers seem to think that Jehovah might have made it fairer and better; but the wiser "Sons of God shouted for joy" over it, as a very miracle of divine wisdom and power. And so it is every way. Consider some of its beneficent aspects and uses to the children of men.

First. *As man's home or dwelling place,* and what a wonder of architecture it is — what foundations, walls, chambers, canopy. How matchless its economy in regard of these great desiderata — warmth, water, ventilation, light. What a heating apparatus, with conductors and registers, and softly tempered airs. What conveniences as to water — the great ocean-reservoir, the cloud-aqueducts, the river-conduits — yea, a distribution into all its chambers of hot and cold water by these mysterious ocean currents. Then its ventilation wherein so many builders fail — how wonderfully is this done through these dynamics of the atmosphere, these tidal trade winds, these land breezes and sea breezes, now cooled by Polar ice-fields, now warmed by Tropic sands. Meantime its appointments for light are more expressive still of the Divine wisdom. Man fails in lighting satisfactorily for a single night any great temple; and a world illumined by human art would be only night rendered hideous by millions of millions of glaring burners in every forest and field. But in God's hand one central solar lamp diffuses its tempered splendor for the day's labor, and innumerable softened lusters along the nocturnal canopy adapt it for repose. And thus every way, this house, builded in God's great city of worlds — in its architecture, its conveniences, its adornments — hath the seeming of a palace for a race of immortals, and well might the stars sing over it, and the great Architect pronounce it very good.

Second. But then this planet is more than a man's home; more significantly still, *it is his school-house,* and, as such, most marvelously supplies all educational desiderata. Observe its situation — seclude (as a seminary should be always) from any constant, sensible intercourse with the heavenly metropolitan life. Note its scientific and philosophic apparatus; what a cabinet of minerals in these geologic chambers, what a prodigal flora in its botanical gardens, what illustrations of physical science in air, light, ocean, the gravitation of mountains, the dynamics of the rivers, the optics of the skies. What a chemistry in these inorganic transmutations, and the processes and phenomena of this vegetable and animal life. What an orrery or planetarium revolves and sparkles in the sky, illustrating astronomy. Here are manifest adaptations and excitants to man's intellectual nature, rendering earth even a better school-house than it is a home; so that the man who limits the significance of life to its sensations and seeks in God's great building only banquet hall and dormitory, is like a foolish child degrading scientific apparatus into playthings, and prostitutes into an aimless palace-life that which God mean to be a glorious pupilage.

Meanwhile, in its aspect of a school-room, these mental appliances are not its chief excellences. Its appointments for man's *moral* culture are still more wonderful. Its condition of seclusion from other worlds, and consequently of ignorance of the higher spiritual life that peoples the universe, compels the soul unto faith. Its great time-keeper — sun and stars, revolving along yon crystalline dial-plate and giving to these fleeting hours the significance of portions of eternity — excites the soul to diligence. Its whole process of man's self-development toward the good or the evil is a lesson of retribution. It is a school, in short, where not even a California Educational Board can separate religion from science; where, indeed, the chair of Theology is better filled and endowed than those of Philosophy or Belles-Letters. Where science seems only rudimental to religion — all its appliances but manifestations of the wonderful thoughts of God. Where everything that the man-child meets in his task discourses precious ethics; the flowers teaching him humility, and the birds singing of faith; and every development, inorganic or vital, demonstrates the great fact of retribution; and all the tremendous processes going on around, urge to activity in well-doing; and above him the burning sun in his strength and the lamping stars in their splendor, all cry aloud like the apocalyptic voice out of heaven. "Come up hither," till the winged spirit seems compelled to aspire and ascend.

We cannot enlarge here; but this simple glance at the manifold adjustment of this earth to the wants of our nature is enough to fill the heart with gratitude unto God, the great World-Builder. It is a fair world in itself, and a fitting world in its ministries. Its creation was in infinite love. Its arrangements and appointments are all in infinite wisdom. It is glorious in its origin and in its destiny. Over it all the angels praised God when it was made; and for it there come to very man the text's inspired call; "Bless the Lord, all his works in all places of his dominion. Bless the Lord, O my soul."

But we are not to rest satisfied with this broad generalization. As we said at the outset, the point of the exhortation is unto individuals and specialties. So, turning still more homeward and heartward, we say—

Secondly, — *Let us praise the Lord for our country.* And here I am not about to exercise, what I claim as a minister's right, the privilege of discoursing somewhat on political questions on these thanksgiving days. I waive that privilege now, for I cannot see any great questions at issue in present political controversies. Today, then, we will let the star-spangled banner float undisturbed and the American eagle nestle, and leave Plymouth Rock alone in its glory. We are looking on our country from a Christian standpoint. From any other, extreme views are sure to be taken, and, instead of Christian gratitude, men will either glory or grumble.

Some men are disposed to grumble. To hear them, one would suppose Almighty God had a special controversy with the American nation. The grumbling politician cries: "Taxation, public debt, bribery, corruption, anarchy, ruin." The grumbling reformer cries: "O, our vices are digging the graves of our liberties. Our institutions have outlived those social virtues which at first created and can alone conserve them. Already are the clouds gathering, and the sea and waves roaring, and thunders uttering their voices, and the great earthquake, by which we are to perish, shaking the nation." But, blessed be God, all this, repeated year after year for half a century, has proved a false alarm. There was not so much of a storm after all. The hail was not so heavy, nor the thunder so loud, nor the earthquake so destructive. The grand social edifice was not rocked into ruins; and our gallant eagle still soars in his pride of place. Even these political antagonisms which now divide and perplex us are only the subsiding waves of that old war-tempest which we have just weathered, and upon which the ship of state has come up to the wind again and goes on her way rejoicing.

Meanwhile, in antitheses to all this grumbling, there are men among us disposed unduly to glory. Listen to them, and one would suppose that this same American eagle were akin to the apocalyptic angle, and this western continent "the new earth whereon dwelleth righteousness." And these men err as widely as the others. Politically and socially, we have not attained unto perfection. Our beloved ally, we have not attained unto perfection. Our beloved nationality is, like all nationalities, not a manufacture, but a growth. A grand germ it surely is. Nevertheless, as a germ it needs earnest culture about its roots, and a pruning knife among its branches, ere it fulfill the old prophetic vision of "a tree whose height reached heaven, and the sight thereof was unto the ends of the earth.'

But to the eye of Christian philosophy this culture is going on. These political excitements we have just referred to are, in this aspect, no more the strong winds amid the branches, causing the roots to shoot deeper and giving strength to the trunk. American practical politics, which, for the time, make us all actors and orators in regard to great questions and principles, are the true means and theatre of American development and discipline. They educate the popular mind to think, and excite the popular heart to feel. They bring men out of the selfish world of trade; they lift men up from the shallow world of fashion to the broader world and healthier airs of a great civil life, fitting them for the franchises and immunities of this grand American citizenship.

The laws of free nations are no more than "another name for the popular common sense and conscience," and their power and beneficence grow with any true, broad popular culture. The theory that men are for institutions, wherewith Solon tortured unto death, on his iron bed of Procustes, the old Grecian liberty, has given place among us to the law of all true civil life — that institutions are for men, to be modified and fashioned to the ever-expanding human shape and stature. Neither our one Federal, nor our several State Constitutions, are as yet perfect. All alike do they need growth and culture, like great trees, downward in the roots, upward in the branches. The English Constitution has been found equal to all crises, just because it is the slow growth of ages; and, therefore, has been justly compared to "an old mansion, often repaired, with quaint additions and seven gables, all differently fashioned." Our own Constitution, on the contrary, which is the work of a lifetime, may be compared to one of these California buildings, extemporized for the occasion, brilliant with new paint, showy with cornices, but in which every earthquake is sure to smash the crockery and frighten the children. What we want is growth; and, surely, we are growing — steadily and rapidly advancing to the fulfillment of the divine ideal. And thus, to a truly Christian faith, our nationality rises today — a consolidated commonwealth, stretching from ocean to ocean athwart this broad continent; a nation of freemen ,self-governed, governed by simple law, without police or soldiery — a nation of five hundred millions of people, covering the land with great cities, and the sea with great fleets; first in arts and learning, and every true product of genius; and thus, even politically, a power before which the war-power of kings can be only as the Philistines to Samson; but, above all, religiously God's almoner of salvation unto all people; the light of the benighted; the refuge of the oppressed; the home of the exile; the hope of the lost. So to the Christian's eye it looks. This is the prerogative of American faith — to exult even from afar over our sure and sublime future; to behold the first spring of the eaglet to the air, that in circles of such amazing swiftness and power is soaring to the sun; yea, to behold here the form of the apocalyptic angle, rising on heavenly pinions to bear abroad the everlasting Gospel of "peace on earth and good will unto men, and glory to God in the highest." And, therefore, our thanksgiving for a land like this should be in the very spirit of the inspired exhortation: "He hath not dealt so with any people. Praise Him in the sanctuary. Praise Him in the firmament of His power. Praise the Lord all ye His angels that excel in strength." "Praise the Lord, O my soul!"

Meanwhile, this exhortation should be still further limited and specialized; therefore let us—

Thirdly—*Praise the Lord for our State.* We are here not merely as Americans, but as Californians, and as such should today be especially thankful. And here, too, there is need of that Christian circumspection which finds truth between extremes. California reproduces, on her own account, the two great national types of life—men who glory, and men who grumble.

First, we have *grumblers* among us. Men and women who have come here expecting to find English agriculture, Parisian social life, and New England piety, in a land where even now the wild bear roams unmolested, and where only twenty years ago the wilder Indian lighted his torch, like Diogenes, at noonday, looking for a man. And as our men and manners do not please them, so nothing pleases them. Our grapes are too sweet and our strawberries too sour; our fish are without flavor, and our coal is sulphurous; our flora is inodorous, and our fauns is tough. We have many negative inferiorities, and as many positive monstrosities. "O these summer winds and fogs; these deluging winter rains; these terrible, terrible earthquakes!" Now we are not disposed to underrate our misfortunes, nor ignore our deficiencies. California is not the old Paradise — certainly not Paradise before the tempter entered it. But we are disposed to recognize our peculiar blessings, and looking on the bright side even of our clouds, to perceive the good that is in the evil. Without these summer winds and winter rains our State would be a Sahara, and our city a lazaretto. Surely his honor the Mayor and our Board of Supervisors ought to join the general thanksgiving, that our streets are cleaned once a year and ventilated every evening. Our earthquakes are, indeed, serious realities, and yet, even with them, are our property and our lives safer than theirs whose exposure is to the havoc and devastation of the old Atlantic elements; indeed, if we only profit by them as we should. If they teach us to build dwellings which any respectable New England snowstorm would be ashamed not to crush and scatter into kindling wood; if they persuade us to leave our waterfronts where Jehovah appointed them, and not to erect "balloon" warehouses on a pasty domain stolen from the playground of Leviathan; above all, if they frighten our young married folks out of these mammoth caravansaries into the properties of separate homes, and our old unmarried folks into a better and brighter life than this miserable monasticism of furnished rooms and restaurants; in short, if these comparatively harmless disturbances teach us a little practical common sense, then the Californians of the next generation will, retrospectively, find in these very earthquakes new matter of thanksgiving.

Certainly, taking all things together, the most unreasonable and unconscionable of grumblers is a Californian grumbler. Meanwhile it must be confessed—

Second. That we have among us Californians who *glory*. Happy as is our present, and bright as seems our future, yet we have not the genii of the Aladdin lamp to achieve for us impracticable miracles, and yet we are projecting work for the whole legion. We have town-lots enough, outlined and in market, to afford the whole population of the three great emporiums of the world sites for grand dwellings. We are forgetting that the law of city-growth is not that of mushrooms — that London was a town of considerable importance in the reign of the Roman Nero; that Julius Caesar found Paris a capital city in his old Gallic conquests;

that New York is the very New Amsterdam, wherein Dutchmen gloried two hundred years ago. We do not consider that great cities are the creatures, and not the creators of states; that gold mines and railroads cannot furnish the elements of the highest social prosperity. If these sand hills were all as richly metalliferous as the White Pine mountains, still wheat fields would be better for us. And even if the entire commerce of the Indies were to pass the Golden Gate, it must pass only on exodus to the Oriental Canaan. But then it will not even enter. Obviously, over our Pacific railroads can be transported only the most precious forms of merchandise. Along God's great water-course, shortened through the Isthmus, must forever pass the aggregate of the world's common and coarser commerce. The future growth of our city depends on men for agriculture and capital for manufactures, and railroads and mines will not furnish either. Though we are unquestionably a marvelous people, yet we have not the rod of Moses, and we cannot work miracles. The Olympian Jupiter has not come down upon our Sierras. The Titanic skeleton that Professor Whitney's fancy discovered in the gold drift of 36,000 years ago is, in fact, only the skull of a rickety Digger Indian, whose flesh was eaten by a bear of the last generation. And, while it is proper, and even scriptural, for "our sons and our daughters to prophesy, and our young men to see visions, and our old men to dream dreams," it is still, perhaps, safest to dismiss from our minds the pleasing illusion that yonder iron road is, in our day, to bring New York over the Sierras that it may be a suburb of San Francisco, or that along it even now the New Jerusalem is coming down out of Heaven, and will "switch off" into Oakland.

And yet, even in the reckonings of sound reason, as Californians and San Franciscans we have abundant ground of thanksgiving. If true to ourselves, we are here, as in the world's future centre, laying the foundations of an immense commercial, intellectual and religious prosperity. San Francisco is to be the great commercial emporium, at least of this coast. And when a noble group of Pacific States shall encircle her as a nucleus, all alive with a busy population, and rich in all agricultural and manufacturing wealth, she will be the New York or London of the Occident.

Meanwhile morally, or as regards her intellectual and religious character, her future is surely hopeful. The fears, felt very widely, occasionally expressed, of the effeminating effects of our delicious climate upon physical and mental vigor are, surely, not justified, nay, are forever dispelled, by the specimens of strong-limbed, red-blooded, graceful, vigorous manhood and womanhood into which children born in California are already developing. In this regard, "Young California" can be, ought to be, a splendid human creature, combining, in matchless composite, northern firmness and southern fire; oriental repose with occidental vigor; the Italian verdure of human nature bright and fair over its Alpine granite; its taste exquisite as this azure firmament; its genius imperial as yonder gigantic mountain and these blue Pacific seas.

Nor, if true to ourselves, are our fears better founded in regard of our moral and religious future. The present popular infidelity, over which the Christian heart sickens, is no more than a short-lived fungus born of the reeking scum which might tides of immigration always cast upon the shore. With the noble band of California pioneers who entered yonder Golden Gate, inspired by ancestral piety, to establish schools, build churches, and organize charities — thus laying broad and deep on these shores the foundations of a genuine Christian civilization — there came the whole motley herd of outlaws and outcasts of the old social life, and they have multiplied and increased and done after their kind, until the air reeks with the breath of their blasphemy. But this current and flippant infidelity is no more an exponent of California moral life than the mushrooms of your kennels are emblems of your magnificent cedars. When yonder iron thoroughfare shall have brought us into contact and vital sympathy with Eastern Christendom all this pretentious and pitiful unbelief will pass away, as the stunted and pigmy wolves that twenty years ago raced and howled on these sand hills have give place to these troops of beloved children, who, today, keep joyous thanksgiving in our streets and homes.

And with these two fears dispelled, surely, as our present is bright, so our future is unbounded.

Shut in by these grand Sierras to these blue Pacific seas, sheltered as by adamantine bulwarks from the thousand special evils of yonder dear old States — their thunder and lightning; their east winds and consumptions; their snows and sun-strokes; their mushroom noblesse and monstrous sea serpents; their uncertain climate and more uncertain currency — sheltered, in short, from that Alp-like climax of mortal life, which, like the mercury of their thermometers, ranges from the twenty degrees below nothing to the whole hundred above. And, meanwhile, shut into a land where soil, climate, atmosphere — each a marvel in itself — combine in phenomena absolutely miraculous; with clusters heavier than Eschol's; and fruits more abundant that Arcadia's; and flowers more wondrously fair than Paestum's or Sharon's; where the winter fields are carpeted with emerald of three-ply, and the summer heavens glow as with lustres flung back from the pinnacles of the city whose foundations are of precious stones; here a city, net yet twenty years old, with a population as large and architecture surpassing all that Paris could show after a thousand years of progress, and all around, spreading away in matchless loveliness, these valleys, where our merchant-princes even now delight to plant gardens like Eden, and to build palaces to embosom a new social life, and enshrine coming types of art fairer than the Greek — we, by occupation, and our children by birth, possessed of such an inheritance, surely a joyous thanksgiving becomes us today. And if the dwellers in other lands obey the exhortation "Praise the Lord all his creatures in all places of his dominion," then, louder and more loving, should our cry be: "Bless the Lord, O my soul."

But, beyond all these common blessings, does the text's exhortation extend. Let us, therefore—

Fourthly — *Bless the Lord for our special individual blessings.* And here, of course, each man must be his own preacher. Mine is not the golden key to enter the sanctuary of every home and heart and point out special mercies. But quite certain I am that every one of us finds reason in past and present experience for fervent thanksgiving. We have, doubtless, our particular trials. It would be strange, nay, it would be disastrous, if we had not; for our life on earth is not a citizenship, but a pilgrimage, and—

"The path of sorrow, and that path alone
Leads to the land where sorrow is unknown."

And we should perceive God's hidden purpose of love even in our sorest afflictions, and know that he who, in a right spirit, opens home and heart to great sorrows, only like the trustful apostle, "entertain angels unawares." Meanwhile, let our trials be many and large as they may, honestly reckoned, our blessings greatly outnumber them. And we have only most cursorily to review the long catalogue — all our bodily blessings, intellectual blessings, family blessings, civil blessings, business blessings, n sanctifying blessings; all our multiform and marvelous experience of good at the hand of our Heavenly Father, who has filled for us with bright forms the whole immeasurable space between non-existence and heaven — and then surely our grateful voices will be loud in thanksgiving, and we shall sit in these seats and go forth to our homes with bright eyes and smiling faces, glad of the present, trustful for the future. If stormy winds wail around ruined fortunes, nevertheless so attuning our hearts to the very blast that they give forth strains soft and sweet as Aeolians; or, if clouds lie heavily along the horizon, still beholding how in faith's blessed sunshine their borders are fringed with silver and golden light. And se shall sit at bright firesides and at festive boards, and share in childhood's sports and friendship's gentle ministries, fully blessed with the beatitude God accords us today, and trustful of God's grace that he will take care of us on the morrow. And our exhortation will not be merely unto others in view of their seeming greater good. "Bless the Lord all ye creatures in all places of his dominion." But, as if placed each one in his own pulpit to preach a sermon to himself, we shall cry more earnestly: "Bless the Lord, O my soul!"

Meanwhile, not even with this thought ends the text's specialization. Hitherto we have been thinking of our general and temporal mercies; and as the objects of our praise have been material, so, to a degree, at least, have been their subject and instruments. Our language has been: "Praise God in his sanctuary; praise him in the firmament of his power. Praise him with the sound of the trumpet; praise him with the timbrel and dance. Praise him with stringed instruments and organs; praise him with loud cymbals. Praise him upon high-sounding cymbals." And it is as if we had been saying each to himself: "God hath given me forms of beauty; bless the Lord, O my eyes.' "God hath ravished me with sounds of harmony; bless the Lord, O my ears." "God hath led me along peaceful paths; bless the Lord, O my feet." "God hath filled my home with love's ministries; bless the Lord, O my heart." The measure and range of the hallelujah has been, to a degree, sublunary and sensuous. But just here at its close, inspired by the text, it should rise purely and grandly into the spiritual. "Bless the Lord, O my soul!"

The word "soul" is to be understood here in its best and truest sense. Not that *Psyche* of the Greek, that principle of animal life which the rich man addressed, when he said: "Soul, take thine ease — eat, drink, and be merry." But that Spirit, that higher spiritual life, of which Paul was cognizant when in that rapture into Paradise he did not know "whether he was in the body or out of it" — that pure emanation from God in-breathed, inspiring the primitive man made in God's image — a principle which the Scripture everywhere distinguishes form the animal life, as allying man with the higher intelligences that people eternity — to this is the Psalmist's last appeal. And in addressing it, we cross at once the boundary of visible and sensuous things, We divest ourselves virtually, for the moment, of all that is merely animal, and are thrown, as purely spiritual beings, into purely spiritual conditions. We pass the threshold of the "earthly tabernacle." We approach, we left the veil, we enter the secret recesses of our own nature. We stand face to face with the essential human self-hood, the immortal human soul — that last made, and most marvelous creature of God — which here, even in its infancy, rocked in its earthly cradle and wrapped in carnal swaddling-bands, works so widely and wondrously; which rules and reigns over nature, extends its survey over creation — yea, rises above all perishable things and dares to cast itself in adoring rapture on the very bosom of God; and which, at last, in its higher development, "clothed upon with the heavenly life and immortality," shall go forth in transcendent ministries when yonder sun shall have burned out all his splendors and the stars have faded as the watch-fires of a night. To this mysterious and mighty creature of God, formed in his image, redeemed by his mediation — "this angel sitting on the bosom" — we are supposed now to come in the text's grand climax, calling upon it last and loudest of all to join in thanksgiving. "O soul," we cry, as if unto a reposeful and slumbering angel. "O soul, O winged and deathless spirit, bless thou the Lord." Praise him for thy creation; praise him for thy marvelous redemption; praise him for thy all-glorious destiny. Praise him for all the mercies wherewith Jehovah hath rounded thy life and beautified thy great paths. For those spiritual benefactions, compared with which all things we have been considering, seem as vanity and nothing — these fair lands only as deserts — these beloved homes only as dungeons — this fair world, rounded into beauty, and hung amid the stars, only as a transient meteor vanishing into night. For a higher world beyond these waters and these graves, for a land which death shall never enter and night never darken, for a city that hath foundations, for a house of many mansions, for raiment white and glistening, for crowns set with unfading stars, for thrones of power whereon we shall reign over angels, for winged feet to walk all those ascending paths of knowledge and holiness and joy and love that loose themselves in Godhead; yea, for that very "partaking of the divine nature" which makes us one with the Incarnate, and so lifts us, as in privilege so in praise, forever above all "the angels that excel in strength," and gives us a seat on God's throne and a rest on God's bosom. O, thou soul! O, thou redeemed and immortal spirit, unto whom the divine gifts of love so immeasurably transcend all gifts unto angels; surely thine should be the loftiest place in creation's choir, the loudest voice in creation's anthem. And while the inspired voice cries: "Bless the Lord ye his angels that excel in strength, that do His commandments, hearkening to the voice of His word; bless ye the Lord all ye hosts, ye ministers of His that do His pleasure; bless the Lord all His works in all places of His dominion." Yet with a louder voice and a stronger emphasis cries that voice in transcendent climax: "Bless the Lord, O MY SOUL!"

ABOUT THE AUTHOR

CHARLES WADSWORTH (May 8, 1814 – April 1, 1882) stands as a distinguished figure in 19th-century American religious history, celebrated for his profound roles as a Presbyterian minister and recognized as one of the most eloquent divines of his time. Born on May 8, 1814, in Litchfield, Connecticut, Wadsworth's life unfolded as a testament to his unwavering commitment to the ministry.

After graduating from Union College in 1837, Wadsworth embarked on a pastoral journey that showcased his dedication to spiritual leadership. He served as the pastor of the 2nd Presbyterian Church in Troy, New York, from 1837 to 1850. Following this, he assumed pastoral responsibilities at the Arch Street Presbyterian Church in Philadelphia, where he served from 1850 to 1862. His eloquence and captivating oratory skills distinguished him as one of the most compelling preachers of his era. In recognition of his contributions, the University of the City of New York conferred upon him the honorary degree of Doctor of Divinity in 1857.

Throughout his career, Wadsworth continued to shepherd congregations, leaving an indelible mark on each community he served. He ministered at a Presbyterian church in San Francisco from 1862 to 1869, followed by leadership roles at the 3rd Reformed Dutch Church in Philadelphia from 1869 to 1873. Subsequently, he served at the Clinton Street Presbyterian Church in Philadelphia from 1873 to 1879 and at the Clinton Street Immanuel Church from 1879 until his passing in 1882.

Wadsworth's sermons, renowned for their depth and eloquence, were published posthumously in three volumes in 1882-1884, along with a memoir that provided insight into the life and impact of this influential divine. His legacy endures as a testament to his dedication to the ministry and his ability to inspire congregations through the power of his words.

Beyond his remarkable career in the ministry, Wadsworth is also remembered for his notable friendship with the renowned poet Emily Dickinson. Their paths crossed during a trip back from Washington, D.C., in 1855, when Dickinson, accompanied by her sister Lavinia, visited their cousin Eliza Coleman in Philadelphia. This encounter sparked a correspondence that endured until Wadsworth's death. Despite the platonic nature of their relationship and Wadsworth's marital status, Dickinson considered him her "dearest earthly friend." This unique connection, while a minor part of Wadsworth's extensive career, adds a fascinating layer to the legacy of this eminent divine. Charles Wadsworth passed away on April 1, 1882, leaving behind a rich tapestry of spiritual leadership, eloquent preaching, and a captivating friendship that transcended the boundaries of time.

FUNERAL ADDRESS

BY THE REV. JOHN DEWITT, D.D.

We have gathered around his lifeless body, to pay the tribute of our respect to the memory of one, who, as a preacher of the Gospel, was both highly honored and widely known; but one, who, in his personal life, was so secluded, that few of his own congregation and few of his professional brethren knew him well or saw him often, elsewhere than in the pulpit. It would not have been surprising if, owing to this seclusion, while Dr. Wadsworth's exceptional gifts and productions called forth admiration, the expression of that admiration had been united with other expressions, evincing a lack of personal interest. But I am sure, that here in Philadelphia and certainly among his brethren of the ministry, whenever his name was mentioned, and that of course was often, he was spoken of in terms of friendly and even of affectionate interest. This high personal regard for Dr. Wadsworth on the part of his professional brethren, most of whom did not know him personally at all, was largely due to the conviction, that his seclusion was not a deliberate choice on his part; that, at any rate, it was not to be regarded as evidence of any want of affection for his co-laborers; that it was due solely to a temperament, as singular, and as powerful in its command over his conduct, as his mode of viewing or his mode of expressing evangelical truth. The fact of this high personal regard for Dr. Wadsworth on the part of his brethren, I know; for it has often been the theme of conversation among them. They have deeply regretted that they could not know one, whom all felt it would have been an advantage to know well. And I have been told that, on more than one occasion, Dr. Wadsworth gave expression to his own great regret, that he found himself unable, without painful and exhausting physical effort, to engage with his brethren, in that conversational interchange of ideas and beliefs and experiences, which nearly all men find so helpful, and which the great majority of men find an absolute necessity. Notwithstanding this lack in Dr. Wadsworth, his career, as a preacher of the Gospel of Christ, was useful and eminent in an extraordinary degree. In Troy, in Philadelphia, and in San Francisco, he was not only admired but loved by his own people; while his singularly eloquent and profoundly spiritual discourses were heard by crowded congregations, whom he never failed to charm, and whose spiritual natures he often profoundly impressed.

You will agree with me, that this is a striking and unusual statement to make in those days, when personal interest in the preacher of the Gospel is dependent largely upon personal acquaintance with him. Inevitably, it carries the mind back to other ages of the Church; as the age in which John Chrysostom was wont to come from the seclusion of his cell in Antioch, into the pulpit of the Cathedral; and, after having delivered his discourse, to disappear as though he were a messenger from another world. The fact that there was this wide and deep personal interest in Dr. Wadsworth, although his personal acquaintances were very few, makes it singularly appropriate, that, before his body is taken for the last time from the scene of his latest labors, the story of his life be told, and the elements of his power be shortly stated.

Charles Wadsworth's ancestors, on both his father's side and his mother's side, were Puritans. All of us know how deep an impression has been made by the Puritans, both of England and of New England, on politics, on literature, on social life and, above all, on theology. In politics, their influence has been on the side of civil liberty and self-government. In literature, they have enriched every department of effort save, perhaps, the department of the Drama. The two greatest works of genius, which England in the seventeenth century gave to the world, were the Paradise Lost of the Puritan John Milton, and the Pilgrim's Progress of the Puritan John Bunyan. From the descendants of this same class, has proceeded the great body of the increasing literary product of our own country. I do not doubt that many of you must have remarked, in connection with the event which we deplore today, that the middle name of the American poet, whose death, within a week or two, has called forth the eulogies of all English-speaking peoples, was the same Puritan name, Wadsworth, that was borne by your pastor. Of the impress of Puritanism on social life, I feel that I have a right to speak. It was my privilege to live for several years, as a pastor, in the capital of New England; and I do not wonder that, when strangers visit our country, they are urged, if they wish to carry back to their homes a favorable impression of the land, to visit, and to study the life, of a characteristic New England village.

But the greatest impression made by the Puritans, of both England and America, has been a religious impression. The reason is not far to find or difficult to state. The name Puritan designates, not a race, but a religious class. Upon the strong foundation of the Anglo-Saxon nature, was built up a character by means of the loftiest religious beliefs and the strongest religious feelings. This was the Puritan character. No writer has more accurately or more eloquently described its broader features, than has Lord Macaulay, in his well-known essay on John Milton. After the statement, which he unfolds at length, that "the Puritan was a man whose mind had derived a peculiar character from the daily contemplation of superior beings and eternal interests," he concludes with this description of the Puritan's view of his own relations to the governing forces of the universe. "He was a being to whose fate a mysterious and terrible importance belonged, on whose slightest actions the spirits of light and darkness looked with intense interest, who had been destined before heaven and earth were created, to enjoy a felicity which should continue when heaven and earth should have passed away. Events, which short-sighted politicians ascribed to earthly causes, had been ordained on his account. For his sake, Empires had risen, flourished, and decayed. For his sake, the Almighty had proclaimed His will by the pen of the evangelist and the harp of the prophet. He had been rescued by no common deliverer from the group of no common foe. He had ben ransomed by the sweat of no vulgar agony, by the blood of no earthly sacrifice. It was for him that the sun had been darkened, that the rocks had been rent, that the dead had arisen, that all nature had shuddered at the sufferings of her expiring God." This was the lofty and religious stock from which Charles Wadsworth's ancestry sprung.

Nor was his ancestry unworthy of the stock. This is not the time to state that ancestry in detail. But I may say that, as on his mother's side a Bradley, and, on his father's side a Wadsworth, there united in his person two currents of the best blood of the New England Colonies. General Wadsworth, his grandfather, was a Brigade Commander in the Revolutionary War; and among his ancestors, was that Captain Wadsworth, who performed no slight service in perpetuating the granted liberties of Connecticut, by hiding, in what has been known as the Charter Oak, the charter of the colony, when the messenger of James II sought, by attempting to secure it for revocation, to enslave a free people.

Of this ancestry, Charles Wadsworth was born, on the 8th of May, 1814. The place of his birth was the well-known and beautiful New England town of Litchfield, Connecticut. He was born during that period of the Republic's life when, as has well been said, "the rich were poor, and the poor had abundance." He was born during the second war with England when, especially in New England, there were few families who did not know from experience the necessity of economy. This necessity, your pastor had special reason to know; for his father died when he had scarcely passed out of infancy into childhood. His mother, on whom the care of the family descended, was a devoted mother, a wise woman and a good Christian. She lived to see her son a distinguished man, and to hear of his reputation in his profession as national; and the son was able to make comfortable and happy her last years, by the glad office of filial piety.

The son inherited from his ancestry the energy and persistence, that we all know as traits of the New England character. These, with his intellectual gifts and tastes, aroused within him a determination to become an educated man, in the special sense in which that phrase is employed. And he set about obtaining an education with a strong New England will. In this matter of securing an education, it is particularly true of a New England boy that "when there is a well, there is a way." There need not here be told, the details of the labors and economies through which he passed, in order to reach the goal of his early ambition, the degree of Bachelor of Arts. It is the same story, in substance, that is told of the large majority of men who rise to eminence in our professions: the story of Presidents, and Judges, and Governors, and of prominent lawyers, and physicians, and clergymen, almost without number. Let us be thankful, that we live in a land where this has been the general rule, and not the mere exception. Young Wadsworth toiled and economized, first at Hamilton College, and then at Union College, where he was graduated in the year 1837.

In his early life, he had been trained in the religion of his ancestors; but somehow, during his college life, his mind strayed away, and that very far. He not only lost his early faith, but lost it entirely. Always a positive man, he was not content with any position halfway between Christianity and blank skepticism. But he did not remain long in skepticism. By means of study and reflection, he was brought back into the light; and he loved it all the more because of the "blackness of darkness;" in which for a time his spirit was imprisoned.

His college life was not undistinguished. His love of literary work soon manifested itself. He wrote and wrote acceptably for the newspapers, both in prose and in poetry. He was the poet of his class; indeed, by eminence the poet of the college in his day. The brilliant fancy, which reveals itself in all his sermons, was active, and its products were striking, and inspiriting to hearers and readers, from the beginning. "I knew him as well as anyone knew him at Union College," said a distinguished clergyman to me, only yesterday, "And the traits of mind and of character, that were conspicuous in his best days, were conspicuous then."

After his college course, he taught awhile. How strong must have been his constitutional tendency to the life of a recluse, is shown by the fact that this occupation, engaged in as it was at a formative period of his life, and involving necessarily, as it did, communion with others, did not teach him how to live in the society of his fellow men. It was probably with a view to awaken within him a love of social life that Alonzo Potter, afterwards a distinguished Bishop in the Episcopal community, but then a tutor at Union College, who had remarked his exceptional endowments, advised him to become a teacher, and recommended him as eminently fitted for the work.

To his brief career as a teacher, succeeded his life as a student in the Theological Seminary at Princeton. I do not know when he determined to become a clergyman, but I may say, that during his Seminary life the subjects in which he seemed most interested, were those great and elemental themes, like the goodness of God and the doctrine of Providence, that would naturally be selected by one, who had lately been brought out of darkness, into the light of that Gospel, which alone makes clearly known to us the living, and holy, and parental God.

He lived a secluded life at Princeton. His home was not in the dormitory, but a little distance from it in the country. From his country home he came regularly to his classes and was a faithful student. But, of course, it was as a preacher that he was best known. When it was known that Wadsworth would preach, the oratory of the Seminary was crowded. Whoever, as a student, has preached to his fellow students from the oratory pulpit in Princeton, needs not to be told that he cannot find a more critical audience, or an audience more generous in the expression of its approval and delight, if only the preacher dares to defy, and be able to disarm, criticism. It was the merit of Wadsworth, that he began his sermon in defiance of criticism by adopting a new and original homiletical method, and ended his sermon by leaving criticism not only disarmed, but charmed and delighted with its own defeat.

But I should do the accounts which I have received of his Seminary life great injustice, if I were to leave the impression that he was only a brilliant rhetorician and speaker. No one who has heard or read his sermons, has failed to remark that a great theological system underlies them all; a system well-known to the preacher, and, obviously, thoroughly believed by him. Nor can anyone have closely studied his sermons, without observing that he was finely familiar with the Book, that is better than all systems of theology; for it is the fountain, from which the one true Christian theology must spring. Dr. Wadsworth's doctrinal and Biblical preaching leads inevitably to the conclusion, which the testimony of his Seminary friends confirm, that during his course at Princeton he was a faithful and able student, both of the Biblical course and of the course in systematic Divinity. Nor was this all. When yesterday at the meeting of his co-Presbyters his death was officially announced, one and another gave feeling expression to their sense of the great loss which the Church had sustained in his death. His classmate, the Rev. Dr. Schenck, of our city, recalled his own impressions of the deep devotional life of your pastor, when preparing as a student for the duties of the sacred ministry; and of the exalted, and yet confiding language in which, in the meetings of prayer, that life was expressed. Dr. Schenck's remarks left on me the impression, that if Charles Wadsworth, the theological student, lived a life secluded from men, he at least did not live a life apart from God.

Though a recluse, he was never cynical. If a fellow-student but surprised him in his cell, or met him during one of his solitary walks, he found him a frank, genial, charitable, Christian brother, full of knowledge and quite ready "to talk," with a rare fund of anecdotes, which he told with find humor; in short, a warm, fraternal Christian, whose only defect seemed to be a "diffidence" which he could not overcome; and which, though he was in all other respects eminently fitted for society, pursued him like a fury, till it drove him back within himself. He remained at Princeton two years. He left with the friendly regard and warm admiration of his fellow-students, and with the respect of his instructors. For one of these last, while he revered them all, he had the highest admiration. Dr. Addison Alexander had no warmer admirer than Charles Wadsworth. He always employed in describing Dr. Alexander the words that Dr. Hodge once employed, "Addison Alexander was the greatest man I have ever known."

When his Seminary course was ended, he was licensed by the Presbytery of Troy. He was invited to supply, during the absence of the pastor, the pulpit of the Second Church of that city. The pulpit becoming vacant soon after by the pastor's resignation, the congregation unanimously and cordially invited him to become their pastor. He accepted the call, and was ordained and installed on the 17th of February, 1842. There he remained for eight years. It is needless to say, that his congregations were immense from the beginning to the close of this pastorate. But mere popularity was not the sole or the chief seal of God's blessing on his ministry. On one occasion, not less than one hundred young men professed their faith in Christ in his Church.

During his life at Troy, he was of course urged to go to other churches; but he remained in his first charge, until the state of his health demanded that he should seek its renovation by a change of pulpits. He came to Philadelphia, and took charge of the Arch Street Presbyterian Church. The congregation was one of the smallest in the city; and the corporation was heavily in debt. The church building was in danger of being sold. Dr. Wadsworth began to preach. Suddenly the church filled. The debt was paid: and a strong congregation was secured to our Church. He was pastor at Arch Street from 1850 to 1862. This was probably the period of his widest popularity and his greatest power. There is no need that I attempt a description, here, of the delivery of one of Dr. Wadsworth's sermons. The testimony is abundant, and is not impeached, that the power which he had over his audience, was the power of the orator in the superlative degree. Nor did this power abate at all either form the beginning to the close of a single sermon, or from the beginning to the close of his entire Arch Street ministry. He preached not only to his own congregation, but to the city; and more, perhaps, than any other minister "to the stranger within the gates." Here, his reputation became national; and whenever throughout the country he occupied a pulpit, the whole community was anxious to hear him. I remember, that when I was a boy, my father, then the pastor at Harrisburg, and Dr. Wadsworth exchanged pulpits for a Sunday. I was too young to make one of the crowded congregation that gathered to hear him. But I remember distinctly the immense throng that came to the church, which stood opposite our house, and the profound impression made by his discourses on the community; an impression which thirty years have not served to efface.

After twelve years of work in Philadelphia, he felt compelled, for reasons connected with his health, again to change his field of labor. He accepted a call from Calvary Church, San Francisco. His pastorate in San Francisco was marked by the same popularity and power, that marked his pastorate in Arch Street. For eight years he remained on the Pacific Coast. At their close he accepted an invitation to return to Philadelphia. Here for ten years he was pastor of the Third Reformed Dutch Church. Finally he preached in this pulpit for three years; first, as pastor of Immanuel Presbyterian Church; and afterwards as pastor of the Church formed by the union of Immanuel and Clinton Street Churches, and known as the Clinton Street Immanuel Presbyterian Church.

That Dr. Wadsworth did not enjoy the wide popularity during his second, that he enjoyed during his first residence in Philadelphia, was obvious to all. To no one was it more obvious than it was to himself. This abatement of his popularity must have been a trial. But he bore it not only with fortitude, but with Christian cheerfulness. He was undoubtedly aided in bearing it, by two circumstances. One of these was the fact, that it was known and conceded, that its abatement was due, in no degree whatever, to any loss in intellectual power, but simply to a diminution of the power of the organs of speech. Everyone who heard Dr. Wadsworth was convinced, that if only his voice could return all of his old power and popularity would return with it. His latest sermons possess all the force and beauty which belonged to the sermons of his best days. Nor were these later sermons, in their formal traits, better suited to the last generation than to the present. They were as well suited to the times in which they were preached, as were the discourses of his most brilliant period. This became evident to the whole community, when the Presbyterian newspaper began the regular publication of his sermons. Through that medium, he found again his old congregation. Indeed, he found a larger congregation. The editor of that journal has told me, of the wide interest which each of these discourses awakened. Strangers, who never heard of him, were charmed by his brilliant and fervid discourses; for they were brilliant and fervid even on the printed page. And his old hearers would pore over the newspaper; and, as they read they would see the impassioned preacher, and hear his noble voice once more, and be rapt away on the wings of his eloquence.

But there was another circumstance, that sustained Dr. Wadsworth in the trial to which I have referred. I mean the unswerving loyalty of the congregation of this Church. I cannot stay to dwell on this loyalty. Nor do you, Christian friends, need any words of commendation from me.

Dr. Wadsworth closed his career, as every minister might well wish to end his life. He was useful and laborious to the last. He preached in the pulpit of his Church on the last Sunday of his life. He conducted the weekly meeting for prayer on the following Wednesday evening. The sermon for the next Lord's day morning was prepared. But on Wednesday evening his condition was such, as to excite the apprehension of his friends, who were at the prayer meeting. On Thursday he was confined to his bed. On last Saturday morning he died. When one of the distinguished physicians, who were attending him, announced to him the grave character of his disease; and told him that if he had any preparations to make in view of what must soon occur, he ought to make them at once, Dr. Wadsworth replied, "I have no preparations ot make. They have been made." Soon afterwards, his mind began to wander; and in his delirium, as though announcing the close of his own work, he said, "Shut the Bible." In a little while he fell into a deep sleep as gentle as the sleep of a little child. And the sleep of a child it was. For when he awoke, he awoke to the open presence of his Heavenly Father.

This is not the time to set forth critically the elements of the great power, which, as a preacher of the Gospel, Dr. Wadsworth wielded for forty years. It is too soon to apply to his work the dissecting knife of literary criticism. We are here to listen to his story, and to find what comfort God offers to us in the loss, which his family, his congregation, the city and the Church of God have suffered. But I should leave far too incomplete this grief address at his burial which I have undertaken to deliver, if I did not at least mention Dr. Wadsworth's profound conviction of the truth of the Gospel of Jesus Christ, as the prime source of his power as a preacher. Eloquence, that has not its root in conviction, is mere elocution and rhetoric, and ends in the mere excitement of the sensibilities. Dr. Wadsworth spoke, above all, because he believed: he spoke that which he believed; and that which he believed the more, because his faith was the termination of an awful struggle of his spirit, upward out of unbelief. I therefore pass by all the special elements of his power, to assert first, that without this deep and abiding conviction he could not have been the mighty preacher he was, and was by all confessed to be.

To this conviction, must be added a well-furnished and well-disciplined mind; a habit of mind that looked at all objects of knowledge from the preacher's point of view, and that subordinated all to the preacher's work; a large and strong Intellect; the special gift of a brilliant fancy of remarkable activity and power; profound spiritual emotions; a sympathetic nature; and laborious and (what may be new to some before me) methodical habits of work. Moreover, he had that which, because we cannot call it anything else, we call a "dash of genius;" the "fine frenzy," as Shakespeare calls it in the poet; "the light that never was on sea or land," which the painter, according to Wordsworth, adds, if he possesses genius, to his picture of land or sky or sea, in calm or storm. Dr. Wadsworth had somewhat of this subtle thing, that eludes analysis; and we perhaps do best, when we speak of it only, as a special and immediate gift of God.

Nor do I think that we ought to regard his secluded life as wholly a misfortune. For his sermons possess some noble and lofty qualities, which probably they would have lacked, had he been called, instead of to do this one thing, to dissipate his energies over that wide and diversified field of pastoral and administrative duties, whose fulfillment exhausts the time and wearies the bodies of so many preachers. There are preachers—and perhaps it is true of the majority of preachers—whose sermons are far better when inspired and moulded by intercourse with their people, than when they are the product solely of hard work in the study. But your pastor's sermons were not of this character. He addressed his subject. He was absorbed by his subject, and by the emotions it enkindled in himself. H seemed to forget his audience. He spoke out like a Hebrew prophet whom his lofty theme was enough to satisfy, and to whom it was unknown whether men heard or did not hear.

The work he did was confessedly a great work; and this great work he did exceptionally well. Great, therefore, is the loss that you sustain. Where will you find comfort? Where can any of us find comfort in the losses and bereavements and agonies of this life? The heaven saith, it is not in me, and the deep saith, it is not in me. The only comfort in earthly loss that I know, is in the Gospel that he preached. This event, to all who, in whatever degree, are afflicted by it and who trust in God, is a part of what Dr. Wadsworth loved to call "that gracious discipline of our heavenly Father, by which He is preparing us for our eternal home." It seems strange that trials like this should befall Christians. "It seems strange sometimes,' he said in one of his noblest sermons, "that at the first moment of repentance and pardon, the justified soul is not taken to glory. But we shall see it by and by, and we ought to see it presently—that, as spirits under discipline for the different allotments of heaven, more precious to us is this pilgrimage with its poor scrip, and its worn sandal, than the instant fire-car of the prophet to translate us to the skies. There are distinctions in the condition of the redeemed in eternity —harps of a more amazing power—and scepters of a wider sway,—and stations nearer in honor to the throne of God! And this wearisome pilgrimage on earth is but a continuance on that wresting arena, where every successful struggle adds to the fair and goodly things that make up eternity."

This is our comfort, friends. This is always our conflict in affliction.

In words like these he would address us, could he speak to us today. And he would bit us, in the pain of our earthly pilgrimage, think of the gory that is sure to be its outcome. He would tell us, as once he told you, that painful even as life is, it is not without abundant blessings. He would tee us, "That along the desert sand falls the heavenly manna, and fast by our side flows the living water, and steadfast in our van abides the Shekinah of glory. And then beyond! Canaan! Canaan, with its royal cities, and its thrones of power, and its diadems of glory! Canaan, as it burst upon the eye of Moses, making his dying hour a triumphant rapture on the heights of Pisgah! Canaan, that house of many mansions! That home of the beloved dead! That dwelling place of Jesus! That glorious Kingdom of God! Canaan lies brought and fair before us; and this path that lies through the desert is the only path that leads to its enrapturing inheritance!

www.ingramcontent.com/pod-product-compliance
Lightning Source LLC
Chambersburg PA
CBHW070443090526
44586CB00046B/1662